# A Faith That Frees

# A Faith That Frees

*Catholic Matters for the 21st Century*

Richard G. Malloy

ORBIS BOOKS
Maryknoll, New York 10545

Founded in 1970, Orbis Books endeavors to publish works that enlighten the mind, nourish the spirit, and challenge the conscience. The publishing arm of the Maryknoll Fathers and Brothers, Orbis seeks to explore the global dimensions of the Christian faith and mission, to invite dialogue with diverse cultures and religious traditions, and to serve the cause of reconciliation and peace. The books published reflect the views of their authors and do not represent the official position of the Maryknoll Society. To learn more about Maryknoll and Orbis Books, please visit our website at www.maryknoll.org.

Library of Congress Cataloging-in-Publication Data

Malloy, Richard G.
  A faith that frees : Catholic matters for the 21st century / Richard
G. Malloy.
      p. cm.
  Includes bibliographical references and index.
  ISBN 978-1-57075-734-1
  1. Catholic Church—Doctrines.  2. Theology, Doctrinal—Popular works.
I. Title.
  BX1751.3.M25 2007
  282—dc22
                            2007008447

*To Eloise Squires, David Niederhauser, and Lillian Santiago,*
*three Camdenites,*
*and*
*Br. Dennis Jude Ryan, SJ, Mr. Joe Grady, SJ,*
*and Br. William Sudzina, SJ,*
*three companions in the Society of Jesus,*
*all of whom have taught me much*
*about a faith that frees.*

*"Blessed be the Lord, the God of Israel;*
*he has come to his people and set them free....*
*This was the oath he swore to our father Abraham:*
*to set us free...*
*free to worship him without fear..."*
    —Luke 1:68 ff.
        *(ICET English translation of the Benedictus)*


*"You will know the truth*
*and the truth will set you free."*
    —John 8:32


*"For freedom Christ has set us free.*
*Stand firm, therefore,*
*and do not submit again to a yoke of slavery....*
*For you were called to freedom..."*
    —Galatians 5:1, 13


*"Lord, by your cross and resurrection*
*you have set us free.*
*You are the savior or the world."*
    —Memorial Acclamation

*"...one could very well describe Christianity*
*as a philosophy of freedom."*
    —Joseph Cardinal Ratzinger (Pope Benedict XVI)

# Contents

# Acknowledgments

Michael Leach, Catherine Costello, and Celine Allen and the entire team at Orbis Books have lavished extraordinary care and dedication on this project. Their expertise has been of great assistance to me in the completion of this book.

# Introduction

*"Jesus spoke to them and said, 'Take heart, it is I; do not be afraid.'
Peter answered him, 'Lord, if it is you, command me to come to you
on the water.' He said, 'Come.'"*
—Matthew 14:27–29

## Walking on Water into the Twenty-first Century

God loves us. This reality of God's actively loving us is the beginning
and the end, and all in between, of our being Catholic. God's love pre-
cedes and inspires our being followers of Jesus, being those persons co-
operating with our transformation in Christ. The real challenge is to
know how to live out the implications of this amazing faith reality of our
lives. Being Catholic is no longer static, simple, or self-evident. Being
Catholic today calls us to be like Peter, engage Jesus, and walk, even
walk on the waves. The question is not only, "What would Jesus do?"
(WWJD). The crucial question today is, "What would Peter and Paul
and Mary Magdalene do?" As Mary did, we must witness to the cross
and the resurrection. As Paul did, we need to adapt and transform cultural practices in order to express and live out our love and faith in
Christ. As Peter did, we must find the trust and courage to get out of the
boat and walk on water. In so doing, we will learn to live a vibrant and
freeing Catholicism. To do so we need to look at things in new ways.

Years ago, as a young Jesuit scholastic, I was sent to the Gesu parish
in North Philadelphia to work in a children's summer program, Reading Is Fundamental (RIF). The way we enticed the kids to do the reading during the hot summer days was to promise swim time in the pool
at the Jesuit high school next door. One day I stood at the edge of the
pool and loudly proclaimed to all the kids that I was going to walk on

water. "No way. You is crazy Mr. Rick," responded Shaquilla, an African American ten-year-old. But the little kids were wide eyed with anticipation. "Can you really do that?" asked Alicia, a little Puerto Rican six year old. At this point, a sixteen-year-old counselor, who was helping out with the program, came up and shoved me in. After climbing out and enduring the laughter of the assembled crowd, I again announced that I was going to walk on water. The kids were loudly arguing, yelling, and screaming. I said, "Ready?" and put my foot out toward the pool's water. Then I swung 180 degrees and walked the other way, splashing in the poolside puddles, saying, "See? I'm walking on water." The kids howled in protest and once again hurled me into the pool. After I had climbed out again and dealt with all the uproar I had caused, a little seven-year-old named Tariq came over and said, "Everyone else thinks that was dumb, but you know, I never thought of walking on water that way." Smart kid.

To live our lives as disciples of Jesus, we need to constantly and consistently find new ways to walk on water. We need to challenge our culture's and cultures' ways of treating women, minorities, and the poor. We need to walk on water, not as Jesus did, but as Peter did. We need to know that when we get out of the boat and stand in the waves, even if our faith falters and fails, the Lord will be there to bolster and uphold us and send us on to build the community. To be authentic Catholics, to be truly free followers of Jesus Christ in the twenty-first century, we must find the courage and freedom of Saints Peter and Paul. Peter had the faith and courage to walk on water, and the freedom to listen to Paul. Paul had the faith and courage to challenge Peter, and together they adapted and changed the cultural practices with which they had lived in order to more faithfully and freely follow the risen Lord. We too must do in our times what they did in their era. As we do so, we will hear the words of Jesus calling to us across the waters, "Take heart, it is I; do not be afraid" (Matthew 14:27). Like Peter, we need to get out of our boats, get out of our comfort zones, and walk on water toward the Lord. Like Paul, we need to name the cultural practices of our times that are in accord with the living of the gospel and challenge the cultural currents of our age that militate against the full expression of God's presence in our personal and communal lives. Like Mary Magdalene, we need to announce the risen Lord.

*"To live our lives as disciples of Jesus, we need to constantly and consistently find new ways to walk on water."*

## Culture Matters: Practicing a Faith That Frees

Understanding our faith and developing cultural practices that will make our living of the faith vibrant and transformative of ourselves, our communities, and our twenty-first-century world means knowing what Peter knew as he stepped over the side of the boat, as he felt the strong winds whipping through the air and the cold waves lapping at his feet and knees. Faith is not something meant for safe harbor. Faith takes us where we do not always plan to go. As we engage the reality of God, we will have to risk getting out of our safe and comfortable cultural boats and be willing to create and incarnate cultural practices that make our faith what it essentially is, a way to experience God and a way to live in love and practice justice. Such a faith frees us, for it is rooted in freedom. Catholic faith exists in a loving relationship founded in the freedom we are given and the freedom God is. Our God graces us with the power of choice and wants us to choose what makes us and others happy and healthy and holy and free. A faith that frees us and fosters justice for all our brothers and sisters is what the practices of Catholicism ought to foster in all cultures and societies on this planet. Paul's letters are exercises in the relating of faith in Jesus Christ to such cultural creation and adaptation.

As the twenty-first century dawns, we need an articulation of Catholicism—what our faith is and why we should live according to this faith—that finds its starting point in the complex, fascinating, and primordial role culture plays in the practices of Catholicism. For the Catholic faith to be truly a faith that frees, we need to start with the reality that human beings are cultural beings. The ways we understand and relate to ourselves, others, and God are primordially contoured and conditioned by who and what we are culturally, and our cultural selves are visible and tangible in our concrete actions and choices, that is, the practices, of our lives. To answer the question, "Why be Catholic?" we need to grasp the truth that culture is that by which we are what we are. If you had been born and raised in a different culture, you would not be who you are, and if I had been born and raised in a different culture, I would not be who I am. Too often, we Catholics cannot give cogent reasons for why we choose to live as Catholics because we have not learned how to relate intellectually the truths we know and accept by faith with the cultural relationships that structure and undergird the daily choices and primary meaning systems of our lives. Culture matters, and one reason we are so mum and numb about Catholicism is because the cultural practices of our faith have become so anemic.

This book begins, not with discarnate philosophies, the traditional starting point for serious reflections on our faith, but rather with the methods and insights of cultural anthropology and applies them to the questions with which we struggle as we strive to live as Catholics in today's increasingly globalized world with its myriad, interpenetrating, complex cultures. This book privileges not theological truths to be disseminated but rather practices and experiences, conversations and dialogues, hoping that the authentic living of our faith, a full and flexible Catholicism, will transform us by persuasion and example, rather than by the hammering home of seemingly self-evident, monological truths.

Faith is "the assurance of things hoped for, the conviction of things not seen" (Hebrews 11:1), and the primordial effect of our practice of faith as Catholics is our being freed from all that keeps us in bondage. Every morning those who engage in the practice of the Liturgy of the Hours pray Zechariah's canticle: "Blessed be the Lord, the God of Israel; he has come to his people and set them free.... This was the oath he swore to our father Abraham: to set us free...free to worship him without fear, holy and righteous in his sight all the days of our life" (Luke 1:68–71; ICET). The psalmist sings, "Out of my distress I called on the Lord; the Lord answered me and set me free" (Psalm 118:5; RSV). "For freedom Christ has set us free," proclaims St. Paul (Galatians 5:1). The central dynamic of the Spiritual Exercises of St. Ignatius of Loyola has been described as being freed from, freed for, freed to be with. Our relationship with Jesus frees us from all in our experience that drags us toward death, from all that constructs and maintains what Thomas Merton calls our false self (Finley 2003). As we practice our faith, we are freed for service to others, freed to make a world of justice and peace wherein everyone can live in hope and harmony, peace and prosperity, joy and justice, love and liberty. Ultimately, our faith frees us to be with God and all our loved ones for all eternity.

Although 85 to 90 percent of those who live in the United States profess a belief in God, the question is, in what kind of God do people in the U.S. believe? *American Piety in the 21st Century*, a study released by the Baylor Institute for Studies of Religion, measured the meaning of Americans' belief in God, constructing a fourfold typology of God: People expressed belief in God as Benevolent, Authoritarian, Distant, or

Critical. The study rated the four images of God on a scale of engagement to anger (Baylor Institute 2006:26). Still, Baylor's massive study didn't specifically mention the image of God that is so empirically demonstrated in the lives of millions daily. The "Higher Power" of the multitude of 12-step programs (e.g., Alcoholics Anonymous, Overeaters Anonymous) is a God who frees, a higher power who salvages, changes, and transforms peoples' lives. The God who frees is the God wanted and needed by millions trapped in the destructive spirals of addictions and diseases of the spirit, mind, and body. The God sought by so many caught in the cynicism and depression of the first world's constantly competitive and harried existence is the God who frees us from being measured and manipulated by the machinations of a godless, capitalistic, materialistic culture. The God desired by the billons in poverty-stricken nations is the God of liberation gracing us with freedom from want, freedom from fear, freedom from an inhumane existence. It is the experience of being redeemed and saved that encourages so many to praise a God who frees. The God experienced in the true practice of Catholicism is always a God who engages us freely and calls us to exercise our freedom in ways that make a sustainable and loving world for one another. We meet this God by risking walking on water as Peter did, by venturing out and walking into new towns and villages as Paul did, by speaking to the apostles as Mary Magdalene did.

Faith is always and in all ways contextualized and lived out in human culture. The practices of faith are always lived in relation to various cultural contexts. Bernard Lonergan writes, "A theology mediates between a cultural matrix and the role of religion in that matrix" (Lonergan 1972:xi). Lonergan's thought concentrates on elucidating the relationship between the practice of faith and the cultural matrix in which we live—our ever more technologized, globalized, and media-ized world of the twenty-first century—and how people of faith can work to make this "pale, blue dot" (Sagan 1994) whirling on the edge of the Milky Way galaxy a world of justice and joy, peace and prosperity, liberty and love. A Faith That Frees is about our relationships to ourselves as free and responsible persons and our relationships to the various communities of which we are members, especially the community we call church. At its core, faith is about the ground and the trajectory of our being human and thus is a

"Faith is the knowledge born of religious love."
(Lonergan 1972:115)

meditation on, and wondering about, our relationship to God, who is love (1 John 4:16). Ultimately, faith is about who and what we really are, who and what we desire and hope to become, who and what we really love, and what that loving does to transform us and our world.

Although much of what is written here about the relationship of faith and culture can apply to many faith traditions, this book concentrates on practicing the Catholic faith in the United States for at least two reasons. One is that the attempt to practice faith as a Catholic has formed the central cultural matrix of my life, and, therefore, I can most cogently comment upon trying to be a person of faith by reflecting on my own experience as a Catholic. And, for all but four years of my life, I have lived in the United States. Being Catholic in this country is what I know best. It is, for better or worse, who and what I am. Second, today Catholics in the United States are alarmingly deficient in understanding the relationships that necessarily exist between faith and culture and in being able to comment confidently and cogently on these issues. The degeneration of the Catholic community's leadership into ever more polarized factions, commonly labeled "conservative" and "liberal," has left the bulk of the church's members anywhere from bemused to bewildered to battered, if not actually bruised.

Such polarization is often bemoaned, but rarely effectively addressed. The only way forward, the only way to transcend the ever more bitter and biting sniping at one another among Catholic elites (often self-appointed), is through dialogue. Authentic dialogue is risky. By entering into true dialogue, we open ourselves to change. It is only through the hard, trusting, committed work of dialogue that we can hope to construct common meaning. And it is only through the conscious construction of religious cultural practices that common meaning can take root and grow into a way of life transformative of ourselves on the personal, communal, and societal levels of our being. The challenge is to strive to hold paradoxes and contradictions in creative tension without allowing them to devolve into destructive polarities. The patient labor of holding things together is what makes the construction of common meaning possible and more probable.

"To reach an understanding in a dialogue is not merely a matter of putting oneself forward and successfully asserting one's own point of view, but being transformed into a communion in which we do not remain what we were."
(Gadamer 1991:378)

Faith communities form around, and are sustained by, common meaning. Lonergan writes, "As common meaning constitutes community, so divergent meaning divides it" (Lonergan 1972:357). According to Lonergan, conversion of heart and mind, or lack thereof, is the root cause of division among people of faith. The way forward is found in practicing our faith in ways that lead to conversion of mind and heart. We need to invite all Catholics to the table and share sustenance and substance. The carping and "put downs" of one another as somehow illegitimate or unworthy Catholics is a recipe for destruction and disaster.

Recently I presided at a marriage of close friends. Both were mature adults in their forties who had been through the paralyzing pain of divorce. Both had gone through the rigors of the tribunal process in their diocese. The groom, a non-Catholic, a faithful, Bible-reading Baptist, accepted the church's teachings on no sexual relations before marriage. After filing the papers with the marriage tribunal, the couple waited eighteen months for the church to annul his previous marriage, which had ended due to his previous wife's infidelities. So, imagine their reaction, two good people who had been through painful and difficult marriages and a somewhat baffling annulment process, when they were told they could not celebrate the sacrament of matrimony in the parish church. They would have to use the chapel, because the multiple divorces "were a source of scandal." To whom? The only scandal was the message received by the seventy-five people attending the wedding that the Catholic Church is an unwelcoming and rule-rigid organization.

The more we stop arbitrarily judging one another and putting one another down for being this type or that kind of Catholic, the more we will discover a faith that frees. The more we insist on castigating and categorizing fellow Catholics, the more we will create a caricature of the faith, not a faith that frees but a faith that freezes. Such a rigor-mortised form of faith stands in need of conversion. Such a frozen faith cannot foster the development of men and women ready to get out of the boat and walk on water toward Jesus.

Many forms of faith stand in need of conversion today. These include unintelligent fundamentalisms of many persuasions: those of terrorists who hijack Islam, those of people who pit religious traditions against science, those of hypercritical Catholics of various ideological bents. But we too often disagree on what such conversions ought to be like, and on what cultural issues such conversions ought to address and remedy. Such disagreements stall conversion and frustrate the ability of the community to live a faith that frees, a faith that contributes to our amelioration and transformation on both personal and social levels.

In this book, I hope to engage in authentic dialogue and address many of the various crises in contemporary Catholicism and, in so doing, address the crisis involved in living religious faiths in general in the twenty-first century. This book is written for those who want to understand Catholicism as a faith that can free, as a faith that can encourage us to walk on water, converse with contemporary Samaritans (Luke 10; John 4), redefine profane and sacred and metaphorically eat foods we've never eaten before (Acts 10:9–42), meet and form community with contemporary lepers, prostitutes, tax collectors, and gentiles. Ultimately, ours is a faith that encourages us to endure the cross in hope of resurrection.

There are many ways to practice Catholicism authentically. Appreciating such diversity will aid the reader in understanding a bit of what has been going on in the Catholic Church for the past forty years in the wake of Vatican II as various groups have reacted and responded differently to cultural changes in society. Such understanding and appreciation will show how we can regroup and move things forward in a way that forms a church more like the one Jesus described in the New Testament, a church as concerned with the parable of the judgment of the nations, "Whatever you did for one of these least brothers of mine, you did for me" (Matthew 25:31-46; NAB), as with Matthew's Petrine proclamation, "You are Peter and on this rock I will build my church" (Matthew 16:18). Courageous dialogue on topics often avoided in theological and ecclesiological discussions (e.g., race, gender, inequality, etc.) will foster a faith that does justice, a faith that is capable of freeing everyone from oppressions and sinful structures antithetical to the glory of God.

For too many in the United States today, the Catholic Church is a woefully misunderstood and underappreciated institution. Rather than seeing it as the largest provider of social services to the nation that it is, too many view the Catholic Church as a guilt-inducing religion whose leaders threaten eternal damnation for those who do not live by its dictates. The reality of the matter is that millions do not find guilt-inducing pro-

> "The Spirit is Freedom, and nothing should be allowed to dim, imperil or weaken in us the consciousness of our Christian freedom."
>
> (von Balthasar 1957:103)

nouncements that patrol and paralyze their relationship with God helpful or healing. Most Catholics know that unjustifiable guilt is a weak motivator and a poor basis on which to establish and maintain a loving relationship with the God who is love, and an even worse basis on which to form and build community. Much better are the realizations that life and all we have are gifts, and that we are invited as the Body of Christ to share our gifts, liberally and lavishly. The gift of faith and the practices of the faith are rooted in loving relationships. Those relationships ought to foster freedom and justice and love. As people see us being the pilgrim people of God, the Body of Christ in the world today, freely loving and serving others, they will be attracted to our communities and want to join us as we worship God and engage with others in establishing social structures that exemplify the values of the kingdom Jesus preached.

A Faith That Frees reaches out to all those of good will who seek to discover and create ways for humans to live in harmony and peace with all creation. One can be a good and loving person of faith in multiple ways, according to many traditions. As Vatican II teaches, the church gives primary consideration to what people of faith "have in common and what promotes fellowship among them.... The Catholic Church rejects nothing which is true and holy in these religions" (Nostra Aetate [Declaration on the Relationship of the Church to Non-Christian Religions], 1–2). This book concentrates on how one can be a person of faith as a Catholic and highlights the strengths of the Catholic tradition—and one of the great strengths of the Catholic Church after Vatican II has been our openness to dialogue with those who embrace other faith traditions.

## What Believing Means

A few years after my having taught his son, an Ivy League–educated psychiatrist engaged me in conversation. Having gotten to know me as both friend and priest, he finally felt comfortable enough to ask me a question that had been burning within him for some time: "Why do you believe?" My questioner, a fifty-something baby boomer, a non-Catholic and a non-Christian, is one of the finer human beings I have had the privilege to know and call friend. He is highly educated and highly principled, a person who has searched long and hard for faith.

In dialogue with many like him, I've come to realize that faith is not so much a matter of content and dogma; it is more a matter of presentation and practice. My answer to his question is that living the Catholic faith has been fascinating and fulfilling, in ways that I little understood as a child, and in ways that I little imagined when I began to get serious about my faith as a young adult. The main thing is to realize that living as a Catholic frees us and makes us conscious of the transformations going on in our life with Christ. Living life and faith freely, responsibly, and lovingly fulfills us and transforms both us and our world. But faith frozen fast and hard in some pre–Vatican II framework cannot be mediated to those who are shaped in the fullness and flexibility of contemporary cultural currents. We have not articulated the meanings and beauties of our beliefs and practices in a manner attractive and compelling for the "post-modernized" generations of the latter twentieth-century United States. In turn, those generations have had little ability to mediate our faith to their children in the twenty-first century. Sculpting an answer for those who in their understanding and living are seeking faith, a full and flexible faith that engages people on an adult level and respects their intelligence, freedom, and good will, is a challenge we must meet. We need to sketch out and implement practices that meet the problems of our day, cultural Catholic practices creatively responding to the cultural complexity of our times. Such practices will be rooted in hope and trust that our loving God will guide us to realize the tremendous potential and opportunities of our times. How to achieve the conditions of intelligence, commitment, and conversion called for by a full and flexible faith is the subject of this book. Part one (chapters 1–3) is a theory of Catholicism. Part two (chapters 4–8) is a set of reflections providing provocative and prophetic practices of Catholicism that lead to conversion and transformation in various social and cultural venues.

Ever since the Israelites were slaves in Egypt, our God has been responding to those who call for freedom (Exodus 3:7). The human community's deep desire and holy longing for freedom is rooted deep in all human hearts: freedom from all oppression and injustice, from all fear and folly, from all that is destructive and death dealing; freedom for becoming all we desire to be as human beings and human communities; freedom to be with our God in play and prayer, in work and worship, in ways that construct and maintain a social order and global culture carrying the values of love and peace and justice for all.

Many recently are raising their voices against organized religion and even faith itself, voices as varied as those of Richard Dawkins (2006), Daniel Dennett (2006), Sam Harris (2005, 2006), and comedians like George Carlin and HBO's *Real Time* denunciator-at-large, Bill Maher. What religion's debunkers fail to understand is that the antidote for bad religion, or the illegitimate ideological cooptation of religion's energies and prophetic power, is not the abandonment of faith and the outlawing of the practices of religion. The response to the controversial religious dynamics of our time must be the practice of good religion and reasonable faith, religion that labors for peace and justice, faith that complements and works with reason (cf. John Paul II's encyclical *Fides et Ratio*). Those who decry religion for the supposed failures—even atrocities—of religious persons and religious organizations would not deal with other sectors of society in the same manner. Just because there are bad governments, we don't call for the abolition of politics. Just because there are some unethical pharmaceutical corporations and unscrupulous doctors, we do not call for the demolition of the practice of medicine. Just because some cops are bad, we don't call for the dismantling of the criminal justice system. And, despite the endless litanies of lawyer jokes, we all thank and trust advocates who shepherd us through legal systems.

> *"Those who decry religion for the supposed failures—even atrocities—of religious persons and religious organizations would not deal with other sectors of society in the same manner."*

Even those who champion science as an alternative world view in supposed contradistinction to religious epistemologies fail to justify their own assumptions. One cannot justify the scientific method using the methods of science. One cannot justify materialism without making an act of faith that there is nothing beyond our physical world. With the mysterious and murky discoveries of quantum mechanics, even science itself demonstrates how tenuous a hold materialism has on our evaluation of our everyday experiences (cf. Greene 2000, 2005). Further, those who advocate the abolition or illegitimacy of faith fail to address some central questions of human existence: Why are we here? From where have we come? What happens when we die? None of these questions can be fully answered by science, although science can contribute much to our appreciation and wonder at the gift our lives are. And a gift implies a giver.

We all believe in something, and, hopefully, someone. We all believe in some ways, many times in ways given to us in and through our cultures. The examination of the ways in which, and the reasons why, we believe, and the practices we culturally embody as we live out our faith, is the goal of this book. Such examination provides us with meaning and mission.

As we begin, let's ask God's blessing:

May our good and gracious God grant you
Joy for the Journey
Courage for the Choices
Faith for the Freeing
Hope for the Healing
and
Love for the Lasting

# PART ONE
# FAITH MATTERS
## A Theory of Catholicism

### Prelude

*Hail to the God who joins us; for through him*
*arise the symbols where we truly live.*
*And, with tiny footsteps, the clocks move*
*separately from authentic time.*

*Though we are unaware of our true status*
*our actions stem from pure relationship.*
*Far away, our antennas hear antennas*
*and the empty distances transmit...*

*Pure readiness. Oh unheard starry music!*
*Isn't your sound protected from all static*
*by the ordinary business of our days?*

*In spite of all the farmer's work and worry,*
*he can't reach down to where the seed is slowly*
*transmuted into summer. The earth bestows.*

—Rainer Maria Rilke
The Sonnets to Orpheus, XII
(Rilke 1995:433)

# 1
# Being Catholic
## *The Great Adventure*

*"For the Son of God became man so that we might become God."*
 *—St. Athanasius*

### The Great Heroic Adventure

Maybe you are one of those post–Vatican II Catholics who doesn't really know what "Vatican II" is, or was. Maybe the minions of the mass media have convinced you that being Catholic is akin to mindless disengagement with the issues of the day. Maybe, when your fundamentalist "Christian neighbor" (using the terms loosely) teaches her children to tell your children they are going to Hell because they are Catholic, you don't have a quick retort ready. (This actually happened to a friend's family in Denver a few years ago.) Personally, I suggest replying, "We're going wherever Mother Teresa went!" Maybe you don't feel very confident in being able to explain to someone what being a Catholic is or means. Maybe the clergy sex scandals have made you radically question your allegiance to the church, if not your very faith itself. Then this book is for you.

Many contemporary Catholics in the United States have little idea of the incredible riches that our faith and its practices offer. In the words of the poet Rilke quoted in the introduction to this section, "Though we are unaware of our true status / our actions stem from pure relationship." Being Catholic bestows a set of relationships upon us, relationships that grant us a status too little appreciated. For many, being Catholic means seemingly trivial pursuits: from annoying requests for money to build yet another parish space, to incomprehensible "feast days of obligation," to "forcing" teenagers to go to a "boring" Mass on Sunday. Yet, the eucharistic celebration isn't boring. The teens are bored. Why? No one has shown them the meaning and power of the Eucharist, or demonstrated for them the intrinsic fascination of practicing Catholicism. "Happy Meals" our kids practice and learn about before pre-school. "Eucharist" they memorize for confirmation class and forget the week after the visit of the bishop (remember that guy? the one in the "cone-head" hat?). Our high school and college age students readily worship at the altars of Budweiser and Jim Beam, convinced that getting "wasted" is preferable to being a person of prayer.

Being Catholic isn't boring. Being Catholic freely, fully, and flexibly is fascinating. Fundraising campaigns for parish spaces involve far less money than building campaigns for country clubs and private universities. "Feast days of obligation" could be viewed as welcome respites, granting us communal permission to stop slaving for the gods of our jobs and to quit worshiping at the altars of commerce—"obligations" we must perform almost every day of our lives. And seriously practicing a full and flexible Catholicism will make us less stressed, happier, and more peaceful than any expensive nights out, tearing up popular clubs and bars. But McDonald's and the country clubs and the private colleges and our commercial culture have done a much better job of selling their products and communicating their meanings to our kids and us than we as church have done. It's time to catch up. It's time to let our children know the value of Catholicism. It's time to work intelligently to instill in them the values of our faith. And those values are better communicated through practices than through CCD classes or required university theology courses

A few years ago, I was at a meeting of Maryland Province Jesuits and lay colleagues. A group of professors from the Loyola College business faculty were facilitating the meeting. One evening, after a long day discussing future apostolic plans, I sat down with several of these facilitators. They had been fascinated by the Jesuits' discussions concerning the issue of "Catholic illiteracy." They themselves readily admitted their own ignorance about multiple aspects of our faith. These people, all with Ph.D.s in their fields, felt they had at best an eighth-grade religious education. This book is for people like those professors, for those who want to know what life is all about, who God is and who we are, how we relate the human and divine, and how we can go about ascertaining the answers to the ultimate questions of our existence. To those who haven't had, or taken, the time to really think about and ponder Catholicism, I offer the practice of a full and flexible Catholicism as a great adventure. For those who feel they haven't had the opportunity to really investigate Catholicism's answers to ultimate questions, I want to make the case that our faith is fascinating and freeing.

Our freeing faith challenges us to relate the sacred to the secular, to be a leaven in society and, by our Catholic practices, to form a world of peace and justice for all. For example, informed Catholics and others of good faith often seriously question capitalism's cultural hegemony over our lives. Even our most sacred icons are now for sale. The Archdiocese of Mexico City allowed corporate sponsors to finance Pope John Paul II's 1998 visit. The Pepsi-owned Sabritas chip company put up $1.8 million dollars, buying the right to place the Pontiff's picture on their packaging: *Las Papas del Papa* (The Potato Chips of the Pope). A Miami-based company sold a Vatican approved John Paul II prepaid phone card. Volvo now offers to "save your soul" and Mercedes-Benz trumpets the slogan, "Sacrifice Nothing" (Budde and Brimlow, 2002). Despite these aberrations, the sacred is not for sale. The fact that something cannot be bought is one of the characteristics that mark it as sacred.

The sacred isn't encountered in trivia. Life isn't all about shopping or golf. Life isn't all about being Number #1, or being better than the next guy or gal. Life isn't about winning the Super Bowl. (Commentator asks, "Bubba, what would you do to win the Super Bowl?" "I'd run over my Grandmother to win the Super Bowl." He asks Bubba's opponent the same question, "What would you do to win?" "I'd run over his Grandmother too"). Life is not about winning the championship at the expense of others. To tell the truth, life is following Jesus and becoming one with God. Everything else is just details. Yet, what does following Jesus as a Catholic really mean? What does living as a Catholic have to do with the realities of life? What does truly being Catholic and practicing a full and flexible Catholicism have to do with the complexities of life in the twenty-first century? Is living as a Catholic just another lifestyle choice in the marketplace of identities one can try on and discard like bargain buys at K-Mart? Is being a Catholic just a cosmic insurance policy (Let's placate the "Big Guy" and keep on his good side, just in case it all really matters somehow)? For too

> *"Life is following Jesus and becoming one with God. Everything else is just details."*

many post–Vatican II Catholics, faith is peripheral to the real issues of life. We aren't really sure if faith matters, and we're not really clear about what faith matters are.

But what if the practices of Catholicism answer questions central to the deepest longings and meanings of our hearts? What if the scriptures (i.e., the Bible) and the sacraments inform the clearest and most central truths of our minds? What if prayer and service in Jesus' name through the Catholic community can be the source of the energy and vibrancy of spirit we so deeply desire? What if revitalizing the rituals and practices and meeting the challenges of practicing a full and flexible Catholicism will feed our souls and form us as persons aware of our deepest, truest, values and meanings? What if being Catholic, if really living the faith, can help us trust our eternal destiny? What if the practicing of Catholicism can lead us to a contentment and peace we never imagined possible? What if our freeing faith can ignite our hearts and fill us with joy and purpose in our lives? What if we could walk on water today?

Being Catholic, really living as intelligent, thoughtful Catholics, is a way to grow and be formed in ways that make us truly happy and holy and healthy and free. *Sr. Mary Ignatius Explains It All for You* and the inane, anti-Catholic characters on *Saturday Night Live* skits are prejudiced caricatures that no other ethnic or religious group would tolerate. Anti-Catholicism and the ridiculing of Catholics run rampant in popular culture (Martin 2000; Massa 2003). Yet, portrayals by Robert DeNiro and Jeremy Irons in *The Mission* are much closer to the mark, and even the Whoopi Goldberg–influenced convent in *Sister Act I & II*, and the Gallagher family in *While You Were Sleeping,* or Fr. Cavanaugh in *Rudy* are much better images of what Catholicism is and can be: a transformative force in our lives, cultures, and societies. Certainly the Oscar-winning performance of Susan Sarandon in *Dead Man Walking* is much closer to the reality of lived Catholicism as it is actually practiced in our times. Come and see. Be part of the great mission. Practicing a full and flexible Catholicism is a fascinating adventure.

## To Be in Relationship unto Transformation

The fundamental idea is this: to be Catholic is to be consciously and freely in relationship with oneself and others, all the while being aware that everything is being transformed by the mercy, grace, and love of

God. To be Catholic is to be aware of one's involvement in a series of great transformations: the transformation of one's self over a lifetime into a person incorporated into the reality of God, the promise made to us all that we may "become participants in the divine nature" (2 Peter 1:4). Our personal transformations are part of a larger cosmic process: the promised transformation of all human history and all creation (Romans 8:21) into the coming kingdom of God, wherein God will be "all in all" (1 Corinthians 15:28). Right at the beginning of *Lumen Gentium*, the great document of Vatican II that describes what the church is and ought to be, we learn what Catholicism is all about: God's plan is "to dignify men [and women] with a participation in His own divine life" (*Lumen Gentium*, 2). *Dei Verbum*, Vatican II's document on revelation, says the same thing: ". . . through Christ, the Word made flesh, men and women have access to the Father in the Holy Spirit and come to share the divine nature" (*Dei Verbum*, 2). This isn't some radical, unorthodox, liberal, Jesuit spin on theology. Back in the early days of the church St. Athanasius said the same thing: "For the Son of God became man so that we might become God." That's a pretty wild claim, but it's what our faith promises us. St. Augustine agrees: "Of his own will he was born for us today, in time, so that he could lead us to his Father's eternity. God became man so that man might become God" (Office of Readings, Saturday before Epiphany). St. Thomas Aquinas says, "Since it is the will of God's only begotten Son that men should share in his divinity, he assumed our nature in order that by becoming man he might make men gods" (Office of Readings, Feast of Corpus Christi). We are destined to be one with God. That's what life is all about. Since we are all destined to be one with God and all else in creation, we live our lives in relationship with God and others, in light of that truth.

The fact that we are destined to be with God forever relates to absolutely everything in our human existence. Our eternal salvation, our being participants in the reality of God, calls us to be the kind of persons that can co-exist with God. We become the persons who can live with God and with others who live in God. That reality doesn't start the day we die; it starts the day we are conceived. From the moment of our creation we are in relationship with God and other persons, all other persons, all who have lived and will live. The creation, maintenance, and fostering of relationships between ourselves and God, and between ourselves and others, are really two sides of the same coin (Mark 12:30–31). In and through the people, events, and realities of our lives, God is present to us. St. Ignatius called this way of relating to everything "finding God in all things." I expand the terminology and suggest that in the twenty-first century we are invited to "Seek God in all realities." To be Catholic is to believe that all realities, and all levels of reality, are imbued with the pulsating presence of the God who creates us, who loves us, and who sustains us. This God saves us from the seeming destruction of death. That salvation is always going on in our lives. We can cooperate with it or ignore it. We can deny it or we can use all the powers of our human consciousness to try and understand the incredible processes in which we're involved.

### A Disciplined Spirituality

To be Catholic is to be consciously choosing how one fashions one's self and one's community unto God. Such choosing operates on various levels of conversion. Longed-for conversions don't just happen. Therefore, Catholicism is disciplined spirituality. Many today make a distinction between "religion" and "spirituality," with "religion" getting the decidedly short end of the stick. To be into "spirituality" is cool; to be "religious" is to be backward, unintelligent, or oppressed. But a spirituality without religious commitment and discipline can easily dissolve into smorgasbord spirituality, the dabbling in this and that for a few months at a time, being everything for a short while, but never becoming fully, deeply, totally, much of anything. By the end of one's experimenting, one has skimmed the surface of spirituality, but failed to plunge radically, that is, to the roots, to the depths of spiritual realities.

David Brooks in his *Bobos in Paradise* questions the depth of religious experience for which the spiritual-but-not-religious folks can realistically hope. He notes that "spiritual individualism" can too easily become "spirituality without obligation" (Brooks 2000:235). Brooks argues that contemporary, upper-middle-class Americans are "Bobos," a curious blend of the 1950s Bourgeois and the 1960s Bohemian cultural styles. This hyper-hip, ever changing, postmodern lifestyle leads to great individualistic, iconoclastic life choices, but such liberty comes at a price, especially in the religious realms of human existence.

> The thing we are in danger of losing with our broad diverse lives is a sense of belonging. A person who limits himself to one community or one spouse is going to have deeper bonds to that community or that spouse than the person who experiments

throughout life. A person who surrenders to a single faith is going to have a deeper commitment to that one faith than the person who zigzags through in a state of curious agnosticism. The monk in the monastery does not lead an experimental life, but perhaps he is able to lead a profound one. And so we get in Bobo life a world of many options, but maybe not a life of do-or-die commitments, and maybe not a life that ever offers access to the profoundest truths, deepest emotions, or highest aspirations. (Brooks 2000:246)

What we need is both vibrant spirituality and the power and presence of the social structures of authentic religious institutions in order to ensure that spirituality's affects and effects will be consolingly sustaining, long lasting, and truly transformative, on both the personal and communal levels of our lives. Spirituality without discipline and commitment to a community is a lake a million miles wide and two inches deep. Religion without vibrant, relational, personal spirituality is a polluted and stagnant pond, an oppressive institution that frustrates, rather than fosters, love and liberty, justice and joy, peace and prosperity. Such a spiritless institution may mouth the truths but it will fail to lead people to the transformations the truths promise. Such a religion is a dry riverbed. Following such a religion may get one to the ocean, but one will be very thirsty on the way.

Spirituality deals with all those parts of us that make us most human: our hopes and dreams, fears and anxieties, loves and longings, worries, fantasies, obsessions, addictions, commitments, images, stories, works, actions, choices, relationships, imaginings—in sum, all those internal aspects of our existence that form our perceptions of the external realities of our lives. Spirituality is about what matters and makes meaning in our lives. Spirituality is about both grace and dis-grace in our personal and social histories. Practicing a full and flexible Catholicism offers ways of ordering our spiritual selves and living out our spiritual lives on both personal and communal levels, ways found tested and true over two thousand years. The rituals and sacraments of our Catholic faith inspire us by the Holy Spirit to live like Jesus, to be the Body of Christ in the world today. At their best, religions and religious institutions harness the power of spirituality and direct it toward the common good. Religions foster

God's plan is "to dignify men [and women] with a participation in His own divine life."

(*Lumen Gentium*, 2)

practices that ensure spirituality's lasting and durable impact on us and others. That lasting impact extends to the institutional configuration of societies and cultures, and to the historical trajectory of the human race. Leo Ryan, a father of eight in Omaha, Nebraska, said at a family Mass, "Religion means caring for God's people." Catholic religious practices and spiritual disciplines over the centuries have created and sustained institutions of caring: schools, hospitals, universities, parish centers, and diocesan social agencies. The Catholic Church is the largest provider of social services in the United States. Catholic Relief Services is one of the most effective and respected agencies of its kind in the world. When someone says to me, "I'm spiritual, not religious," I'm always tempted to point out that there are no "spiritual" community's inner city schools or hospitals for the poor.

A full and flexible Catholicism, intelligently and authentically practiced, can be such a transformative religion for the twenty-first century. Yet today many contemporary Catholics are confused as to what practicing Catholicism both entails and promises. Many Catholics have too little an intellectual grasp of the truths of our faith, too little heartfelt allegiance to our Catholic myths and stories, and even less commitment to our faith and its practices as a way of life. More and more, the mission for the Catholic Church in the United States as we enter the new millennium is the conversion of Catholics. Thousands (dare I opine millions?) of baptized Catholics have no idea of the beauty and power of the gift we were given when water was poured on our heads. A distressingly high percentage of Catholics are unable to explain even simple, central ideas and truths of the faith, let alone articulate the notion that we are destined to participate in the very life of God. We Catholics just don't know too much about our faith. A great gift from God is sitting in our hearts, waiting to be opened and operative in our lives. To be converted is to open that gift. Yet not many Catholics realize that we stand in need of conversion. We all know we need to lose weight to get our bodies in shape, but we have woefully little understanding of what we need to get and keep our spirits and our souls in shape. We know the signs of being physically unfit; we are less able to gauge our spiritual fitness.

Engage in a thought experiment for a moment. If you were accused of being a Catholic, would there be enough evidence to convict you? If we as a community were accused of being Catholics, would there be enough evidence to convict us? If there is not enough evidence to convict us, if a sharp lawyer could help us "beat the rap," what would that say about our living of the Catholic faith? And what evidence would get us convicted?

### Catholicism as a Pathway to God

Religion, the communal expression and living of faith, matters because, at its best, good religion gets us to God. The authentic practice of the Catholic faith ushers forth in the experience of God. The integration of Catholic perspectives and practices into our personal lives, our communities, and our social systems makes for a world of love and life, faith and freedom, peace and prosperity, hope and healing, joy and justice for all. But too often our Catholic sacraments and rituals, our papal encyclicals and multitude of social services, our schools, our rich history and spirituality, are like matches near the wood: they sit there waiting for someone to spark the fire and flame forth the experience of God in our lives.

The experience of God is mediated in our experiences of love and life, justice and joy, service and sacrifice, consolation and contentment, challenge and choice, tenuousness and transformation. When God is at the center of our hearts and our communities, we are transformative folk, converted and converting people, men and women on fire with a message of hope, loving persons filled with the faith that human existence is ultimately generous, graceful, and good. When we know God, when we experience God, we trust that the universe is user friendly, despite any and all evidence to the contrary.

## The Norm of Authenticity

We can experience God by practicing the Catholic faith. Like all religions, Catholicism, lived poorly or wrongly, can be an elaborately employed means of staving off transformative love and humble, self-sacrificing service. Religion lived unauthentically can be a means of avoiding or blocking the experience of the true and living God. Think of C. S. Lewis as portrayed by Anthony Hopkins in *Shadowlands* (1993). Pre-conversion, Lewis is religious, but not converted to the point where God rules his heart. He has all the answers to the "problem of pain," the title of one of his early books. Yet he structures his life so that pain cannot touch him. Sadly, a life closed to the possibility of pain is often closed to the possibility of joy and pure pleasure. Through the experience of his relationship with Joy Gresham, Lewis becomes a man of God, a man who experiences God in the opening of his heart to life and love and even the pain that such opening may entail. Instead of choosing safety and avoiding suffering, he enters into the suffering of being human and emerges a man of faith and love. In the process he becomes capable of joy. Through his life, C. S. Lewis became authentically a man in relationship with God and others.

There are parts of us that desperately want the reality of God in our lives. There are also parts of each and every person that resist with tremendous force, and often ingeniously devious methods (think of addictions, for example) awareness of the presence and action of God. The practice of a full and flexible Catholicism is an invitation to enter into the conversions through which one becomes consciously and freely engaged in the experience of God. Conversion is a *metanoia*, a "turning toward." When we risk getting out of our boats and walking on water, we change. True conversion leads to freeing faith, a full and flexible faith that is open to questions while holding in trust the truths of tradition, all the while allowing traditions to be transformed when placed in dialogue with grace coursing through contemporary cultural currents.

A full, flexible, freeing faith challenges one to ask himself or herself, to what am I really oriented, toward what am I tending with my life? What is the direction and goal of my life? Am I moving toward or away from God? Further, in what direction is my community moving? Are we moving toward or away from God? The answers to such questions are demonstrated by the way we live our lives, the practices of our days. Individually and communally, as a church and as a culture, we are what we are. It is evident if we are serious about finding God in our lives. It also is evident if we are insincere in such efforts. Following Bernard Lonergan's thought, what I call the "Norm of Authenticity" reveals us to ourselves, others, and God. The truth of our lives is manifest in the way we live and the loves we display in our lives. Those ways and loves are made manifest in the daily practices of our existence. If, like the average American, I watch television for thirty-two hours a week and spend only one hour a week in prayer, my priorities are rather clear. I've joked that "I go to the gym three times a week, once a year." The results are sadly evidenced by the size of my waistline.

Authenticity is demonstrated by what we do and are. Being a life-long Philadelphia Phillies fan, I can name some of the players on both the infamous 1964 "collapse" squad and the 1980 World Champions of baseball. I listened to Richie Ashburn's play by play on the radio for years until that former Whiz Kid passed on to the great center field in the sky. I've followed the Fightin' Phils all my life and could easily prove it. If I were accused of being a Phillies fan, I could point to the things I do that demonstrate my allegiance and loyalty. But I could not claim to be as much of a fanatic about the Phillies as I am about fishing. I love to fish. I fish some thirty to forty times a year, if only for an hour of urban fishing in the evening on the Wissahickon creek in Philadelphia. I'd fish three hundred times a year, if I could. My friends know that my life exemplifies the saying, "Fishing is not a matter of life and death. It is much more important than that." So, I am a more or less committed Phillies fan, and a bona fide Fisherman. What I am is evident in the practices of my life. To a large degree, we are what we do.

We return to the question asked above: If I were accused of being Catholic, would there be enough evidence to convict me? That depends on what the definition of "Catholic" is and, even more important, what practices—what daily, weekly, and lifelong actions and attitudes—really demonstrate one's being Catholic. Being a Jesuit priest, celebrating the sacraments and presiding at the liturgical rites of the church, teaching in a Jesuit university, having lived and worked for fif-teen years as a member of the Jesuit Urban Ser-vice Team in North Camden, New Jersey, may seem to make it easy for me to assert and defend my claim to be Catholic. If I'm not Catholic, who is?

> *"If I were accused of being Catholic, would there be enough evidence to convict me?"*

But authentic Catholicism is elusive and difficult for intelligent, thinking people to define. Both "cranky conservatives" and "loose liber-als" may have their litmus tests, but true and vibrant Catholicism, a full and flexible practice of the faith, has always had a healthy respect for the mystery of each and every human person. Each and every one of us is a locus of freedom, and we must freely choose to be who and what we are, and are becoming. Ever since Jesus spoke to the woman caught in adul-tery (John 8:1–11) and Zacchaeus (Luke 19:1–10), the church has had (or ought to have had) deep trust in the processes of conversion and a reluctance to champion itself or its members as the sinless elect, able to easily condemn and judge others. On the other hand, ever since Jesus told the parable of the judgment of the nations (Matthew 25:31–46), it has been clear that we all share the duty to serve those in need, and that there are consequences for those who fail to do so. The Christian community formed by the baptized, the church, has the privilege and power to proclaim the good news that God loves us, and the prophetic task of standing up to those who fail to love others. Prophets call for conversion and change on the part of those who oppress others.

## A Call to Conversion

Deeply reflecting on our Catholic faith, hopefully, will lead us to awareness, to consciousness, of the conversions God invites everyone to experience. Such conversions will ultimately lead us to living as authentic Catholics, persons practicing a full and flexible faith, persons who truly and operatively experience the reality of God in our lives. Such a relationship with God changes us, changes the ways we experience life, love, . . . everything! Being authentically Catholic affects the way we relate as men and women, as economic actors, as constructors of the cultures in which we live. Being Catholic calls us to continually grow in becoming, and in being, more and more converted persons, women and men who form communities wherein we know and love God and one another and express that love in outward, visible signs of worship and service. Full and flexible Catholicism, living Catholicism, breathes into us the Spirit of Jesus, making us happy and healthy and holy and free. Being Catholic means finding God in all the realities of our lives. In words attributed to Pedro Arrupe, SJ, the former superior general of the Society of Jesus:

> Nothing is more practical than finding God, that is, than falling in love in a quite absolute, final way. What you are in love with, what seizes your imagination, will affect everything. It will decide what will get you out of bed in the morning, what you do with your evenings, how you spend your weekends, what you read, who you know, what breaks your heart, and what amazes you with joy and gratitude. Fall in love, stay in love, and it will decide everything.

Conversion is all about falling in love, about being in love, about staying in love. Conversion occurs at different times and on different levels. That is why it is so difficult and dangerous to judge where others are on their journey toward God. It is truly difficult to examine and evaluate where we ourselves are in our own conversion processes. But, just because something is difficult does not mean we should shirk from attempting it. After all, if we can master computers, the exploration of the galaxies, the mysteries of modern medicine, and the incredible dynamics of quantum physics, we should feel some confidence in tackling an even greater challenge: the understanding of how we operate as human beings, and of how we are called to fashion ourselves, our communities, and our cultures according to the norms inherent in the functioning of our own hearts and minds. Such understanding will convert us in ways we can hardly imagine at the start of the journey. Following the lead of Jesuit theologian Bernard Lonergan, subsequent chapters explore the revelations communicated in the way our hearts and minds operate, revelations of who and what we are and ought to be, how we can judge the degree to which we are living our lives authentically, and the degrees to which our cultures are authentic.

### Conversion and Culture

Conversion is profoundly influenced by cultural realities. Becoming culturally conscious will serve the members of the Catholic Church well as we strive to live as true and committed Catholics, as Catholics searching for, and finding, the power and presence of the living God in our midst in the twenty-first century. Since culture so pervades and frames the perceptions of our minds and hearts, conversion is not easy when cultural realities undermine and militate against gospel values and practices. Still, freely entering into and undergoing the rigors and realities of transformations on spiritual and cultural levels may lead us to be more than we ever imagined we could be. We may become a rose.

## The Yellow Flower and the Rose

*Once upon a time, there was a garden. All the flowers in the garden were competing to see which one would be the prettiest. One very beautiful Yellow Flower, a rather immature and conceited flower, woke up one morning and announced to all the other flowers that she was going to become a rose. A hush came over the other flowers, because for a flower to claim that she wants to be a rose is a very serious matter, since everyone knows that, without a doubt, the Rose is the most beautiful flower of all.*

*This Yellow Flower, which claimed to want to be a rose, fluffed her petals, turned to the morning sun and evening waters, and spoke her case. She asked to be turned into a rose. The sun and water listened and smiled benignly and decided to respond to the immature and conceited Yellow Flower's delusions of grandeur. They recognized that she knew little about becoming and being a rose.*

*The sun sent a bush to be planted next to the immature and conceited Yellow Flower. At first, the bush was nothing more than a bundle of bare branches, stuck in a heap of pungent manure. The Yellow Flower cursed the stench and wailed that her fragrance would be marred by the bush's smell. Then waters came and turned the manure into a stinky, sodden, sickening mess. Then the branches of the bush sprouted thorns, ugly and sharp thorns. The Yellow Flower felt quite superior to her neighbor, the poor, ugly, thorny bush. The Yellow Flower ridiculed the thorns of the bare bush and told all the other flowers to have nothing to do with her.*

*By and by, the bare bush, covered with jagged and grotesque thorns and rooted deep in the sticky and smelly manure, sprouted a little bud. The Yellow Flower looked on curiously and with growing fright as the bud blossomed into a beautiful Rose. The Yellow Flower experienced many different emotions as the Rose became recognized by all the other flowers as the most beautiful flower the garden had ever seen.*

*At last the Yellow Flower swallowed her pride and spoke to the Rose, asking how she too could become a beautiful rose. The Rose looked at her kindly, and gently told her this truth: A flower cannot blossom and be truly beautiful unless she roots herself in manure and bears the humiliation of her thorns.*

One way of realizing one is not yet a rose is to look at the somewhat un-aromatic aspects of one's community and world. Throughout this book, I'll be referring to information about our culture(s) and society, information taken mostly from readily accessible sources (e.g., best sellers, common college textbooks, popular magazines, and easily accessible websites). I want the reader to know that most of the information found here is not hidden away in obscure academic journals, or posted only on arcane, erudite websites. Such problems as economic inequality, sexist practices, and racism both personal and institutional are well known to a few but ignored by many. Too often we fail to pay attention to social problems and how our practice of the faith fails to address these issues. Practicing a full and flexible Catholicism encourages and entails one's facing up to the realities of aspects in both our personal and social lives that contradict the gospel. Such realities call us to conversion. On the feast of Christ the King, we pray, "As king he claims dominion over all creation, that he may present to you, his almighty Father… a kingdom of truth and life, a kingdom of holiness and grace, a kingdom of justice, love and peace" (Preface for the Feast of Christ the King). To be Catholic is to live and serve in ways that make the reign of God more operative in our lives.

In this book I'm speaking mainly to Catholics and those who want to be Catholic. I in no way intend to denigrate or deny the ways in which God works in other communions, faiths, or religions. I simply want to stress some aspects of the Catholic faith that too often have been muted by our times and culture. Much of what I'm saying here could apply to any part of the world. Still, given who and what I am, in this work, I concentrate on the practicing of Catholicism in the United States. In the year 2006, according to the BBC news, some 66.3 million people or roughly 22 percent of the population identified themselves as Catholic. The Catholic Church in the United States was one of the very few religious bodies to evidence a double-digit increase in membership in the 1990s (Glenmary Research Center 2002). More than two decades ago, in the conclusion of their magisterial study of mainline religions in the United States, Wade Clark Roof and William McKinney wrote:

> Partly because of the elevated social position of Catholics, partly because of the changes following Vatican II, partly because of Protestantism's weakened hold on the culture, the American Catholic church has entered into a new and fuller involvement in national affairs. Always involved in "Catholic" issues (e.g., birth control, immigration policy, rights of working people), the new activism and visibility of Catholic bishops on issues of nuclear disarmament and economic justice signals a shift toward greater public participation in issues facing the entire national

community. *The Catholic church appears to us to be in its best position ever to assume a custodial role for American culture at large.* (Roof and McKinney 1987:237; italics added)

The same year in which Roof and McKinney's study was published, Richard John Neuhaus, no "liberal" Catholic, argued in *The Catholic Moment* that the late twentieth century was the time for the Roman Catholic Church to be "the lead church in proclaiming and exemplifying the Gospel" (Neuhaus 1987:283). Neuhaus argued that the main crisis confronting the age is one of unbelief, and the Roman Catholic Church's seizing the moment would make more probable the triumph of freedom and justice over the forces of slavery and tyranny in the world (Neuhaus 1987:286–87). The esteemed Jesuit sociologist John Coleman noted that, along with Neuhaus, Martin Marty and Robert Bellah also recognized that the time was ripe for "just such a new Catholic moment in American history" (Coleman 1988:245). All along the continuum, two decades ago, articulate observers were calling for the Catholic Church to take the lead in the direction of the cultural currents of our times.

Almost twenty years later, in the wake of the clergy sex scandals of 2002, the church in the United States is far from fulfilling the promise of directing the cultural currents of our age. In 2006, the Catholic Church in this country claimed some 69 million members, 23 percent of the population (Kenedy and Sons 2006). But an American Religious Identification Survey in 2001 found 56 million declaring themselves to be Catholic, while another 9.5 million reported that they had "left the Church" (Grossman 2002:5D). Greeley finds that 34 percent of people in the United States are raised Catholic, but only 25 percent remain so throughout their lives (Greeley 2004:100).

So, of the present 69 million Catholics, how many are deeply connected to the church? The ubiquitous term "Recovering Catholic" poses more than a challenge to the Catholic Church. The fact that the church has such a weak and tenuous hold on so many of its members intimates that the church's effectiveness as an institution, working to ameliorate social conditions in the United States and in the world, is in jeopardy. The clergy sex abuse scandals of the past decades have made the difficult task of attracting alienated Catholics immeasurably more arduous. Despite the shame and horror of the scan-

"Be what you is, because if you ain't what you is, you is what you ain't."

(Words of wisdom from an inner city street man)

dals, Jenkins (1996) and others have demonstrated that the number of priest pedophiles is a small percentage of the clergy. In 2004, the National Review Board reported that 4 percent of Catholic clergy, 4,392 priests out of 109,694, had been "accused of engaging in sexual abuse of a minor" between 1950 and 2002 (National Review Board 2004:11). According to some experts, that is a lower rate than exists in the general population of American males. Attorney L. Martin Nussbaum reports that the rates of sexual abuse of children in public institutions such as schools, foster homes, and juvenile detention centers is much worse than (his word is "dwarfs") anything seen in Catholic parishes and schools (Nussbaum 2006). Still, the scandals have understandably caused an as yet undetermined amount of disaffection, distrust, and disgust among both Catholics and non-Catholics.

Even more, the failure of the bishops of the church to deal with sexual predators and abusers among the clergy has caused incalculable harm to the church's prestige and credibility. There exists a crisis of leadership in the Catholic Church that undermines people's ability to believe and decreases the authority church teachings enjoy both among Catholics and non-Catholics. The bishops' consistent and courageous stand against George W. Bush's war with Iraq, and their well researched and well presented prophetic pronouncements on issues as diverse as the criminal justice system and issues relating to immigration have a hard time getting a hearing when district attorneys and grand juries in Boston and Philadelphia make front page news with their exposés of bishops' gross failures in confronting priests guilty of crimes.

## A Call to Heroism

I want to make a case that, despite the recent scandals, the following of Christ as a Catholic in the twenty-first century, truly practicing a full and flexible Catholicism, is ultimately more than simply a meaningful way to live our lives. The vast majority of priests are men who live holy and generous lives. Such priests and the thousands and thousands of sisters and lay men and women who sacrifice their lives to staff Catholic schools and hospitals and social service agencies are the basic reality of the Catholic Church. The millions who practice the faith should know what these servants of the Lord already realize: our lives as Catholics should call us to heroism.

I think that today Christianity is in trouble not because its myths are dead, but because it does not offer its ideal of heroic sainthood as an immediate personal one to be lived by all believers. In a perverse way, the churches have turned their backs both on the miraculousness of creation *and* on the need to do something heroic in this world. The early promise of Christianity was to bring about once and for all the social justice that the ancient world was crying for; Christianity never fulfilled this promise, and is as far from it today as ever. No wonder it has trouble taking itself seriously as a hero system. (Becker 1975:164)

What we are about as Catholics living a faith that frees is immersing ourselves in the processes of becoming and being heroes. The nuns and lay teachers who tutor antsy little kids on sweaty, hot, inner city summer afternoons are heroes. Two parents struggling to keep their marriage alive and vibrant as they care for three children, one in a wheelchair, are heroes. Businesspeople trying to marshal the powers of the economy to eradicate poverty and make a world more just for all are heroes. Those laboring to demolish inequality, racism, and sexism in our society and in our hearts are heroes. Those teaching rambunctious teenagers in confirmation classes, visiting the aged, and bringing the Eucharist to those in hospitals are heroes. These heroes step out of the boat like Peter and walk on water.

You, in whatever you do with your life, can be in relationship to God and others in a heroic manner. Such heroism may not be noticed. It will often go unrewarded and be underpaid. Nevertheless, such heroic responses to Christ's invitation to follow him (Mark 10:21) lead to the conversion of our hearts and minds and the transformation of our world. A full and flexible following of Jesus can make us heroic persons who are transformed by our faith and thus usher forth in our world the kingdom inaugurated and proclaimed by Jesus Christ. The faith of heroic people is not simply about what they believe, or what they think and feel. It's more than that. As Dan Berrigan, SJ, once said: "Your faith is rarely where your head is at and rarely where you heart is at. Your faith is where your ass is at! Inside what commitments are you sitting? Within what reality do you anchor yourself?" (Rolheiser 2002:6). We demonstrate our faith by where we are, by what we are, and by what we do. In that lies the quiet, daily heroism of our lives.

A faith that frees does not concentrate on the "pelvic issues" that have caused so much controversy in Catholic circles, but these issues do enter into any broad discussion of matters pertaining to faith. Even though I think God is much more concerned with what happens in corporate boardrooms than with what happens in our bedrooms, I recognize that both venues are arenas within which grace and dis-grace can abound. Given the fact that so much of Catholic sexual teaching is ignored (85 percent of U.S. Catholics ignore the teachings on artificial means of birth control [Greeley 2004:73]) and that scandals perpetrated by Catholic priests were too often swept under the rug by clueless Catholic bishops, we must admit that the church's credibility in matters pertaining to sex is at an all-time low. A frank and forthright discussion of sexuality is urgently needed throughout the church. In the final chapter of this book I extrapolate from the meaning and messages of Catholicism what a sane and sensible sexuality could look like when viewed through the lens of cultural anthropology. A full and flexible Catholicism will avoid the extremes of a nasty, judgmental legalism in matters sexual, while maintaining a clear gospel challenge to the sexual ethic underlying the messages communicated in those parts of contemporary culture devoted to a heated hedonism and idiosyncratic individualism. Jesus truly does not want us to live our lives according to the mores of movies like *American Pie* and websites like *drunkuniversity.com* or *collegehumor.com*. Still, we may hope for as much flexibility and respect for a Catholic's individual choices in matters sexual as we allow for in matters economic, assuming of course that such choices are informed by a responsible conscience.

Pedro Arrupe, SJ, once characterized our global community as "A Planet to Heal." The practice of a full and flexible Catholicism offers an alternative to a twenty-first-century, postmodern world that has lost its bearings and harmed too many of our brothers and sisters on this planet. Our contemporary weakened social institutions and crumbling cultures too little teach us how to be truly human, and therefore undercut the probability of our lives being a journey through transcendence unto union with God. By revitalizing and reinvigorating the practices of the Catholic faith in this new millennium, we can chart a course through the turbulent currents and rough waters of our times. There is safe harbor. Our God wants to lead us to those tranquil waters, in the same way God

"The Christian lives by love and, therefore, by freedom."
(Merton 1961:182)

led the Israelites out of slavery into the Promised Land. But in order to negotiate the distance between slavery and freedom, we must carefully choose and discerningly direct the conscious, deliberate patterns of our personal and social lives. Ultimately, our ships are not meant for dry land or safe harbors. We are invited to sail forth on high seas and even walk on water in order to convert our world and ourselves more and more into the pilgrim people of God, striving to serve Christ's mission.

# 2
# Catholicism Is *Not* for Dummies
## *Culturally Conscious Conversion*

*"Progress is a nice word. But change is its motivator, and change has its enemies."*
   —Robert F. Kennedy

Catholicism is not for Dummies! Conversion is not for ignorant wimps. Contemporary cultural conundrums call us to be intelligent and astute as we practice a full and flexible Catholicism in the twenty-first century. To be authentic Roman Catholics at the dawn of this new millennium will necessitate personal and institutional conversion on the intellectual, moral, and religious levels. Such conversion is not easy, nor can such conversion be mandated or reduced to simple formulaic lists of rules. Proverbial "dos" and "don'ts" are inadequate. Authentic conversion must be ongoing and progressive if the faith we profess and strive to enact is to survive and flourish in human hearts and minds and communities. The reasons why such ongoing conversion is crucial are both simple and complex. Simply stated, it is obvious that cultural change today occurs at a pace and depth never before experienced by human beings, and cultural change necessitates conversion.

Catholicism is a pathway to God and walking that path necessitates conversion, a *metanoia* from slavery to freedom, from inauthenticity to authenticity. Bernard Lonergan sees that those who are open and honest move from conversion on the intellectual level (Is it true?) to the moral level (Is it good?) to the religious level (Is it loving?). Lonergan argues that the converted are better able to discern the direction in which communities ought to move. Converted persons and communities will have to sift through the various theoretical paradigms available and consider and choose according to a clearly defined and articulated method for discerning and choosing things both material and spiritual. Creative and authentic conversion will have to be culturally conscious conversion in the minds and hearts of all people of good will, especially prayerfully committed Catholics.

Such conversions will not be easy for those who are used to, or desire, a simple, never-changing Catholicism. But, the days of "pay, pray, and obey" Catholicism are long gone. Catholicism was born and grew in an agricultural world wherein news traveled slowly and things changed at a snail's pace. We live in a world where this morning is ancient history and choices must be made with an eye to a future filled with ever more unpredictable and rapid social and cultural transformations. Catholicism was fashioned in a world where new information arrived slowly and was digested over centuries. We live in a world were we are bombarded by literally thousands of bits of information each day, and the flood of information flows across the planet at the speed of light. Early missionaries could float on a boat for months, or walk for weeks, to get to their destination. We can get in a plane and be on the other side of the globe in less than a day. Catholicism was articulated over centuries in worlds where elites could control the flow of images and symbols. Today, mass media and the Internet have erupted as prime constructors of our symbol systems and communal imaginations. In the twenty-first century, anyone with a computer and a web page can produce and promulgate his or her own views on literally any aspect of the Catholic faith. In our own personal lives we experience this often unsettling and startlingly new rate of cultural change.

> *Item one:* A few years ago, my parish church—the church building in which I was raised in the faith, where I received First Communion, where as a boy I first served Mass, where I said my first Mass as a priest—was to be remodeled. This elicited fierce opposition from older parishioners. Many who had been there for years did not want the pastor "messing with the church." In one memorable exchange with the pastor, an Irishman asked in a rich brogue he'd never lost after four decades in this country, "Tell me, Father, how long have you been here at Our Mother of Good Counsel?" The pastor replied, "Seven years." "Well, Father, I've been here forty. You'll be gone in a few years, and I'll still be here. You have no right to destroy my church." After the work

was finished, I went to the eucharistic liturgy celebrating the re-modeling. The interior "worship space" had been completely re-done, beautifully and radically, according to the latest dictates of liturgists and church architects. But I have to admit that it was, and is, a bit disconcerting to no longer be able to enter and sit in the church I remember from my childhood. That church interior is gone forever.

*Item two:* During a confirmation ceremony, a bishop asks the young teens how many sacraments there are. One of those to be confirmed replies, "Seven for men and six for women." Conservative Catholics may try to ignore one of the key revolutions of the twentieth century, the transformation of women's roles and positions in society, but ignoring reality has never advanced the cause of Catholicism. Many college educated, liberal Catholics too easily assume that all in the pews really want what elite feminists and academics desire. But, even though most Catholics are not willing to go to the wall over women's ordination, the days of treating women as second-class citizens in the church are long gone. The plummeting vocations to women's religious orders (from 179,954 in 1965 to 67,773 [Kenedy and Sons 2006]) are clear evidence that women will not give their lives to a church that relegates them to subservient status.

*Item three:* In 1968, Pope Paul VI issued *Humanae Vitae*, an encyclical in which he went against the recommendation of his own commission and reiterated the church's traditional stance against the use of artificial means of birth control. In the encyclical, the pope warned that the use of the pill and other contraceptive devices would create a contraceptive mentality, severely harming the human family, especially women. Today a vast majority of Catholics observe the church's teachings on sexual morality, if they do at all, "cafeteria style," picking what they wish and leaving the rest. The teaching authority of the church on matters sexual has become ineffectual at best, a joke at worst. The clergy scandals have devastated the credibility of the church on anything having to do with sex. In my years of ordained ministry, I've only rarely been asked about the church's teaching on the use of artificial means of birth control.

I've heard many more agonizing questions about the atrocious priest pedophile scandals.

*Item four:* The United States Catholic bishops' pastoral letters on peace (1981) and the economy (1986) received mixed receptions among U.S. Catholics. Mostly, American Catholics have little awareness of the pastorals and less, if any, understanding of the biblical, philosophical, and theological basis on which the pastorals challenge North American culture. At St. Joseph's University in Philadelphia, I once preached on the principles articulated in the 1986 pastoral letter on the economy, *Economic Justice for All*. It was during the mid-1990s debate on welfare reform, and the gospel for that Sunday was the beatitudes from the sixth chapter of Luke: "Blessed are you poor; woe to you that are rich." One student strode out in the middle of the homily and wrote a strident letter to the school paper denouncing me, claiming that I had abused the privilege of the pulpit because I dared to side with the Gospel of St. Luke instead of the opinions of Rush Limbaugh. I responded with a letter quoting the bishops' document *Salt and Light*, which clearly instructs priests to connect in the Sunday homily the gospel's message with contemporary issues of social justice.

*Item five:* Most young Catholics have a meager grasp of the contents of the gospels, let alone the rest of the Bible. But they do have "scriptures." With a group of college students from Saint Joseph's University, I spend a spring break working to build houses in the Appalachian mountains near Neon, Kentucky. For eight days, the CD player runs constantly. All the college students can immediately recognize virtually hundreds of songs on hearing little more than a tune's first three notes. They know not only their own music but also the "oldies." "I did it my way" is Frank Sinatra's signature, and every college student knows it. To hear "Everybody in old cell block / was dancing to the Jailhouse Rock" makes Elvis present. To say "Yesterday" immediately conjures the Beatles song. "It's five o'clock on a Saturday / the regular crowd shuffles in," and we're with Billy Joel. Gloria Estefan, Mariah Carey, Boyz to Men, on and on: these troubadours are contemporary evangelists. The songs are scripture. Students who cannot name the four gospels, let alone recognize scriptural quotations or even biblical allusions, know immediately, without any studying for the test, who sang what, and when. They know all the words. And those words carry messages and meanings intimately related to feelings. What's more, the students know all my baby boomer generation's tunes, but I have little awareness of the songs of the 1990s and 2000s that fill their consciousnesses. Everyone laughs when I express surprise at learning that the group Bare Naked Ladies of "If I had a million dollars" fame is composed of three guys.

All five items can be understood as examples of cultural conundrums. A cultural conundrum is a "paradoxical, insoluble, or difficult problem; a dilemma" in the cultural sphere. How to remodel older churches, how to respond to the challenges of women's transforming roles in society, how to encourage Catholics to enflesh the church's teachings on sexual morality, how to call Catholics to put into practice church teachings on social justice, how to get young people really familiar with scripture, are all cultural problems without clear-cut, simple solutions.

*"Trying to solve cultural conundrums by theological fiat is like trying to cure dandruff by pronouncing 'Rome does not allow it.'"*

Trying to solve cultural conundrums by theological fiat is like trying to cure dandruff by pronouncing "Rome does not allow it." Trying to connect the rich heritage of Catholicism with contemporary cultural changes happening at the speed of light is often like trying to herd cats backward. Item number one, remodeling a church, deals with power and authority, especially power and authority over matters of aesthetics and taste, realities filled through and through with deeply felt cultural assumptions. Item number two, the ordination of women, evidences the profound shifts of meaning around the realities of gender and what it means to be male and female in society. Item number three, artificial means of birth control, deals with adaptation to cultural change and the clash of cultural values that occurs when technology changes how humans go about fundamental ways of doing things. Item number four, the impact of bishops' pastoral letters, deals with how the church effectively operates in a complex society, while trying to influence that society and form it in the light of Catholic teachings. Item number five, popular culture's effects, looks at what exactly runs through the hearts and minds of contemporary people, to what words, images, and songs folks actually pay attention. All five items are examples of cultural issues confronting and confounding church ministers and members. Theological pronouncements will not settle such problems. Only conversion, and conversion consciously aware of the relationships that constitute culture, can help us here. Catholicism calls for understanding, creating, and enacting cultural conversion.

Conversion results in authentic living. Authentic Catholics will lead the way in addressing the pressing issues facing the church in this century. To grasp and respond to cultural conundrums we need to know what the problems actually are. What is it that truly threatens us?

### What Is Really Going on in Contemporary Church Battles

We are dealing with greater and deeper and more rapid cultural change than at any time in human history. I doubt the thought of women priests ever crossed my grandmother's mind, yet I know my mother has to explain to her granddaughters why women cannot be priests. For the first time in the forty-thousand-year history of *Homo sapiens sapiens,* the control of natural processes like birth is possible, and, with genetic engineering and right to die movements, we haven't seen the tip of the iceberg of this revolution. These are huge changes, and such changes affect many aspects of culture. All these cultural changes, with their astonishing speed and depth, affect theological understandings of humankind's relationship with God. Churches that have stood unchanged for centuries need new ways to think about change and new cultural practices with which to respond to the cultural transformations happening at rates faster and at more levels than at any time in human history. Church communities must consciously choose how and why they will be what they are in relationship to these overwhelming and swift cultural currents in which we, they, and all else swirl.

*"Actually, most theological debates today are not about theological problems at all."*

Actually, most theological debates today are not about theological problems at all. We rarely get into heated arguments concerning whether the Holy Spirit proceeds from the Father and the Son, or just the Father. Rarely do we argue the distinction between the supernatural and the natural. Our battles have to do with how we actually act on the tenets of the faith we do hold in common. We do not argue about abolishing priesthood (a theological issue). We do argue over the exclusion of women from ordination (a cultural issue). We little argue over whether God desires social justice (a theological issue); yet we are quite at sea over what social justice actually is, in other words, how much everyone ought to receive and what the rules of distribution ought to be (cultural issues). We do not have knock-down drag-out fights over what we mean theologically by "real presence." But we do agonize over whether to tell our best friend at the wedding that she should not receive communion. The exclusion of someone from the table of the Lord may make sense theologically, but culturally it feels offensive and exclusionary.

Our arguments are about the *practices of the faith*, and often such arguments about practices betray deep confusion about the theological meanings of such practices and the appropriate cultural expressions of those meanings. At their roots, much of what we term theological problems today are cultural problems, problems of practice, problems that result from rapid, confusing cultural change. As one Jesuit commenting on another Jesuit's liturgical style once said, "I'm not sure if what Fr. Jones is doing is wrong, or if I just don't like it."

Cultural change lies at the heart of most problems, or conundrums, facing Catholics as we enter the new millennium. As we cross the threshold of the third millennium, most theological battles are really rooted in confusions about deep cultural changes never before confronted by the human race. No other humans ever had to deal with changes like electric light, atomic weapons, the ubiquitous presence of television with the coded messages contained in its advertising, a capitalist system infiltrating and formatting every aspect of human relationships, computers collapsing centuries-old distinctions of time and space, an ever increasing population, and a radically new issue, the large percentage of the elderly in society. All of this is occurring at a time when we are learning more about Jesus and his times than any previous generation of Christians ever imagined knowing (e.g., Chilton 2000; Crossan 1995; Horsley and Silberman 1997; Malina 2001; Pilch 1995, 1996, 1997, 2002; Wright 1997).

The cultural and sociological changes in the Roman Catholic Church in the United States in the past quarter century have been seismic. Look at some of the numbers from *The Official Catholic Directory* (Kenedy and Sons 1965, 1985, 2006):

|                                              | 1965         | 1985         | 2006         |
|----------------------------------------------|--------------|--------------|--------------|
| Catholics in the USA                         | 45.6 million | 52.2 million | 69.1 million |
| % of Population of USA                       | 24%          | 22.5%        | 23%          |
| Parishes                                     | 17,367       | 19,244       | 18,992       |
| Grade Schools                                | 10,931       | 7,957        | 6,511        |
| # of grade school pupils                     | 4,566,809    | 2,162,955    | 1,762,401    |
| High Schools                                 | 2,465        | 1,425        | 1,354        |
| # of high school pupils                      | 1,095,519    | 794,028      | 679,506      |
| Catholic Colleges and Universities           | 304          | 242          | 231          |
| # of students in those universities          | 384,526      | 549,540      | 763,757      |
| Catholic Hospitals                           | 952          | 731          | 965          |
| # of patients treated annually               | 17 million   | 37 million   | 91 million   |
| Number of Priests                            | 58,132       | 57,317       | 42,271       |
| Total Seminarians                            | 48,992       | 11,028       | 5,642        |
| Sisters in Religious Orders                  | 179,954      | 115,386      | 67,773       |
| Brothers in Religious Orders                 | 12,271       | 7,544        | 5,252        |
| Permanent Deacons                            | none         | 7,204        | 14,995       |
| Converts/ Accepted into Full Communion       | 126,209      | 91,750       | 73,684       |

Notice that in 1965 there were 48,992 seminarians preparing for priesthood; by 2006, there were only 5,642. Peter Steinfels reports that in 1965 there was one priest for every eight hundred Catholics; by 2002, one for every fourteen hundred. Priests are aging. In 1965, almost 50 percent of diocesan priests were under forty-five years of age. In 2002 only 20 percent were under forty-five. In 1965 there were 994 priests ordained; in 2002 only 479. In 1965 Catholics gave 2.2 percent of their income to the church. By 2002 that had decreased 50 percent to 1.1 percent of income. In 1965, there were virtually no lay persons working full time as pastoral ministers. By 2002 there were fourteen thousand lay people serving in full-time ministry (Steinfels 2003:28–29).

## Culture Shock

Cultural anthropologists describe the experience of being suddenly thrust into another cultural world as "culture shock." I began informally studying cultural anthropology during my years of training as a Jesuit priest. Between my study of philosophy and theology, in the early 1980s, I was sent to teach English and religion in Osorno, Chile, a small city in the southern part of the country. While I was there, I ran head-on into cultural differences, culture shock, and how deeply culture permeates our being. The mastering of the Spanish language takes a lifetime. Proficiency takes at least a year. Until you have tried to teach a class of fifty high school sophomores using a second language in which you are barely competent, you never fully realize the simple joy of having the ability to speak and use a language well.

In my first week at Colegio San Mateo, I was conducting an English class. The phrase the boys were learning was, "We are going to play in the field." What I should have said in explaining the phrase in Spanish was, "*Vamos a jugar en la cancha.*" Instead, I mispronounced the word "*cancha*," replacing the first "a" in "*cancha*" with an "o." Doing so transformed the word "*cancha*" to "*concha*" (literally shell), the grossest "dirty" word in Chilean Spanish. "*Concha*" refers to the female genitalia. I had just told fifty thirteen-year-old boys, "We are going to play in the female sexual organs." The boys were rolling in the aisles laughing, yelling, "*No, Meester, no! Nunca Diga eso!*" ("No, Mister, no! Don't ever say that!"). Language creates and permeates culture. To understand what is happening to us we have to understand the words we use and their effects on us and others.

Culture shock comes in many ways, both large and small. What is "normal" and "given" in one's home culture is repugnant and unacceptable in another. In Chile, eggs are prepared by filling the bottom of a skillet with a quarter inch of cooking oil and heating the oil. Eggs are then cracked and floated on the oil to cook. Frankly, I found the eggs in Chile to be really a pretty greasy affair, and I avoided eating them if I could. I had always put a little dab of butter in a pan and, when it melted, added the eggs. One weekend, I took a group of twenty high school kids, all juniors and seniors, to a rustic retreat house. For dinner, we had planned to cook up some eggs and *tallerines* (spaghetti). We had forgotten to pack the oil and were nowhere near a store. So I cooked up the eggs using butter. The boys didn't say anything, but they were exchanging apprehensive looks. The kids gobbled up the *tallerines*, but barely touched the eggs. Later, a few of the guys informed me that cooking eggs with butter just seemed wrong to the group. One other suggestion for getting along in Chile: never use the word for egg, *huevo*. There are endless double entendres connected to the image of the egg (e.g., testicle, etc.) that give Chileans endless mirth as clueless gringos order breakfast.

The poverty of Chile had a deep impact on me. I would walk through the nearby *población* and talk with families who lived in small *hogar de Cristo* houses: small, four-wooden-walled, zinc roofed shacks, about eight feet high by fifteen feet wide and twenty feet long. I had seen poverty in the United States, but nothing on the scale of the poverty that existed in Latin America in the 1980s. Still, when I asked about the causes of poverty in Chile, middle- to upper-class Chileans would sometimes downplay the matter. "That's just the way it is." "*Qué lastima* [what a shame], but there is little that can really be done about it," was the resigned attitude among some. Yet Chileans would often ask about racism in the United States. For me with my cultural background, poverty was a more pressing issue than racism. For the Chileans, racism in the United States seemed a much greater affront to the just order of things on a vast scale than did poverty (even though I did and do care deeply about eradicating racism in the United States, and the vast majority of Chileans would sincerely love to eradicate poverty in their midst). Maybe my perceptions and attitudes would have been different had I been an African American from the United States. Maybe the middle- to upper-class Chileans' attitudes and perceptions would have been different if they themselves had lived in the *poblaciones*.

The years I was in Chile, 1981–1984, saw the last attempts of General Pinochet to brutally impose his will on the Chilean people. Torture reached such epidemic proportions in the early 1980s in Chile that the bishops of the Catholic Church excommunicated all those in the Chilean army and society who ordered, participated in, or simply knew about and did nothing to stop torture. Although Chileans were eventually able to throw off the shackles of this U.S. government placed and supported brutal dictator, the fact that Pinochet ruled and terrorized from 1973 until the late 1980s made me face the fact that "the bad guys can win," at least for a long while. Moving from Chile to theology studies in Cambridge, Massachusetts, I was filled with questions as to why a good God would allow such ongoing evil to triumph. And I was forced to question what I was to do about my government in the United States that so routinely supported and taught the dictators of Latin America.

In January 2006, it was a deep consolation to millions to see a woman elected president of Chile. During the 1970s Michelle Bachelet, like thousands of other Chileans, had been imprisoned and tortured under Pinochet's dictatorship. Her father had been killed by Pinochet's army. Eventually she had been forced into exile with her family. On March, 11, 2006, Chile celebrated her inauguration. She is the first woman directly elected president of a Latin American country. Still, even though by 2006 Pinochet was a ruined old man and one of his victims now occupied his position of power, the suffering and pain of so many Chileans—and of so many millions who suffer poverty, injustice, terror, and genocide—force us to ask how we as a church are to respond. How we are to feel and what we are to do about situations as diverse and confusing as Rwanda, Darfur, and Iraq? This is a question we all must confront. Feeling at a loss and unable to respond adequately is a subtle sign of cultural confusion.

Over time, as I reflected on my three years in Chile, on the simple cultural differences, the experiences of attitudes toward poverty and racism, toward overt governmental corruption and torture, I began to wonder if some of the cultural differences that are so apparent when we are thrust into a totally "other" culture are not in fact also operating in less conspicuous, less conscious manners in the complex societies we all live in "at home." I wonder if many pre–Vatican II Catholics (and those appropriating the pre–Vatican II traditions in the present) are still experiencing some mild (or extreme) form of culture shock four decades after Vatican II. The cultural world of the pre–Vatican II era was seemingly more stable, more easily engaged and understood, and changed much more slowly than the cultural world(s) we inhabit at the end of the second millennium.

Culture shock is much more pervasive and difficult to address and change through rational analysis than what Radcliffe refers to as "root shock" (Radcliffe 2005:169). Root shock is when one's "emotional ecosystem" is in disarray due to the machinations of outside forces, like a city building a highway through

> "The arc of the moral universe is long, but it bends toward justice."
> —Martin Luther King, Jr.

your neighborhood (as happened to Camden, New Jersey, when Route 676 was built, splitting the city in half and destroying neighborhoods and property values). Culture shock occurs when one's and a community's most deeply held meanings and values are misunderstood, ignored, devalued, and/or abandoned. Culture shock is obvious when one is flown halfway round the world and plunged into another culture. The shock is more subtle and erosive when brought on by deep, rapid, and constant cultural change in one's and a community's life history.

As a post–Vatican II Catholic, I have experienced constant change through virtually all my religious life. Born in 1955, I was among the first group of altar boys in my parish who did not have to learn Latin. Throughout my school years, the practices of the church had been in flux: in grade school, we had guitar masses with "Sons of God, Hear His Holy Word"; in high school, Simon and Garfunkel's "Bridge Over Troubled Waters" was a must for all post-communion moments. During freshman year at Jesuit-run St. Joe's Prep in Philadelphia, we read the documents of Vatican II and demythologized the Bible. In sophomore year we studied the Dutch Catechism. During junior year we listened to Webber and Rice's *Jesus Christ Superstar* and studied other religions. In senior year we studied the psychology of religion and sacraments and broached the topic of marriage. Entering the Society of Jesus in 1976, I became a Jesuit at the moment the order was rearticulating our mission as "the service of faith, of which the promotion of justice is an absolute requirement" (Society of Jesus, 32). During the twelve years of preparation for ordination as a Jesuit priest, I saw liberation theology rise and fall out of favor with some, feminist theologies come and go with even fewer adherents, and the emergence of a virulent, vindictive conservatism on the part of a very small, but influential, minority of Catholics in a movement grasping for a tenuous foothold in the U.S. church. But for most people in the pews, these storms came and went with little comprehension or, frankly, much interest. John Paul II's steady and charismatic leadership, and the U.S. bishops walking a quiet, middle pathway between the extreme, loose liberal coalitions and cranky conservative groups have helped steer the institutional church through turbulent waters in the past quarter century.

Still, the ideological battles have taken their toll. Many mainstream Catholics are confused and wearied by the decades-old bickering and backbiting among the intelligentsia in the church. Most just don't pay attention anymore to the NCR (*National Catholic Reporter*) versus NCR

(*National Catholic Register*) battles. Fr. Timothy Radcliffe, OP, the former head of the Dominican order, argues it is time for what he terms "Kingdom Catholics" to reconcile with what he calls "Communion Catholics." Kingdom Catholics are those who read theologians like Rahner, Schillebeeckx, and Gutiérrez while Communion Catholics read von Balthasar and Ratzinger (Radcliffe 2005:166 ff.; 2006). According to Radcliffe, both groups have felt betrayed: Communion Catholics by the sea changes of Vatican II and Kingdom Catholics by the restorationist energies and successes of movements like Opus Dei. Some have taken to characterizing the split as *Gaudium et Spes* Catholics versus *Lumen Gentium* Catholics. Yet, while the battles have raged, a baby boomer generation (those born between 1946 and 1964) has come of age both theologically and, more important, religiously illiterate about the truths, meanings, and practices of the faith. Boomers not only do not know any *theology*; they no longer know the *practices of the faith*. The boomers' children, the tattooed, pierced, and cynical Generations "X" and "Y," see the church and its claims as one more lifestyle option held up in a Cosmic Mall, an option you can purchase, consume, and discard when no longer wanted or found interesting. The boomers' youngest kids, the millennials, are even more difficult to describe, but there seems to be among them a significant contingent more open and committed to living the faith (Howe and Strauss 2000).

Even more erosive of Catholic vision, faith, and practice has been the juggernaut of an overly individualistic and materialistic U.S. culture. At Saint Joseph's University in Philadelphia, I teach Introduction to Sociology classes of anywhere from fifty to sixty students. When we get to the chapter on religion in society, I run a thought experiment. I ask the students, who are overwhelmingly at least nominally Catholic, "Would you take 'Catholic' off your resumé if the law firm where you want to get a job subtly communicated to you that you should tone down the fact that you attend Mass every Sunday and teach CCD? The lawyers would say to you: 'Look. We really want you in this law firm. $121,000 a year to start. Pick the color of your Beemer. You'll get two weeks a year at the firm's condo in Barbados. But there is one small glitch on your resumé here. You say you're a lector at your church and a member of your parish

> "Would you take 'Catholic' off your resumé if the law firm where you wanted to get a job subtly communicated to you that you should?"

council. We don't care what you do on Sundays if and when you're not needed here. Go to church. Get your kids baptized. But just don't mention it at work." Eighty percent of the students say they would drop the mention of Catholicism from their resume.

I find that appalling. Students who would gladly suffer crucifixion before giving up their allegiance to their favorite football team or music group will immediately drop overt public proclamation of their Catholicism, the religion in which most of them were confirmed several short years before. The students find religion to be simply a personal choice with no ramifications for a larger social context. Some argue, "I could still go to Mass. Nobody at the law firm has to know about it. Religion has nothing to do with what I do the rest of the week." Amazing. When I was their age, the great criticism of the church was that Sunday was too disconnected from what went on during the rest of the week. The cardinal sin for baby boomers was hypocrisy. For too many "Gen Xers," hypocrisy is "normal." In their experience, society's leaders cannot be trusted. The shortcomings and shenanigans of Bill Clinton, the crimes of Enron executives, the lies of George W. "weapons of mass destruction" Bush, and Catholic bishops shuttling predatory, pedophile priests from parish to parish do little to counter their youthful cynicism. But, before we too easily condemn these lukewarm members of our community, we need to remember that they are products of a time witnessing the deepest and most intense cultural change ever experienced by human beings. Meanings metamorphose at warp speed, and the felt sense of what is important, sacred, and of ultimate value changes every decade, if not every year.

## Meaning Meltdown

The result of this tidal wave of constant and ongoing cultural change and confusion washing over us has been what I am calling "meaning meltdown." Less and less do we know what the central realities of our Catholic faith mean. My grandmother knew exactly "what was what" in the Catholic Church. She knew the rituals and the rules, the stories of the faith and the practices one could perform to give meaning and spiritual sustenance to life. She knew the prayers one could say when and for what, and the saint to whom any prayer should be directed. "You lose something? Saint Anthony always works for me!" She knew which religious practices helped us cope with the tragedy and pain of human existence and which ones enabled us to express the celebration of life's joys. A rosary at a wake was a must. Midnight Mass was at Midnight, not 8:00 PM. Ascension Thursday was on Thursday, not on Sunday, and everyone knew the stories of the saint for whom they were named. For the immigrant and then "ghetto" Catholics, the Catholic faith was *THE* true faith which would never change, and the church was an institution that commanded respect, allegiance, and cooperation.

Their grandchildren live in another ecclesial universe. A friend a couple of years younger than myself, a lifelong Catholic, once called and cried as she spoke about a little neighbor boy who had died after a long battle with cancer. For her, it was a consolation to know he had died on August 15, the feast of the "Ascension." Ascension, Assumption . . . whatever, close enough for the "good enough Catholic." Her Irish immigrant grandmother had played the organ at their local parish church. For the grandmother, the differences between the feasts of the Ascension and the Assumption were as self-evident, well known, and important as the differences between K-Mart and Gap are for her granddaughter and great-granddaughters.

Meaning meltdown must be confronted by a concerted effort at creating (or, better said, re-creating), common meaning. Common meaning is not law that can be legislated and enforced, nor is common meaning the imposition of what I like on people who find my likes debatable to detestable. Common meaning is the struggle to find common ground around symbols, rituals, and religious realities in order that those symbols, rituals, and religious realities may enliven and empower us rather than leave us weary of the constant bickering and battling.

The creative, culturally conscious re-creation of common meaning is the only solution to the destructive polarities on the elite level and the gross ignorance on the popular level into which the church has descended. Getting to both those who want to impose a rigid uniformity of action and creed, and to those who see their Catholicism as being no more consequential than their choice of name brands, as well as getting to all those between the two extremes, necessitates having Catholics become "culturally conscious."

Becoming conscious of culture and how cultures play through the attitudes, world views, and choices churches and members make is not the same as a simplistic "multiculturalism." It is not enough to have diocesan celebrations where people appear in their traditional dress, petitions are prayed in several languages, and typical ethnic foods are shared at the reception following the Mass, as good as such exercises are. Becoming culturally conscious is striving to bring to awareness the reasons behind or beneath the multicultural celebrations. *We are all inhabiting many different cultures.* We are all multicultural, or, allow me to coin a neologism, "pluricultural," whether we realize it or not. I live in one culture at work, in another in my neighborhood at home, and in another when I interact with those who are radically different from me in outlook, attitude, and actions.

Culturally conscious Catholics will freely choose to be Catholic and will understand the implications of that choice and commitment. Adept disciples must be culturally conscious, that is, aware of the cultural components that affect our practice of Catholicism. Being culturally conscious enables us to navigate better the complex and confusing cultural changes occurring today. That means we will pay attention to and understand the cultural relationships that contour and configure our lives. Culturally conscious Catholics will be better able to prayerfully discern how to live out the gospel in different contexts and milieus.

Failure to become culturally conscious will result in an ever more confused community, a community mired in the morass of multiple, and, too often, contradictory meanings. Those who hear Jesus' call to serve our brothers and sisters living in poverty cannot both approve the machinations of unbridled capitalism and think capitalism will eliminate poverty. Those who live by the commandment "Thou shall not kill" cannot both condemn abortion and champion capital punishment. If one group of people in the church wants liturgical dance and another group wants people to kneel before receiving communion, there is a problem, made more painful because we do not all truly share common practices that express our meanings about Jesus Christ, priesthood, and authority in the church and gender roles in worship. But too often we argue over the legitimacy of liturgical dance, or

"The cultural environment associated with the latest era of capitalism, dominated as that environment is by the global culture industries, presents new and imposing barriers (beyond those of typical earlier eras) to the formation of deep religious convictions.... What is at risk is not any particular interpretation of the gospel or the tradition of the church but the capacity to think, feel and experience in ways formed by the Christian story."          (Budde 1997:15) the importance of kneeling before communion, while failing to get to the heart of the matter: we do not share common meanings and practices about the bedrock realities of Catholicism. Too often, the vast majority of Catholics bracket issues like abortion, capital punishment, and our treatment of the poor as beyond our understanding of the teachings of Christ. Today we are being called to go beyond a simplistic Catholicism. This will not be easy. This is a challenge. As I have said, Catholicism, just like living a truly authentic human life, is not for dummies.

## The Transcultural Method of Bernard Lonergan, SJ

To approach and deal with such confusions necessitates informed cultural choices made by converted and converting persons. Bernard J. F. Lonergan, SJ, arguably the most brilliant Jesuit philosopher-theologian in the history of the Society of Jesus, named the problem that results from too much cultural dissonance: a seriously divided community.

> Finally, the divided community, their conflicting actions, and the messy situation are headed for disaster. For the messy situation is diagnosed differently by the divided community; action is ever more at cross purposes; and the situation becomes still messier to provoke still sharper differences in diagnosis and policy, more radical criticism of one another's actions, and an ever deeper crisis in the situation. (Lonergan 1972:358)

To confront such destructive divisions, Lonergan discerned and described a method for becoming more authentically human. This method is based in the processes of knowing rooted in the intrinsic operations of our human minds and hearts. Lonergan notes that any human person experiences, strives to understand experiences, makes judgments based on such understandings, and makes decisions based on such judgments.

Take a simple example. I go to the store to buy a diet soda. The sticker says the 20-ounce bottle costs $2.99. Because I purchased a soda last week, I know that Pepsi costs a lot less than that. I judge that the sticker price is mistaken and take the bottle to the counter. The person at the counter checks, and sure enough the sticker price is incorrect. I pay $1.09 for the soda. My experience of the cost of Pepsi led me to the insight, the act of understanding, that the marked sticker price was much too high in relation to the cost of the same product the week before. I judged that such a price rise was unlikely and decided to ask for a price check. This pattern of Experiencing-Understanding-Judging-Deciding is the bedrock of our humanity. To be human is to be someone who Experiences, Understands, Judges, Decides. This recurrent pattern of human being leads to actions that create and define us and our world.

These operations—experiencing, understanding, judging, deciding, and acting—have inherent rules, or precepts, that correspond to their successful completion. Tad Dunne describes these precepts as the "Be-Attitudes" (cf. Dunne 1985:115–16).

### LONERGAN'S "BE-ATTITUDES" (i.e., TRANSCENDENTAL PRECEPTS)

| | |
|---|---|
| EXPERIENCING | BE ATTENTIVE |
| UNDERSTANDING | BE INTELLIGENT |
| JUDGING | BE REASONABLE |
| DECIDING | BE RESPONSIBLE |
| ACTING | BE LOVING |

According to Lonergan, the canons of the transcendental precepts (Dunne's "Be-Attitudes") are inherent in the operations we spontaneously experience as humans. The spontaneous desires of our hearts and minds impel us to be aware rather than oblivious; to be intelligent rather than stupid; to have reasons for what we choose and do, rather than doing and choosing for no reason at all; to accept responsibility for our choices and actions; to act lovingly rather than apathetically, selfishly, or hatefully.

For Lonergan, conversion is key. Conversion on the intellectual, moral and religious levels of our personhood leads us and our communities to authenticity. Authenticity is the result of our meeting the challenges of the "Be-Attitudes." Unauthenticity is a retreat from the demands of the "Be-Attitudes." Authenticity leads to progress on the personal, communal, societal, and global levels. Unauthenticity leads to decline on the personal, communal, societal, and global levels. Conversion on the intellectual, moral, and religious levels of existence leads to progress. Lack of conversion leads to decline. Converted communities and converted people change the world. Converted communities and converted people can transform our age.

Converted persons and converted communities stand a chance of confronting and changing the cultural conundrums within which we are stuck into ongoing solutions that will lead to the creation of common meaning(s). Culturally conscious communities, converted and converting communities, can cogently and confidently confront the cultural conundrums of our age. Both the unconverted and the converted engage in the same pattern of operations that makes us human. Yet they come to different conclusions. The good news is that the pattern of operations is self-correcting. The corrections are more likely to proceed on the communal level than on the personal level. In other words, the "we" affects "me" more strongly and directly than the "I" affects "us." Lonergan writes, "...development is dialectical. It is not a struggle between any opposites whatsoever but the very precise opposition between authenticity and unauthenticiy" (Lonergan 1972:111).

An authentic, rather than unauthentic, experience of God methodologically produces communities of believers dedicated to not just knowing, but also lovingly living the truths and teachings of the faith. Lonergan's method provides a basis by which to judge and differentiate which religious communities are fostering progress and which are dedicated to decline: "...a religion that promotes self-transcendence to the point, not merely of justice, but of self-sacrificing love, will have a redemptive role in society inasmuch as such love can undo the mischief of decline and restore the cumulative process of progress" (Lonergan 1972:55).

A most concrete example of what Lonergan is talking about is the civil rights movement in the United States in the 1950s and 1960s. At that time the churches authentically put into practice the justice called for by the gospels and were willing to pay the price of such a commitment. John Lewis, one of the great student heroes of the movement, who went on to become a congressman from Georgia, describes in his memoir, *Walking with the Wind* how integral the African American churches were to the advances of the civil rights movement. Lewis argues that the young adults in SNCC, the Student Nonviolent Coordinating Committee, the backbone of the civil rights movement, "were a lot like members of the early Christian church, going out with virtually nothing but the clothes on our backs to bring the gospel of Freedom to the people.... There was a great deal of faith involved in all this. We were venturing out basically on our own, becoming missionaries in a sense" (Lewis 1998:187). Lewis continues, speaking of the small Protestant churches of Alabama and Mississippi:

> The church, in a very real way, was the major gateway for the movement. It was the point of access in almost every community. By giving its blessing to movement organizers, the church opened the door to its membership, who may not have known or understood at first what we were about but who had complete faith in what church elders told them. No matter what it was, if it was coming out of their church, then the people were ready to climb aboard. If the church said it was all right, then it must be all right. (Lewis 1998:400)

The church is an institution aimed at transforming the world in the light of the mystery of Christ. By its words and actions, the church can call the unconverted to conversion, and the converted to fullness of life in the Spirit of Christ. The church forms a community of communities to bring the kingdom of God ever more into reality. Lonergan writes:

> ...the ideal basis of society is community. Without a large measure of community, human society and sovereign states cannot function.... There are needed, then, individuals and groups and, in the modern world, organizations that labor to persuade people to intellectual, moral and religious conversion and that work systematically to undo the mischief brought about by alienation and ideology. Among such bodies should be the Christian church...." (Lonergan 1972:361)

As I said in the introduction, a faith that frees, a full and flexible Catholicism lived by continuously converting Catholic communities, releases in us the energies of the experience of God. So too does the realization of Lonergan's project. Lonergan writes:

> ...being in love with God is the basic fulfillment of our conscious intentionality. That fulfillment brings a deep-set joy that can remain despite humiliation, failure, privation, pain, betrayal, desertion. That fulfillment brings a radical peace, the

peace the world cannot give. *That fulfillment bears fruit in a love of one's neighbor that strives mightily to bring about the kingdom of God on this earth.* On the other hand, the absence of that fulfillment opens the way to the trivialization of human life in the pursuit of fun, to the harshness of human life arising from the ruthless exercise of power, to despair about human welfare springing from the conviction that the universe is absurd. (Lonergan 1972:105; italics added)

## Cultural Anthropology as a Tool for Conversion

From the mix of cultural awareness and theology, imbued with attention to the experience of Catholics, will emerge a church striving to be authentic, and church practices both faithful to tradition and open to the needs of men and women in this age. As we struggle to find and fathom God's presence and action in our lives, understanding the relationship between religion and culture will be much more necessary than understanding the relationship between theology and psychology. Theology studies the relationship between human persons and God, and mediates between cultural patterns and the practices of religion (cf. Lonergan 1972:xi). In the same way that twentieth-century theology was greatly ameliorated by the incorporation of insights from psychology, so will twenty-first-century theology and religious practice become more true to their tasks and mission by incorporating insights from the methodology and study of cultural anthropology.

In the twenty-first century, the church would do well to see cultural anthropology become the prime dialogue partner of theology and pastoral practice. I refer, half jokingly, to cultural anthropology as "theology with facts."

To understand what I mean by culture, we need to pay attention to the shift Lonergan notes between a classicist notion of culture and an empirical notion of culture (cf. Lonergan 1972:xi). The church has for too long clung to a sense of culture as normative, a set of rules and regulations to which our lives must conform. The reality of our lives,

> "In the twenty-first century, the church would do well to see cultural anthropology become the prime dialogue partner of theology and pastoral practice. I refer, half jokingly, to cultural anthropology as 'theology with facts.'"

and the living of a full and flexible Catholicism, necessitate our embracing the empirical notion of culture as "the set of meanings and values that informs a way of life" (Lonergan 1972:xi). Lonergan continues to specify culture's relationship to the human good when he writes: "It is the function of culture to discover, express, validate, criticize, correct, develop, improve such meaning and value" (Lonergan 1972:32).

### A Definition of Culture

Cultural anthropology studies all that forms and continues to form us as human beings. In focusing on the study of culture, cultural anthropology studies how humans adapt to the environment, both the material and spiritual worlds. I define culture as *those relationships whereby we and our community establish identity, i.e., knowledge of ourselves and others; knowledge of the world and of how I/we are to be in the world, i.e., what the world and various versions of the worlds mean to me/us.* Cultural anthropology takes a wide, expansive view of the human condition and attempts to elucidate relationships between various aspects of our historical, multifaceted human experience. To grasp the meanings of culture, imagery often communicates more clearly than definitions. Patrick Chun Wah Tam, a layman working to form lay church leadership among the Yup'ik people on the Yukon Kuskokwim Delta of southwestern Alaska, writes:

> It is fitting, then, to move from various definitions of culture to the diversity of metaphors and images of culture, for these can take us to where words cannot. Culture is like the ocean in which we live as fish; the air we breathe without thinking; a lens which both permits and restricts our seeing; a filter that selects our images of what is normal; a set of codes which we have learned by heart; a set of traffic signals that tell us what to pay attention to; a language made up of spoken words and unspoken messages; a set of blinkers censoring what we see; an invisible cage we can sense around us; a flight recorder holding the memories of our species' journey: a hidden agenda controlling "the conversation about existence"; a womb providing a sense of security and belonging; an accumulation of responses and habits like an unrecognized addiction; "a conspiracy of silence, imposed by the past"; "a menu of existence" offering options with their limits; "a playground of possibilities" opening up to

creativity; "an ever-present horizon, beyond which one cannot see." (Chun Wah Tam 2002:9–10; quoted phrases in the citation are attributed by Chun Wah Tam to Cote 1996:4).

Culture is central to human personhood. When I teach undergraduate students I say to them: You are your culture. You live in a society. You can be on a plane tonight and land in a completely different society tomorrow, but you will culturally still be "you." If you had been raised in another culture, you would not be "you." If I had been born in Mexico or China, I would literally not be the person I am today. The language I speak, the foods I like, my felt sense of right and wrong would all differ to a greater or lesser degree. For example, in the United States, eating dog flesh is repugnant. Not so in all parts of the world. Yet, the sight of me digging into a steak would sicken some people from India. Cultural anthropology studies the ways we are put together culturally. Most important, cultural anthropology disciplines us to see the world from the viewpoint of another culture, revealing and freeing us from our own cultural ethnocentrism, the idea that the way our home culture sees and does things is the "right" way. Culture is crucial to understanding religion, for religion is through and through a cultural reality. Catholicism strives to inculturate itself into all cultures. Although theological realities about Jesus Christ are always and everywhere much the same, the cultural practices we enact to follow and worship Jesus in the United States will differ from the cultural practices used to follow and worship Jesus in other cultures and parts of the world.

This lesson was impressed upon me in my first year as a priest at Holy Name Church in Camden, New Jersey, where I lived and engaged in pastoral work for fifteen years (1988–2003). When Christmas rolled around I found the largely Puerto Rican community served by the parish more focused on the feast of the Three Kings, January 6, than on the feast of Christ's birth, December 25. In Puerto Rico, little kids get their presents on January 6. They leave out *arroz con hibicuelas* (rice and beans) for *Los Tres Reyes* (three kings) and grass for their camels on January 5, much the way that when we were little my brother and sisters and I left milk and cookies for Santa and carrots for the reindeer on December 24. In many ways, the Catholicism I had lived and practiced growing up was very different culturally (but not theologically) from the Catholicism practiced by Puerto Ricans in Camden, less than three miles from where I went to the Jesuit high school in Philadelphia.

Relationships are key to understanding culture. In order to understand one's own or another's culture (i.e., the anthropological enterprise), one must understand the relationships that make up that person's life. For example, to understand me, you have to have some notion of what a Jesuit is, what the Catholic Church is, and what cultural anthropology is, for I am a Jesuit priest and an anthropologist. These are key relationships in my life. To know and understand me more, you may want to know my acquaintances and co-workers; the way I love fishing; how amateurishly, but loudly and joyfully, I play the saxophone in the St. Joe's University Pep Band, and so forth. To really know me, you would have to know my friends and family. To know me truly, you'd have to appreciate how real Jesus is for me, and how central I think and feel prayer is for my very existence, no matter how well or poorly I am actually praying at any point in my life.

*"To know anything, the rules of baseball, algebraic equations, a person, the church, Catholicism, whatever, you must understand the relationships that make up that 'thing's' reality, and be able to integrate that knowledge into other patterns of your knowing."*

To know anything, the rules of baseball, algebraic equations, a person, the church, Catholicism, whatever, you must understand the relationships that make up that "thing's" reality, and be able to integrate that knowledge into other patterns of your knowing. Ponder what Joseph Flanagan is getting at here in his book on Lonergan's philosophy: "If to know a thing concretely is to know that thing in the totality of its relations to other things, then to know the thing completely we must understand all the different ways that things can be known and be able to integrate these different patterns" (Flanagan 1997:115).

In order to understand another culture (and one's own), the key relationships that make up that culture have to be experienced and understood. For example, to understand Chileans, it is probably necessary to speak Spanish, to realize that for Chileans community takes precedence over the individual, to comprehend that their small country welcomes sojourners in their midst, to know that they love a good time, and to have more than a passing awareness of the fall of the Allende government in 1973 and the subsequent years of the Pinochet dictatorship.

To understand deeply the United States of America, most likely you will need to speak English, to recognize that individualism runs deep in

American hearts and bones, to know that immigrants have to scratch and claw their way to acceptance in our society, to realize that Americans work hard and thus value hard work, to be somewhat conscious that the post–World War II United States was the most powerful country on earth and that the Vietnam War dealt a dramatic blow to that sense of power, to be aware that racism is our most persistent and intractable moral and social problem, to realize that abortion is the moral issue on which we are most deeply divided, to recognize that we are profoundly ambivalent in our attitudes toward the economically poor and that since 1968 the nation has swung back and forth between the malaise spoken of by President Carter and the boasting of Ronald Reagan that "America is Back!" More recently, halfway through the first decade of a new century, Americans are still feeling the aftereffects of the September 11, 2001, terrorist attacks on New York and Washington, DC, and grow ever more perplexed and divided over President's Bush's handling of the war on terror and the horrific situation his administration has created in Iraq.

Key cultural relationships are ever more global, even if local. The processes of globalization are increasing exponentially as we enter the new millennium. To be the "Body of Christ," the "Pilgrim People of God," in the next hundred years on this ever more interconnected planet, we will have to be astute and converted Catholics, skilled at being cultural anthropologists as well as informed theologians. The cultural stasis that may have existed in some imagined halcyon past is no longer an option for apostles in the twenty-first century. Cultural change, cultural transformation, cultural conversion, and cultural construction are the challenging tasks we face as we enter this truly new era.

In subsequent chapters of this book, I meditate on the relationship between culture(s) and cultural understandings and the practices of our faith. In Part two I will lay out concrete ways in which we, as Catholics, can live our faith authentically in our ever more complex and globalized world. I want to examine how the community called church can more adequately fulfill its mission by understanding cultural currents coursing through key societal relationships. In order to do that, it will be necessary to spend some time thinking about how to create Catholic culture (chapter 3).

# 3
# Creating Catholic Culture
# Leads to a Freeing Faith

*"The split between the Gospel and culture is without doubt the drama of our time, just as it was in other times. Therefore, every effort must be made to ensure a full evangelization of culture, or more correctly, of cultures. They have to be regenerated by an encounter with the Gospel."*
—*Pope Paul VI*, Evangelii Nuntiandi #20

To live as authentic Catholics, and to articulate and understand our faith as a faith that frees, we need to grasp what culture is, how we understand culture, and how we discern and develop cultural practices that form us as faithful followers of Christ. Such cultural practices lead to conversion.

Cultural anthropology studies culture. As water is to fish, so culture is to humans. A fish does not notice water until it is thrown into water very different from its natural environment as, for example, when a trout is released in salt water, or a cold-water fish is placed in very warm water. We rarely notice our culture until we are thrown into a situation where all the cultural cues confuse us, or where our own cultural cues are not comprehended by those with whom we are interacting. When we bump into, or are thrown into, another culture, we must come to grips with the reality of the "other" in relation to ourselves.

Culture is what we know by the gut reaction it elicits in us when we bump up against cultural realities different from our own. Once, after a long school year in Osorno, Chile, where it rains three hundred days a year, the entire faculty of Colegio San Mateo climbed aboard a bus on a beautiful, early summer sunny day in late December (yes, that's right, December, the start of summer in Chile). Off we went for a day at one of the beautiful lakes that dot the landscape of southern Chile. In the back of the bus filled with chatting and laughing teachers, I noticed a live lamb lying on its side with all four of its feet bound together. I assumed the lamb belonged to the bus driver and that he would be taking it home with him. Wrong. The lamb was the Chilean version of hot dogs and hamburgers. The lamb was lunch. When we arrived at the lake, the men threw a rope up over a tree branch, tied it to the hind leg of the squealing, kicking animal, and hoisted the lamb four feet off the ground. Javier grabbed the lamb's head and quickly slit the animal's throat. Women immediately placed pans beneath the dying animal and caught the hot blood pouring from the wound. They mixed chopped onions, herbs, and spices with the steaming blood and began to pour it into glasses. When they handed me a glass filled with the warm liquid, all eyes turned to watch this gringo's reaction. Not wanting to insult my hosts, or betray myself as less than *macho*, I gulped down the "drink." It wasn't too bad. Actually, it tasted much like the "juice" I like to pour on a baked potato from the "juice" my mother used to collect in a bowl when she cooked roast beef. Culture is just the unquestioned way things are done, and when you bump into another way of doing things, you know it.

Cultural anthropology is the study of the "other" and "others," the striving to comprehend their ways of understanding and responding to human experiences from their perspective. To some degree, cultural anthropology, the attempt to understand those different from some "us," has been present since the dawn of humankind. As the church spread through time and centuries, Christians had to adapt the story of Jesus to many different peoples and cultures.

For example, the early Jesuits in the Americas often functioned as de facto anthropologists. Jesuit Jean Brebeuf's "The Huron Carol" evidences an attempt to translate the meanings and message of the gospel in cultures quite distinct and different from his own French culture. The words and music still appear in the Catholic hymnal *Worship* (GIA Publications, 1986). Notice how Brebeuf changes the details of the infancy narrative in order to make the mystery comprehensible to the Huron and Iroquois peoples. A contemporary Roman Catholic hymnal changes Brebuef's use of the native people's word for God, showing the ongoing struggle over whose culture takes precedence in cultural clashes.

### The Huron Carol ('Twas in the Moon of Winter Time)

'Twas in the moon of wintertime when all the birds had fled
That God the Lord of all the earth ["mighty Gitchi Manitou"
    in many versions] sent angel choirs instead;
Before their light the stars grew dim and wondering hunters
    heard the hymn,
Jesus your King is born, Jesus is born, in excelsis gloria.

Within a lodge of broken bark the tender babe was found;
A ragged robe of rabbit skin enwrapped his beauty round
But as the hunter braves drew nigh the angel song rang
    loud and high,
Jesus your King is born, Jesus is born, in excelsis gloria.

The earliest moon of wintertime is not so round and fair
As was the ring of glory on the helpless infant there.
The chiefs from far before him knelt with gifts of fox
    and beaver pelt.
Jesus your King is born, Jesus is born, in excelsis gloria.

O children of the forest free, O seed of Manitou
The holy Child of earth and heaven is born today for you.
Come kneel before the radiant boy who brings you beauty,
    peace, and joy.
Jesus your King is born, Jesus is born, in excelsis gloria.

Words: Jean de Brebeuf, ca. 1643; trans. Jesse Edgar Middleton, 1926. Music: French Canadian melody (tune name: Jesous Ahatonhia) Worship, GIA Publications, 1986, #380.

Academic cultural anthropology developed as Westerners moved out of Europe and carried European religious and economic systems to the far corners of the earth (but of course those corners were not "far" for those already there). From roughly 1950 to 2000, the interaction of people from various places on the planet, the ability of people in one spot on the globe to significantly affect the lives of others thousands of miles away, has increased beyond the most fervent imaginations of science fiction writers of the nineteenth century.

In struggling to understand various cultures and cultural interactions, there are several prime components cultural anthropologists explore: (1) language, (2) a culture's sense of time and space, (3) power and authority, (4) gender relationships, (5) economic relations, (6) kinship, membership, and community, (7) meaning and world view, and (8) religion, myths, and meanings.

## 1. Language

To understand any culture, one must understand a culture's language, that is, its systems of communication. The mystery of God is that within which we "live and move and have our being" (cf. Acts 17:28), but in order to comprehend, appreciate, appropriate, and communicate this mystery of God, we need to use the gift of language. The ability to speak words, to communicate thoughts and feelings by means of spoken and written symbols is that which connects us to one another and to God. Language, how we use it, what the words we use mean, how the meanings of words change, how words affect our human being and being human: all these aspects of language intimately contour our experience of God. Even to call an experience an experience of God is of itself an act rooted in language. To understand what language is, how we use and are using it, will greatly improve communication among church members.

Language is in large part about the power to name. Processes of naming reveal reality and what groups have the power to name what is real (Bourdieu 1985:203).

One umpire says, "I call 'em as I see 'em." Another umpire says, "I call 'em as they are." The third umpire says, "They ain't nothing 'til I call 'em." Umpires "make" balls and strikes in their naming (i.e., calling) them. Reality and meaning are defined for us, by us, in communication with others. What we say something or someone is soon becomes our notion of what that someone or something is. It is in the processes of naming that most crucial religious matters are settled. Take liturgy, for example. Do we "celebrate the Eucharist" or do we "have Mass"? For some, the celebration of the Eucharist is "exciting," a cel-

> *"One umpire says,*
> *'I call 'em as I see 'em.'*
> *Another umpire says,*
> *'I call 'em as they are.'*
> *The third umpire says,*
> *'They ain't nothing*
> *'til I call 'em.'"*

ebration of Christ's continuing transformative presence among us. For others, many times the young people of our communities, Mass is "boring." Who defined the Mass, which is given gratis, as "boring," and rock concerts, which cost big bucks, as "exciting"? What one really wants to participate in and attend depends on what one's culture names as "exciting" and what it condemns as "boring." Would having the teens name the event "Eucharist" make "Mass" more exciting? Only if, culturally, the words "exciting" and "interesting" get connected to what we do as we listen to the scripture readings and raise up bread and wine in prayer.

Language reveals that all experience is mediated. Only mystics experience God directly, and they constantly attest to the fact that such mystical experiences are indescribable, utterly beyond language's ability to communicate. But language can communicate and mediate a vast array of human experience that can help human persons draw ever closer to one another and to God. The ways we speak matter, because the ways we speak are laced with power to create and maintain cultural and social realities.

## 2. Notions of Time/Space/Reality

Two central constructs of reality are our notions of time and space, of what is present here and now and then and there.

Various cultures have differing notions of time and space. When ideas about time and space are modified, cultures are deeply affected, for our notions of what is real are directly tied to our sense of time and space.

During the first meeting of my cultural anthropology courses, I'll often begin to speak to an empty seat as if my little friend "McGillicuddy" is sitting there. I'll urge students to address "McGillicuddy" because he's feeling a little left out of things. I'll ask if they can see and hear "McGillicuddy." Some brave souls, figuring that I'm not entirely crazy (a somewhat dubious assumption), begin to ask what "McGillicuddy" looks like. I say that he's a little green leprechaun in a black derby hat and a St. Joe's U. sweatshirt, and that in his mouth he has a tobacco pipe that he cannot smoke inside the building. The exercise is intended to make the students think: If all of us agree that "McGillicuddy" is really there, in a sense he becomes present. If we live in a society that agrees "McGillicuddy" is there, and someone disagrees with the "fact" of McGillicuddy's existence, society labels that person insane. Once the students have some grasp of the social construction of reality, I spring the question, "So, what's the difference between our manufacturing of "McGillicuddy" and our "faith" in Jesus? Lively discussion ensues. Is "McGillicuddy" real, and really "here," "now"? Is Jesus really in the chapel when we celebrate the liturgy? When? Where? Is Jesus still there when we go some other place? Is Jesus not there if someone doesn't believe in him?

We believe Jesus is real because we believe he entered our time and our space and still exists among us as risen Lord. The reality of Jesus is affected by how we imagine time and space, and how we imagine that time and space operate. Darwin, Einstein, and Bohr changed everything when their ideas began to filter into the ways we understand the relationships that structure our lives and matter in them (cf. the movie *What the Bleep Do We Really Know*). Evolution, relativity, and quantum mechanics color the ways we understand life and the time given us, even if we aren't well versed in the intricacies of science.

Life is the time between birth and death. That time is "spent" (i.e., lived) some-"where." While we are "here," we envision (i.e., imagine) some "there" to which we will get. Einstein's notions of relativity have completely "relativized" our ordinary notions of time and space. Ideas of the meaning and processes of salvation are impacted when we learn that space and time are relative to the observer of space and time. Such reordering of our thinking about what "now" and "then" mean in relation to "here" and "there" has enormous implications for Christians. Simplistically, we can believe that Jesus saved us from a "there" ("Hell") in order to open the gates for another "there" ("Heaven"), both of which are modes of existence different from the "now" and "here" where we presently are. We believe that our beloved dead are "now" with God. But we wonder, and maybe we even worry about, "where" and "when" we will again meet with them. My grandparents, I imagine, had much firmer, if more simplistic, notions of Heaven, Hell, eternity, and so on. Today, we are leery of too easily pronouncing exactly what the words "Heaven" and "Hell" mean. Such theological ambiguity makes it difficulty for thinking Catholics to articulate what we mean when we assert that we all one "day" be with God "forever."

Contemporary notions of space and time are changing our culture, making the core meanings of our cultural worlds more scientific and technological. We can more easily understand and run computers with such notions of space and time. But this new undertanding of the relativity of time and space makes facile explanations of salvation inadequate and ineffective. Theological reflection on the meaning of our Catholic faith's central assertion, "Jesus Christ has saved us," needs to be culturally and linguistically re-presented for the Einsteinian age, just as Thomas Aquinas had to rethink and re-present the truths of the Catholic faith when Aristotle's ideas became central to Europeans' explanations of experience. The vast majority of Catholics have not yet fully come to grips with the immense cultural changes science has worked on our being human and our religious world views, but such work at becoming aware of science's cultural impact on us is needed, for science alone is inadequate to ground a human response to the mystery of our existence (cf. Appleyard 1992).

Most important for most of us is that fact that, in our daily experience, mass media have virtually obliterated previous notions of time and space. Television is the most significant cultural development since the discovery of fire. Ultimately, the twentieth century will be remembered for having put the small screen everywhere. Our culture and our deepest cultural meanings were radically transformed as soon as we were able to view them through the technology of television. Unlike movies, which in pre-VCR days demanded a certain movement of our bodies in time and space to another location (the "movie palaces" were the twentieth century's "cathedrals"), television is ubiquitous. TV is now present in almost every home on the planet. That change has occurred in less than fifty years. If in 1900 someone had predicted the invention of a little box that would enable us to see in real time across space, and had said that everyone on earth would be watching that box three to six hours daily by the end of the century, people would have taken him to the insane asylum. But, as we crossed the threshold of the year 2000, we found that we are becoming TV and TV is becoming us. Television, with its visual images overwhelming the power of the philosophers to name and interpret our world, is what most affects our ways of being, both with ourselves and with others. Readers of this book may object that TV's overwhelming presence is not such a significant change, that TV is not having as large an effect as I suggest. But note Morris Berman's finding that 60 percent of adult Americans have never read a book of any kind and only 6 percent of the population of the United States reads as much as a book a year (Berman 2000:36). The 2004 National Endowment for the Arts (NEA) study, *Reading at Risk* (NEA 2004), found that the practice of reading for pleasure was in drastic decline, especially among the young (even if J. K. Rowlings's Harry Potter sells millions of copies).

Television therefore cannot *not* affect our ways of being with God. TV affects so much of our life, how can it not affect the way we relate to and understand God? It is also important to note here that computers are basically the same technology as television, with the added bonus of allowing us to have the power to place our own material on the screen. The same goes for DVDs and VCRs (and now iPods). Television has changed the ways we experience time and space. In the centuries preceding this one, life was slower. We had time for God and for learning the issues of the day. But the hour-long sermon or the hours-long Lincoln-Douglas debates (Postman 1985:44–49) have been replaced by the seven-minute homily and the thirty-second TV commercial demanded by our split-second attention spans.

### How Much Time Do You Spend Watching TV?

In *The (Magic) Kingdom of God: Christianity and the Global Culture Industries,* Michael Budde reports that we spend somewhere between one fifth and one third of our lives watching TV (and the poor spend even more time in front of the boob tube). Children and teens are interacting with TV and radio twenty to forty-five hours a week. Budde further reports that toddlers and young children watch from three and a half to four hours a day, and some 33 percent of those under seventeen years of age watch five hours a day. "[T]he average child will have logged between 19,000 and 24,000 hours of television time before his or her 19th birthday. That compares to 12,000 hours of schooling" and sees about forty thousand TV ads a year (Budde 1997: 73–74). Budde calculates that today's teen will spend some thirteen years of his or her first seventy-five years of life in front of the tube (Budde 1997:73-74). And Budde was saying all this before the advent of video games, which have increased astronomically the hours kids, albeit mostly boys, spend in front of the screen. Budde also finds similar rates of viewing in Japan and Europe.

**Do the Math**

The average North American watches four hours and thirty-five minutes of TV a day (<www.nielsenmedia.com>, accessed Sept 21, 2006). This means that, if you're an average American, you spend one out of every six years watching TV. In sixty years, you'll have spent ten years of your life watching TV and two and a half of those years (twelve of every sixty minutes) watching commercials.

Another provocative observer of contemporary culture's effect on us, James Twitchell, argues that commercial modes of framing, articulating, and communicating meaning are supplanting the traditional role of religion.

> Commercial culture is now playing out what was the historic role of organized religion.... The House of Worship has become the Marketplace of Commerce.... In 1997, more than $200 billion was spent on advertising; in 1915 that figure was about $1 billion. The A. C. Nielsen company reports that two-to-five-year-olds average more than 28 hours of television a week, which is 40 school days a year. In 1915 it was entirely possible to go a week without seeing an ad. The average adult today sees some 3000 ads each day. (Twitchell 1999:48–51)

Television has become our source of news and information. Those who produce what is on and the advertisers who pay for it are more and more the authorities of our age.

## 3. Power and Authority

Any culture will define who and what is invested with authority within that culture. On a football team, the quarterbacks and linebackers are usually invested with more authority than the wide receivers and tackles. At work, "the boss" decides what is, and is not, done. Cultural anthropology looks at societal and cultural groups and asks: Who has power and authority? How do they get it? How do they maintain their position? How do they use their power?

It is not only shifts in language use and in the experience of time/space but also other twentieth-century developments that have eroded the traditional authority invested in church and scripture. In a multi-image world, where we and others are mediated to one another at the speed of light—and mediated more as commodities than as human persons—what garners power and authority is whatever can attract attention and make money. And in this commodified world, Christianity takes second place at best, because true worship and service of God rarely have making money as an ultimate objective, at least if the worship and service are authentic.

Christianity is all about encountering the Word of God and responding accordingly. Since God's first communications with human beings, the central issue has always been the same: Will we worship the true and living God, or will we succumb to idols? Authentic worship of the true God leads to freedom, truth, and love. Adulation of idols leads to slavery, deception, and apathy. Remember that it is apathy, not hate, that is the real opposite of love. In his writings, Central American Jesuit theologian Jon Sobrino regularly speaks of the battle between idols and the living God. Worship and service of the idols leads to death; commitment to and service of the Living God leads to life (Sobrino 1984:146, 166).

> "Remember that it is apathy, not hate, that is the real opposite of love."

Lonergan argues that "[a]uthority is the legitimate use of power" and "the source of power is cooperation" (Lonergan 1985:5). When those wielding authority are converted, the community cooperates and progress results. When those wielding authority are not converted, the community's cooperation contributes to inevitable decline. In a time like ours, when people are experiencing such tremendous and deep cultural change, simple assertions of authority will be counterproductive. Only authentic persons and communities will be able to exercise authority in Christ's name. "Religion ... in an era of crisis has to think less of issuing commands and decrees and more of fostering the self-sacrificing love that alone is capable of providing the solution to the evil of decline and reinstating the beneficent progress that is entailed by sustained authenticity" (Lonergan 1985:10-11).

Power and authority in the church are ultimately about being able to name what is true worship of God and what is truly service of others in God's name. That is why we are witnessing such bitter battles over the ways we name and practice our worship: Do you use the term "liturgy" or "the Mass"? Are you part of the "liberal" or the "conservative" wings of the church? Further, power and authority in the church have to do with naming the loving actions that truly and authentically express our love of God and God's love of the world and all within it. Truly loving service of others is what authentically incarnates Christ today. In a full and flexible Catholicism, loving service is the only source of authority and the only means of authentic power. A faith that frees is one that empowers us to authoritatively decide what we deeply and truly desire. In the discernment of such holy desires God communicates with us.

Throughout salvation history, what God has communicated is clear. From Micah's recognition that we are called "to do justice, and to love kindness, and to walk humbly with our God" (Micah 6:8) to Matthew's instruction that what we have done for the least of our sisters and brothers we have done for Christ (Matthew 25:40), the message is clear: authentic followers of Christ freely practice a faith that does justice.

The call to enact social justice is the great strength of the Catholic Church's sacramental view of reality. Catholicism is not the "Me and Jesus" show. Being Catholic is all about "We and Jesus." We are the Body of Christ. Our Catechism teaches: "The duty of making oneself a neighbor to others and actively serving them becomes even more urgent when it involves the disadvantaged, in whatever area this may be" (*Catechism of the Catholic Church*, #1932). Our duty to serve others transcends the level of personal preference. John Paul II called us to construct a civilization of love, and real love is shown in the elimination of unjust inequalities. "There exist also *sinful inequalities* that affect millions of men and women. These are in open contradiction of the Gospel" (*Catechism of the Catholic Church*, #1938).

Power and authority in the church should accrue to those individuals and institutions that carry out the church's social teachings as stringently as they carry out the church's teachings on dogma and liturgical practice and sexual morality. The linking of living as moral persons in matters sexual and the construction of a socially just society is rooted in the depths of Catholic social teaching. The reason people have to be faithful in marriage isn't that God is against the supposed "fun" of illicit love affairs. God wants us to be happy and healthy and holy and free. The more we are faithful to the transcendental precepts (Be Attentive, Be Intelligent, Be Reasonable, Be Responsible), both in our sexual lives and in our business/economic lives, and the more loving we are in both those realms, the more just and peaceful the world will be.

> *"Power and authority in the church should accrue to those individuals and institutions that carry out the church's social teachings as stringently as they carry out the church's teachings on dogma and liturgical practice and sexual morality."*

Solidarity is the principle that should shape the ways in which power and authority are exercised in the Catholic Church. "The principle of solidarity, also articulated in terms of 'friendship' or 'social charity,' is a direct demand of human and Christian brotherhood (cf. John Paul II, *SRS* 38–40; *CA* 10)" (*Catechism of the Catholic Church*, #1939). Solidarity is not some airy, spiritual principle easy to ignore. Solidarity has teeth and calls Catholics to bite into the issues and problems of society. "The equal dignity of human persons requires the effort to reduce excessive social and economic inequalities" (*Catechism of the Catholic Church*, #1947). Catholic social teaching argues against the notion that people can do whatever they want to do with their money. Money in our culture is power, and the church teaches that money and power, like all else, must be subject to the norms of the kingdom of God. "Solidarity is manifested in the first place by the distribution of goods and remuneration for work. It also presupposes the effort for a more just social order where tensions are better able to be reduced and conflicts more readily settled by negotiation" (*Catechism of the Catholic Church*, #1940). Solidarity binds us together and helps us to bridge borders. Solidarity informs the ways in which powerful Catholics in the church and in positions of leadership and influence in society should work to make a better world for all.

## 4. Gender Relations

The need for solidarity today is perhaps greatest in the area of the relationships between men and women. All cultures communicate rules for relationships between men and women. Cultural anthropology investigates how men's and women's roles differ and why. In the past century, the rules of gender relations have been challenged and greatly changed worldwide by women's refusal to accept second-class citizenship in their societies and communities. Sex is a biological category, and men and women obviously differ biologically. Gender has to do with the meanings various cultures attribute to those biological differences. More and more women (and many men) refuse to cooperate with systems and customs that discriminate against women. Although few in the United States would want to take the vote away from women, a "right" women were granted less than ninety years ago in 1920, and few would want to challenge the Mia Hamms of the world on the soccer field, gender equality is still far from an actuality in the United States and in the world.

Sexism is the belief that one sex is better than the other and that, therefore, one sex has the right to dominate the other sex. In the United States, sexism has led to women being called the 52 percent minority

(Gelles and Levine 1999:367). The Equal Pay Act of 1963 and the Civil Rights Act of 1964 made it illegal to pay a member of a particular group or category less than another person for the same job. But women with equal education and experience continue to consistently earn less than men. In 1980 in this country a woman earned 60 cents for every $1.00 earned by a man (Macionis 2007:291); in 2007 James Henslin reported that women working full time earn only 68 percent of what men make (Henslin 2007:314). On a global scale, gender discrimination is even more pronounced. "[W]omen make up about 60 percent of the world's population and perform nearly two thirds of all work hours, but receive only one-tenth of world income and own less than one percent of world property" (U.N. Commission on the Status of Women, in Renzetti and Curran 1998:252).

Sexism is not a good deal for men. Gender inequity may give men more power, wealth, and prestige, but men have three times the suicide rate of women, are three times more likely to suffer severe mental illness, and are six times more likely to be alcoholics. Eighty percent of serious crimes are committed by males and 90 percent of prison populations are male. Men are much more likely to suffer stress-related illnesses such as ulcers, hypertension, or asthma (cf. Robertson 1989:228–29)

The Catholic Church teaches that all men and women share the same human nature (Galatians 3:28). We all have the same origin, and we all hope to share the same life of the Triune God. "All therefore enjoy an equal dignity" (*Catechism of the Catholic Church*, #1934). The work of the church is to convert people to the truth and practice of gender equality—not an easy task for an institution that will not ordain women priests. But a strong argument can be made that, down through the ages, the church has been a site where women were able to advance and hold positions they would not have been able to attain in the secular realms. Sisters were running hospitals and universities long before women were admitted to medical schools and doctoral programs in ivy league universities. Kathleen Norris, in her superb book *The Cloister Walk*, presents a stunningly new reading of women's position in the church with her reflections on the virgin martyrs and St. Maria Goretti (Norris 1996). Far from being simply a bastion of male domination and oppres-

"You could cure a toothache or make snowshoes using the original Britannica, of 1768–71. (You could also imbibe a lot of prejudice and superstition. The entry on 'Woman' was just six words: 'The female of man. See HOMO.')"

(Schiff 2006)

sion, the church in many ways was the springboard for resistance against a patriarchal society. It could still be such a springboard today.

## 5. Economic Relations

Gender relationships and power and authority issues cut across and through cultural realities. A young woman and young man met at an East Coast Catholic college. Both were third-generation Irish Catholics from suburban East Coast metropolitan areas. A couple of years after graduation, they married. You would say they are from the same culture. But even within cultures, cultural differences can be quite problematic. This young couple's marriage almost foundered on the issue of Christmas gifts. What is a proper amount to spend on a Christmas gift for a family member? She had been brought up the daughter of a divorced, single mother, who had provided for her family by working as a school nurse. Money was tight in the family. Christmas was a "spiritual" celebration, and you would spend somewhere between ten and fifteen, maybe twenty, dollars on a Christmas present for a family member. The gift was supposed to be a small token of affection and love. She now expects to give and receive gifts of comparable value from her mother and siblings. His family, on the other hand, sees Christmas as a time to really pull out all the stops. He wants to buy his dad a DVD player and his mother a five-hundred-dollar leather coat. His family members will be giving him and his wife comparable gifts. Two things to note here: one, nowhere in the Bible or in any of the church's social teachings is there any instruction whatsoever on how much we should spend on Christmas gifts. Two, our young couple cannot simply compromise on the gifts. To spend one hundred dollars on a gift is way too expensive for her, way too cheap for him.

It is especially in the giving and receiving of gifts that culture is created and sustained. Economics, the distribution of scarce resources among alternative uses, can be seen as a system of giving and receiving. Any society and culture will be tremendously affected by the ways and systems in which people are involved in the production of goods and services and their distribution. Cultural anthropology asks: What are the rules that govern these economic processes? Who owns the land and the means of production? Who has the power and authority to distribute what is produced? How is labor divided? Who gives jobs? What groups control the economy? How do people reciprocate economically? When someone dies, who gets their wealth? Who has the power and position to answer these questions, to make decisions on these issues (and enforce the rules they make)? Most important, what are the meanings of these economic realities?

The challenge for contemporary Catholics is to know that all of life, and all that is life giving, is gift of and from God. The more we slide into the morass of thinking ourselves self-sufficient, the more we mock the basic structure of reality: We are creatures, created by a loving God, creatures unable to sustain ourselves without great assistance from those around us. Life is a gift we co-create with God for others. God is God and we are not God. The old Baltimore Catechism answer, "God made me to know Him, to love Him, and to serve Him in this world, and to be happy with Him for ever in heaven," is rooted in the recognition of this central relationship in our lives. When we forget this relationship to God and begin to imagine the idols of our times as the source of life, then our lives, cultures, and societies go quite askew. The General Electric corporation's old ad, "GE, we bring good things to life," does more than miss the point. The ad distorts reality. The gift of life is ultimately of, from, and for, God.

In the 1995 movie *First Knight* (starring Sean Connery, Richard Gere, and Julia Ormond), there is a fascinating scene where King Arthur is challenged by his archenemy Malagant, a former knight of the round table, who has revolted against the ideals and laws of Camelot. He invades Camelot and appeals to the people to "free" themselves from King Arthur. In the movie's climactic scene, Malagant declares, "I am the law now. The strong rule the weak. That is how your God made the world." King Arthur replies, "God makes us strong only for a while, so we can help each other." Malagant loudly boasts, "My God makes me strong so that I can live my life. Arthur says to you, 'Serve one another.' When are you going to start living for yourselves? Now this is the freedom I bring you. Freedom from Arthur's tyrannical dream, from Arthur's tyrannical law, from Arthur's tyrannical God." King Arthur knows that the ultimate economic resource is a community imbued with practices of justice and fairness. Malagant's world is not a gift; it's a trap, a trap that ensnares us all in a game of never-ending grab and get, protect and defend, kill or be killed. King Arthur's world opens us to a reality of gift and grace, rooted in service and love. It is interesting that in this telling of the ancient tale, although

Guinevere is tempted to infidelity, she remains true to Arthur, and Lancelot accepts her choice.

Ignatian spirituality is rooted in the discernment of choices, and the most important choices we make have to do with how to share our gifts. The core of the New Testament's teachings are rooted in the belief that all is gift. The more we authentically live out and practice that gift-centered spirituality, the more we become a eucharistic people capable of creating loving and just communities.

The practice of Catholicism should lead to a world more and more like the one described by the philosopher John Rawls in his seminal work *A Theory of Justice* (1971). Rawls argues that in a just world people would be able to be placed in any position in society and know that life was fair. If placed behind a veil of ignorance, not knowing where they would be in society, people would choose a fair and equitable distribution of goods and opportunities, for only thus would they be able to trust the world in which they would find themselves. Rawls allows for two principles that would guide a just social order. First, the principle of equal liberty holds that everyone is granted the same rights along with corresponding duties. Second, the difference principle ensures that (a) any economic and social inequities that are allowed must be to the greatest benefit of all, especially to the "least advantaged members of society" and (b) any position granting unequal authority or goods must be open to all, in the sense that anyone can compete for and attain such a position (Rawls 1971:302). If the values and practices of Catholic social teaching, and of philosophers like Rawls, were put into practice, we would not have a planet like the one we have today where there are so many drastic economic inequities.

> "John Rawls . . . argues that in a just world people would be able to be placed in any position in society and know that life was fair."

## 6. Kinship, Membership, and Community

We often hear the old adage, "It's not what you know; it's who you know." Economic relationships very often influence, if not determine, a person's position in society. Even in a somewhat mobile society like that of the United States, where many people change their economic position during their lifetimes, the vast majority of people live and die in the same class into which they were born. Poor people remain poor. Middle-class people live and die in the middle class. Children of the rich tend to stay rich. When John F. Kennedy, Jr., died in a plane crash, his fortune was reportedly worth one hundred million dollars, although he never "earned" a lot of money. At the time of his death, his magazine *George* was barely afloat. He made money the way his father did, the way many really rich people make money: they inherit it. It is no accident that President George H. W. Bush's sons were governors of Texas and Florida and that "W" became president. Those "born on third" often make it home.

Cultural anthropologists and sociologists study how people gain entrance to certain groups in society, how they maintain their membership in such groups, and how they exclude others from entering. Throughout history, the central institution that conferred identity, status, and role on persons was the family. How families are constructed and how they operate are crucial issues for any society and culture. As I have said, cultural change has been more rapid in our times than at any time in history, and it is in familial relations that this pace of change is excruciatingly evident. As families of choice replace families of origin, as the ancient model of the patriarchal family gives way to new forms and modes of being family, the Catholic Church, which often uses the metaphor of family to describe itself, is deeply affected.

Divorce and remarriage are the norm for over half of the people of the United States. According to the 2000 census, more than 25 percent of Americans now live alone. The *Ozzie and Harriet* family model (Dad works, Mom stays at home with the kids) now comprises less than 10 percent of families in the United States. In 1900, 4 percent of the population was over sixty-five years of age. By 2000, that percentage had risen to 12.4 percent. In 2004 there were 36 million people over sixty-five years of age, and by 2030 that number will almost double, reaching 71 million (Macionis 2007:394). For the first time in history, we will have a society in which a very large proportion of "families" will be made up of senior citizens over the age of sixty-five. Children are more and more raised by grandparents, or gay couples, or stepmoms and stepdads. "Family" is no longer a simple or univocal concept or experience.

One deep and pervasive social change in the past few decades is the pattern of the dual-earner family. In 2005, The National Partnership for Women and Families reported that 78 percent of homes of married-couple families with children have both parents working outside the home (Newman 2006:230). In 1976, this was true of only 32 percent of married couples. "By 2002, the percentage of households that consisted of a married couple dependent on a sole male breadwinner had dropped to about 20%, from a high of almost 60% in 1950" (Newman 2006:230).

---

DIVERSITY OF AMERICAN HOUSEHOLDS

| | |
|---|---|
| Married couple with children under 18 | 23.3% |
| Single female family with children under 18 | 7.3% |
| Single male parent with children under 18 | 1.7% |
| "Child free"/post–child rearing couple | 28.2% |
| People living alone | 26.4% |
| Other households (various family configurations) | 7.5% |
| Non-family households | 5.6% |

(Newman 2006:218)

---

## 7. Meaning and World View

Family is crucial because family, however it is constructed and lived out, mediates culture to individual persons. We learn our culture as we drink our mother's milk. No Italian baby ever spontaneously started speaking Chinese. No child raised a Buddhist ever spontaneously began to chant "Jesus Christ is Lord." We accept the culture we are given as children. We may grow to incorporate aspects of other cultures to complement and modify the cultural self we became as a result of living in a certain culture as children, but we always fundamentally remain, culturally, that into which we were born, even if we spend a great deal of energy in disassociating our self from our culture of origin. Even becoming fluent in another language means that the second language remains a second language. Very few people are completely bilingual.

Along with one's culture come certain ideas, assumptions, ways of doing things that seem "natural" and "right." I was surprised in Chile to find that playing cards are dealt counter-clockwise. I had always thought that cards are dealt clockwise. Again, it is completely arbitrary

which way cards get into player's hands (unless you're illegitimately trying to increase the value of your poker hand), but different cultures do
things differently. In some cultures it is unacceptable to wear shoes inside the house; in others, shoes inside are no problem. In some cultures,
dogs are considered almost a part of the family; in other cultures dogs
are treated like rats. In one Papua New Guinea culture, the pig was
found to hold much the same meaning as lambs in the Mediterranean
and Western worlds (Renzetti and Curran 2000:83). Should we, therefore, elevate the consecrated host and say "Behold the *Pig* of God" before receiving communion in that culture?

Religions are laced through and through with cultural assumptions.
The whole celebration of the liturgical year threw me for a loop in Chile.
I distinctly remember walking down into the plaza in Osorno on a
rainy, cold (35° F) July 4 and entering the cathedral to attend Mass. For
some reason, the instrumental music being played on the sound system
was *Adeste Fideles* (O Come All Ye Faithful). In a curious way, it felt
right, but the calendar in my head made me recognize what for me was
a cultural incongruity. In Chile, Lent begins at the end of the summer
holidays in February or early March and Easter comes as autumn is beginning. Christmas is celebrated in spring as the school year ends and
summer is beginning. Western Europe devised the liturgical year to follow the Northern Hemisphere's seasonal cycle. In the Southern Hemisphere, where the majority of Christians now reside, the entire schema
is reversed. The Chileans would talk about how fitting it is that Jesus is
born as the year is in full swing, and Easter comes to strengthen our
hope when we are heading into the dark days of autumn. In the United
States, I was always taught that Jesus is born at the darkest time of the
year to bring light to the darkness, and that Lent, which comes from the
idea of the days "lengthening," means the days are getting longer and
the light is returning. Easter is all about celebrating the spring planting
in anticipation of the fall harvest. Obviously, in the Southern Hemisphere, this understanding of the liturgical cycle has to be re-imagined.

## 8. Religion, Myths, and Meanings

Cultures are formed and held together by the stories we tell one another about where we came from, who we are, and where we are going.
The bedrock stories are the religious stories we articulate and share.

Religions are belief systems that tie everything together. The word "religion" comes from the Latin, *religare*, "to bind together, to tie fast." Cultures are held together to the degree that members of the culture share the same beliefs and accept the same values. Obviously, in a time of great cultural change, such accepted, shared values will come under increasing pressure. As I said earlier, many of the bitter battles in the Catholic Church in the United States today revolve not around theological truths, but around cultural meanings that are shifting and transforming so rapidly.

Myth and our religious traditions relate us to realities far beyond our limited personal experience. As children we are told something about who and what God is, how to live and love, and what death means—and we believe what the adults tell us. In adolescence and young adulthood, we have to come to some acceptance of the truths we have been told, or, if we find our experiences conflicting with what we were told was the "truth," we often painfully wrestle with our inherited beliefs and possible modifications of those beliefs. Eventually people either accept the beliefs of their childhood in an adult version or strike out looking for meaning elsewhere. But, however we develop, reshape, or form faith, we humans must find myths and meanings to live by (cf. Parks 2000).

Myth, in the sociological and anthropological sense, is a story that orients our life. It may be as simple a story as, "If I make more money, I will be happy." "Money equals happiness" is the operative philosophy in the Horatio Alger myth: "If I just work hard, I will be successful."

Cultures are full of myths. In the United States, people my age will readily recognize the myth of George Washington and the cherry tree, which teaches young children to tell the truth. Whether or not little George ever actually cut down the tree doesn't diminish the truth of the moral point of the tale: tell the truth! (especially if you are a politician). Democracy is a myth, in the sense that we do not really see democracy walking down the street, but we will literally sacrifice our lives, or politicians will sacrifice young people's lives, in order to preserve its presence in this country and elsewhere. We believe that our votes count (or at least we did until the Gore-Bush election of November 2000. "Don't blame me. I voted with the majority," a bumper sticker announced in the aftermath of the election). If

"Most people know what they do. Most people know why they do what they do. But what most people don't know is what what they do, does."

(Michel Foucault, as quoted in Dreyfus and Rabinow 1983:187)

voting becomes too much of a sham and simply ratifies what the big donors want from the candidates, we lose "faith" in democracy.

Movies are becoming our most powerful myths and creators of myths. Few baby boomers in the United States fail to recognize Jimmy Stewart's George Bailey, who learns that "No man is poor who has friends." And Steven Spielberg is the unparalleled master of myth à la Hollywood. When the kids flew on their bikes in *E.T.*, I immediately remembered our fervent desire to make our twenty-inch-wheel bikes fly in the 1960s. No one asks whether Spielberg movies are scientifically "true." The operative questions are: What do they mean? How do they make us feel? What do they impel us to do? The *Star Wars* and *Lord of the Rings* trilogies imbue our imaginations with multiple levels of meaning and, along with the Harry Potter books and movies, enchant and entertain millions of people. On some level, many of us believe that these tales of adventure and battles between good and evil relate to the stories of our lives.

*"No one asks whether Spielberg movies are scientifically 'true.' The operative questions are: What do they mean? How do they make us feel? What do they impel us to do?"*

In this sense, myth is truer than true. It operates as the truth-making, meaning-making mechanism of our lives. I challenge my college students by saying to them, "You all are living a myth at this minute." That statement is greeted with blank stares. I then go on to outline the myth for them: "You all are here at St. Joe's University. You think that getting a good education will get you a good job, and that that will make for a happy life. Do any of you have any evidence for the myth you're living? Are you sure college and a high-paying job will make you happy? What if being a manager at IHOP would really make you happy? Or being a forest ranger in Yellowstone National Park?"

College students often ask if Catholicism is "true." It is. Actually it is more than simply true. Like all good myths, Catholicism is truer than true. I prove this to my students by making them analyze their own experience of one of our culture's most powerful myths: Santa Claus. Students readily agree that "Santa Claus" does not "really" exist and is not "true." But they immediately recognize the power of the Santa Claus "myth" when I point out that 25 percent of retail sales in the United States are related directly to Christmas spending. Jesus truly is the "reason for the season," but get rid of Santa, and our malls go under. And virtually all of the students admit they will tell their children that Santa is "real." The reality and truth of Jesus Christ, of course, far exceed that of Santa. But in a way similar to that of the Santa myth, which means we will place presents under the tree, we will live our lives as followers of Jesus based on the myths and meanings that emerged in the community based on the historical realities of the life and death of Jesus of Nazareth and faith in the resurrection of Christ. Our faith facts about Jesus are based on more than just something that happened back then. Our faith is based on our lived experience of the sacraments and service done in Jesus' name by the community of the baptized (cf. L. T. Johnson 1997). Our faith frees us to live lives that are happy and healthy and holy and free.

In this book, I contend that the myths of our consumer culture are woefully inadequate to help us live lives in ways that make us happy and healthy and holy and free. One of the main thrusts of my argument is that the myths of science and the myths given by the bulk of the mainstream consumerist media-ized culture are inadequate to construct authentic cultures that help us be fully human and fully alive. As good and powerful as the myths of science are, as entertaining and life-giving as a percentage of what is presented in the mass media can be, I contend that humanity stands in desperate need of articulating, communicating, and living out religious myths and stories, narratives that can truly form us as intelligent and loving people who can construct caring and efficacious communities dedicated to fostering the well-being of all on earth, that is, the kingdom of God.

The "truth" of myths rests on the degree of authenticity they inspire in human minds, hearts, and lives. If the myth I am living really makes me energetic and joyful, it will and ought to be the truth by which I live my life. The gospel, the good news of the life, death, and resurrection of Jesus, is true. We know that by faith. But what that life, death, and resurrection mean for you, for me, for us, is only as strong as the mythic hold it has on our hearts and minds and actions. Myth leads our hearts and minds through many processes of conversion. The principal process of conversion by which we become converted to Jesus Christ and form church communities that practice a full and flexible Catholicism is prayer. The more I pray, the more I open my heart to God who wants to be active in the center of my being, the more I put on the mind of Christ and begin to act as he would act and as he would have me act.

Prayer is the making of myself, my person, my/our world, and my/our history more and more like the kingdom Jesus proclaimed. The degree to which the reality of Jesus Christ informs and directs the contents of my/our imagination is the degree to which I am (and we are) actually converted and actually Christian. Prayer leads to service of others, and service can't be faked. Our authenticity as "servants of Christ's mission" is there for all to see. The cultural practices of Catholicism must be about fostering those conversions that make us truly prayerful Christians, truly servants of Christ's kingdom.

Most important, myths inform our imaginations. In many ways, I've come to believe that the primary mission of the church is to transform the imaginations of people. It was only after many years of practicing Ignatian contemplation, a form of prayer in which the exercise of the imagination is crucial, that I finally articulated for myself what it is I mean by imagination.

---

### IMAGINATION IS BOTH PERSONAL AND SOCIAL

Imagination =

Pictures in our Heads
↑ ↓
Words in our Minds
↑ ↓
Feelings in our Hearts
↑ ↓
Actions in our Lives
↑ ↓
Meaning in our World

---

The images we have in our heads are the basis of the words in our minds and feelings in our hearts. Those feelings and words become actions in our lives and make meaning in our world. Grace is basically experienced through our imagination, or it is not experienced at all. Imagination is everything. Gandhi said, "We must be the change we wish to see in the world." It is the power of the imagination that drives and motivates us to be who and what we are. If we are to be converted

Catholics, Christians totally committed to Jesus and God's kingdom, the transformation of ourselves and our world begins in, is rooted in, and tends toward the ongoing investigation and transformation of our imagination, both personal and social. That social and personal imagination is the source and ground of our culture(s).

Imagination is the fountain from which religion flows. Religion's role in the creation, maintenance, and transformation of myths is central because ritual gives myth power. We are the stories we tell and do. Liturgical ritual re-presents, multiple times, the story we are. Sacraments remind us of who we are and offer us the power to actually be ourselves. The practices of our faith, from participating in Mass on Sundays to serving in the soup kitchen, enact our myths and make them operative.

The ills we face as a culture and as a society stand in great need of the transformative remedy of faith lived fully, flexibly, freely. To live in a world where faith and justice are paid more than lip service, where hope and love are attainable, is not an airy fantasy. We need to empower true myths. Empowering true myths is our mission for the twenty-first century. Myths make and sustain community and converted communities heal the earth.

## Being Catholic in an Ever More Global, Culturally Diverse World

Albert Einstein said, "The unleashed power of the atom has changed everything save our modes of thinking, and we thus drift towards unparalleled catastrophes." The Catholic Church as an institution of over one billion people on this planet could make a huge contribution by working to avoid such catastrophes. Karl Rahner cogently recognized that Vatican II transformed the Roman Catholic Church into a World Church. In May of 1987, while I was studying theology before ordination, for the first time in history there were more Christians in the Southern Hemisphere than in the Northern. In ways unable to be imagined by my Jesuit predecessors of the 1900–1975 era, my Jesuit life from 1976 to 2045 (if I'm lucky enough to live that long) will be lived in a totally different world, a much larger, more all-encompassing global community.

Dartmouth professor of environmental studies Dr. Donella Meadows's "State of the Village Report" appeared in 1990. Although the numbers have obviously changed over the past decade and a half, the thought experiment is still helpful. The imaginative jolt one gets from pondering the village's updated statistics makes this a favorite item added to many social science textbooks and thousands of websites. One popular textbook summarizes the data on today's village: If our planet's population of 6.5 billion were reduced to the size of a village of 1,000 persons, 50 villagers would have a college degree. Two hundred people would receive 80 percent of the village's income. One third of the villagers would be unable to read or write. Two hundred villagers would not have decent shelter or access to clean water; 610 villagers would be Asian, 140 would be Africans, 110 would be Europeans, 85 would be Latin Americans, and 45 would be from the USA (Macionis 2007:8).

The vast economic inequities evident in our global village call for nothing less than great intellectual, moral, and religious conversions. Those who claim to follow the Lord who told the story of the Good Samaritan (Luke 10:29–37) and the parable of Lazarus and the rich man (Luke 16:19–31) cannot ignore the realities of global injustice.

"If you have never experienced the danger of battle, the fear of loneliness or imprisonment, the agony of torture, or the pain of starvation…you are better off than 500 million people in the world. If you have food in the refrigerator, clothes on your back, a roof overhead and a place to sleep …you are more comfortable than 75% of the people in this world. If you have money in the bank, in your wallet, and spare change in a dish somewhere …you are among the top 8% of the world's wealthy. If you can read this you are more blessed than the over two billion people in the world who cannot read at all." (State of the Village Report, inspired by Donella H. Meadows. <www.odt.org/popvillage.htm>)

Vatican II recognized that making an earth hospitable for all is an important aspect of practicing Catholicism. "Earthly progress must be carefully distinguished from the growth of Christ's kingdom (a kingdom of truth and life, of holiness and grace, of justice, love and peace). Nevertheless, to the extent that the former can contribute to the better ordering of human society, it is of vital concern to the kingdom of God" (*Guadium et Spes*, 39).

Conscious of this ever increasing global society, Lonergan lays out the communal ramifications of conversion. To be converted on the intellectual, moral, and religious levels of our social and personal being will create community. But conversion proceeds at a different pace in different communities. Lack of conversion among peoples leads to the breakdown of common meaning, and on a global scale such breakdown threatens destruction of the fragile creation society is.

As common meaning constitutes community, so divergent meaning divides it.... The serious division is the one that arises from the presence and absence of intellectual, moral, or religious conversion. For a man is his true self inasmuch as he is self-transcending. Conversion is the way to self-transcendence. Inversely, man is alienated from his true self inasmuch as he refuses self-transcendence, and the basic form of ideology is the self-justification of alienated man. (Lonergan 1972: 357)

Conversion is the key. Real amelioration of conditions on this planet, from the local to the global levels and at all levels in between, necessitates culturally conscious persons struggling to create, construct, and continue communities. Lack of such persons and community portends a bleak future. Communities divided about the core meanings of their culture are in dire straits.

Lonergan calls for the church to be a community dedicated to the conversion of our world and all who live in it. The church's mission is the realization of the kingdom of God. God's will is clear: That the kingdom come! "Its [i.e., the church's] aim is the realization of the kingdom of God not only within its own organization but in the whole of human society and not only in the after life *but also in this life*" (Lonergan 1972:364; italics added). Catholics converted to and cognizant of the church's mission will find meaning and purpose in the practice of our faith and the living of their lives. In the living out of a vibrant, intelligent Catholicism we will find, ultimately, what our hearts most deeply desire—love.

### Society Is a Gift We Give One Another

Catholicism has a clearly thought out and articulated vision of how society can and ought to be. To be Catholic is to know that vision and strive to make it operative and effective in our daily lives. To strive to give each other the gift of a just and loving society will fill our lives with meaning. But in order to give each other the gift, we have to know what it is. Unfortunately too many Catholics have an anemic awareness and understanding of the full ramifications of the faith into which we were baptized. Achieving such awareness is not easy.

Alan Wolfe articulates why it is so difficult to be a modern person. "To be modern is to face the consequences of decisions made by complete strangers while making decisions that will affect the lives of people one will never know" (A. Wolfe 1989:3). To be Catholic today is to be part of a global community in which members strive to be conscious and aware of how their actions affect others. To be Catholic today is to struggle to convert persons and institutions on the intellectual, moral, and religious levels. To be Catholic today is to strive to make all persons enjoy true freedom, *freedom from* want, and *freedom for* love. "We are free only when others are also free, and they are free when we are" (Wolfe 1989:261).

> *"To be Catholic today is to strive to make all persons enjoy true freedom, freedom from want, and freedom for love."*

The following chapters will build upon ideas hinted at in these first chapters by exploring ways in which we can think about applying the principles of Catholicism in the various cultural arenas of our lives. This is the difficult and delicate task of inculturation, not only in cultures far different from our home culture, but also in our own culture.

Ethnocentrism is the assumption that one's home culture is normal, right, and best. The way "we" do things is the way things ought to be done. Such attitudes have been challenged consistently and cogently since tribe met tribe early in human history and certainly since the beginning of the Christian faith. Peter and Paul had to navigate the turbulent waters of articulating the relationship between Jewish people and gentiles as both groups came to faith in Jesus and began to live out that faith in light of their own cultures' values and practices (cf. Acts 15:28). Western European Christian missionaries have at times been blind to their own ethnocentric paradigms and, at other times, incredibly sensitive to the need for adapting to local cultural practices so that the faith could be understood and embraced by different cultures. The life of Matteo Ricci gives exquisite testimony to the ability of the church to adapt to other cultures; the inability of some in the church to follow Ricci's example and advice shows the tension involved in allowing for appropriate adaptations while maintaining the faith (Spence 1985).

Cultural relativism does not justify moral relativism. Awareness of ethnocentrism guards us from falling into the trap of assuming that appeals to culture justify any and every choice, behavior, or practice. All cultures exhibit values and disvalues. The fact that cultures are relative in relation to one another does not justify inhumane or unjust practices, discriminatory attitudes, or deeply held prejudices. Justice is always better than injustice. The strong should be opposed when they mistreat the weak. The truth is always better than falsehood. All persons are entitled to have their human rights respected and honored regardless of the cultural circumstance.

In order to make a good world for one another, we have to raise our awareness of our own ethnocentric viewpoints and stances and strive to see things from the position of people whose lives and social circumstances differ markedly from our own. This has ever been the work of those who announce the good news of Jesus Christ, the art of applying the gospel's healing and life-enhancing message to the multicultural realities of human communities.

PART TWO

# JUSTICE MATTERS
## The Righting of Relationships
## through the Practices of Catholicism

*We recognize, along with many others, that without faith, without the eye of love, the human world seems too evil for God to be good, for a good God to exist. But faith recognizes that God is acting through Christ's love and the power of the Holy Spirit ....*

*This faith in God is inescapably social in its implications, because it is directed towards how people relate to one another and how society should be ordered.... When a society has no moral and spiritual basis, the result is conflicting ideologies of hatreds which provoke nationalistic, racial, economic and sexual violence. This in turn multiplies the abuses that breed resentments and conflict.... Society then falls prey to the powerful and manipulative.*

*But a faith that looks to the Kingdom generates communities which counter social conflict and disintegration. From faith comes the justice willed by God.... religious faith, as the inspiration of the human and social good found in God's Kingdom, that alone can take the human family beyond decline and destructive conflict.*

*Justice can truly flourish only when it involves the transformation of cultures, since the roots of injustice are imbedded in cultural attitudes as well as in economic structures. In Jesus Christ, we can accept the magnitude of this challenge.*

*—The 34th General Congregation of the Society of Jesus (1995)*

# Introduction to Part Two

*"The common good concerns the life of all.... It consists of* three essential elements. *First, the common good presupposes* respect for the person *as such.... Second, the common good requires the* social well-being *and* development *of the group itself.... Finally, the common good requires* peace, *that is, the stability and security of a just order."*
—Catechism of the Catholic Church, ##1906–1909

### Intelligent Inculturation: Meaning Meltdown and the Re-creation of Meaning

The great task facing the church in the United States is the need to consciously choose the meanings of our faith and develop practices that will deepen and solidify those meanings in our daily living. Walking on water in today's world and living a faith that frees are graced gifts of our relationship with the God who leads us from slavery to freedom, free to live the love and liberty of daughters and sons transformed and divinized in Christ Jesus.

We must never forget that it all began with slaves. Centuries ago, the children of Israel were cruelly oppressed by their Egyptian rulers. One of their own, miraculously saved and then educated in the practices of the Pharaoh's household, discovers his true identity and unites himself with his oppressed brethren. He quickly learns that the way of violence is not the way to lasting liberation. Moses wanders in the desert and eventually discovers his mission in an encounter with a burning bush. He and his brother return to rescue their people. For forty years, the Israelites stumble their way to full freedom and the Promised Land. God makes a covenant with the community formed in the desert. The dynasty of David and his infidelities are precursors of the success and failure of the people of God to heed the prophets' calls for justice and right relationship with God and neighbor.

Jesus is born into this history, culture, and tradition. He utilizes the practices of his inherited religion and culture while challenging and transforming his home culture's deepest values and meanings. His preaching and teaching reveal a God who is love, the Father, "Abba," who wants to give us the fullness of life. But we reject the gift. God with us and God for us, Jesus is nailed to a cross, is murdered and dies at our hands, for we too, in ways muddled and mysterious, are just like the Roman soldiers and religious authorities who found Jesus a profound threat to social stability and the existing hierarchical order. In Moses and in Jesus we see lived out, in bold outline, the pattern of our relationship to others and to God.

We too must do what Moses and Jesus have done before us. We must understand and challenge, critique and transform, the cultural and religious practices of our times. In so doing we will again and again know the truth that God is with us, that God is love, that God desires us to be transformed into the actual freedom wherein we experience the very essence of divinity. To aid us in our quest and mission, we are given the Holy Spirit of God, the advocate who comes as a result of Jesus' resurrection. We too must do what Peter and Paul did, walk on water and preach this good news of the Lord's transformative presence among us. We too must do what Mary Magdalene did and go to the tomb, meet the risen Lord, and proclaim him to all.

> "The central message is simple: our faith is profoundly social. We cannot be called truly 'Catholic' unless we hear and heed the church's call to serve those in need and work for justice and peace. We cannot call ourselves followers of Jesus unless we take up his mission of bringing 'good news to the poor, liberty to captives, and new sight to the blind' (cf. Lk 4:18)."
>
> —*Communities of Salt and Light* (USCCB 1993b)

The practice of a faith that frees offers to unchain us from all that hinders and harms our being our deepest truest self, from all that enslaves and addicts us, from all that keeps us from the realization that God is real and working in and through the experiences of our lives. The practice of a faith that frees offers to free us for the justice and joy we all desire and hope for as members of the human family; for all the hard, soul-satisfying work of healing our planet and eradicating racism, sexism, classism, and all the other "isms" that tie and bind us. The practice of a faith that frees offers to free us to be with ourselves, others, and God in the ways of peace and prosperity, the ways of wisdom and wit, the ways of prayer, pleasure, and possession without possessiveness.

The practices of a faith that frees are nothing radically new, but responses to the particular challenges of our time and place in the early years of the twenty-first century. We are called and led to do what followers of Christ have always done. A faith that frees does justice, that is, it engages in the righting of relationships. At the start of this book I noted that faith is "the assurance of things hoped for, the conviction of things not seen" (Hebrews 11:1), and the primordial effect of our practice of faith as Catholics is our being freed from all that keeps us in bondage. The freedom that we enjoy as the sons and daughters of God by its very nature invites us to transcend ourselves and our communities and reach out to all our sisters and brothers on our planet to form a world of peace and prosperity, justice and joy, liberty and love. Faith that stays sterile and satisfied, bolstering our self image while leaving unchallenged and untouched the social conditions oppressing millions of our fellow human beings, is not faith in the transformative power of Jesus Christ.

Bringing good news today means analyzing our practices, the ways we use media, the manner in which we analyze and confront deep-seated dynamics of injustice, such as classism, sexism, and racism, the ways we choose to live our sexual lives, the practices of prayer. All of these are profoundly pervasive social realities that contour and condition our personal relationship with God. That is the way it should be for us as Catholics: faith is always "both/and," both utterly personal and pervasively social.

Jon Sobrino, SJ, following Moltmann, prophetically points out that the question is not, Does the church have a mission? Rather, the question is, Does the mission have a church? (cf. Sobrino 1984:117). The Catholic Church is a church on mission. One of the hallmarks of the mission is service. The largest provider of social services in the United States is the Roman Catholic Church. Since 1970 Catholics through the Catholic Campaign for Human Development have given hundreds of millions of dollars in grants to more than 7,800 self-help initiatives throughout the United States (USCCB 2007a).

The Catholic Church's social teaching articulates a way of life based on the needs of the human person. Society, the economy and business, family, church, political bodies, schools, all institutions are to be measured by whether they make the world a better place for human beings. Life and freedom are to be fostered and protected. Injustice and inequity are to be denounced and eradicated. In preaching the gospel, in celebrating sacraments, and in practicing the precepts of Catholic social teaching, Catholics participate in Christ's mission. Here is a brief outline of key aspects of Catholic social teaching:

---

PRINCIPLES OF CATHOLIC SOCIAL TEACHING

| | |
|---|---|
| 1. Link of the Religious and Social Dimensions | 8. Political Participation |
| 2. Dignity of the Human Person | 9. Economic Justice |
| 3. Political and Economic Rights | 10. Stewardship |
| 4. Option for the Poor | 11. Solidarity |
| 5. Link of Love and Justice | 12. Promotion of Peace |
| 6. Promotion of the Common Good | 13. Work |
| 7. Subsidiarity | 14. Liberation |

(Henriot et al. 1998:22–25)

---

Catholic social teaching articulates a vision and way of life based on the principles listed above, principles and lessons that, when applied and lived in our lives and implemented in our institutions, make for a world based on the needs of human persons, and dedicated to the establishment of social justice.

## A Call to Conversion to a Kingdom Way of Life

Jesus' mission was to preach and call for the establishment of the kingdom of God. This is not the imposition of one religious vision over another. It is a striving to discern how the social structures, cultural values, and meanings of our society and age measure up against the gospel message of life and liberty, truth and love, freedom and hope. The kingdom is the bringing forth of what is best in human hearts and lives. The kingdom stands opposed to all that diminishes, devalues, and destroys what is truly human.

Far from imposing a way of life on people, the kingdom allows for real freedom; the freedom from fear and worry about how I'm doing in life (are we keeping up with the Joneses?), and freedom from a God of terror and retribution, a God who is a "bogeyman" out to get us. The kingdom frees us for the living of a loving relationship with God who cares for us, gifts us, and calls us to use our talents and gifts for the amelioration of our world. Living consciously committed to the kingdom of God frees us and allows God to be God in our lives. It enables us to resist the inherent human temptation to try and play God. The root of most addictions is the perverse attitude that "I am God and God is not." The first step to freeing and healing ourselves and our culture from addictive behaviors is to admit we are powerless and that something has got a hold of us and won't let go. The second step to healing and freedom is to place ourselves in the hands of a higher power.

Seeing addictions and social problems as problems rooted in the same soil accentuates one of the key attitudes underlying the Catholic way of life. I teach college students that social problems are personal problems and personal problems are social problems. Seeing our brothers' and sisters' problems as our problems and our blessings as their inheritance to share frees us from a sterile, immobilizing individualism. Seeing our problems as connected to wider societal and cultural deficiencies allows us to reach out to others so that together we can search for solutions. Nowhere is this more acute and actual for the Catholic Church in the United States than in the debate over immigration. The issue is not new. At the start of the twentieth century, 15 percent of the population of this country was foreign born. Today that number stands at 11.5 percent. And the idea that immigrants make no contribution to us is quite mistaken. Somewhere between $90 and $140 billion a year comes into the coffers of local, state, and federal taxes from the earnings of immigrants. "Undocumented immigrants pay income taxes as well, as evidenced by the Social Security Administration's 'suspense file' (taxes that cannot be matched to workers' names and social security numbers), which grew by $20 billion between 1990 and 1998" (JFI 2007).

If all peoples could be converted to this kingdom way of life, to use the words of the old

> "A change of mentality is needed, no longer seeing the poor as a burden, or as intruders trying to profit from others, but as people seeking to share the goods of the world so that we can create a just and prosperous world for all."
>
> —*Centesimus Annus* (The Hundredth Year) John Paul II, 1991, #28

Louie Armstrong song, "what a wonderful world" this would be. To realize that the kingdom of God truly takes precedence over the kingdoms of this world would mean the end of war, the end of insane piling up and hoarding of wealth, the end to divisions based on race, creed, religion, or nation of origin. To realize that God's reign truly is primordial and paramount in our lives would free us to order our days in accordance with the desires of God and laugh at the attempts of others to impose their vision and way of life upon us.

One of our most articulate, provocative, and prophetic public intellectuals is Princeton philosopher Cornel West. A radical Christian social democrat, he has raised our awareness of crucial social and political issues in his popular books *Race Matters* (1993) and *Democracy Matters* (2004). Following his lead, I suggest that all that forms us as cultural and social beings, "matters."

# 4
# Leadership Matters
## Catholicism as the Practice of the Loving Exercise
## of Power and Authority

*"They were astounded at his teaching, for he taught them as one having authority, and not as the scribes.... They were all amazed, and they kept on asking one another, 'What is this? A new teaching—with authority! He commands even the unclean spirits, and they obey him.'"*
—Mark 1:22, 2

There is an oft-repeated tale in anthropological circles of the anthropologist who asks the tribal chief how he maintains his position. "I tell the warriors to do what they want to do," he answers. "What would happen if you told them to do what they didn't want to do?" "Oh, I wouldn't be chief for long."

Chiefs who impose unnecessary burdens on people are soon no longer powerful. But a religion that is charged with transforming the world according to the insights and ideas of the kingdom of God cannot simply tell all people what they want to hear. Power and authority in the church run the risk of being on the one hand too lenient, simply telling people what they want to hear and do, and, on the other hand, being too strident, telling people what they do not need to do or hear. Jesus said to scholars of the law, "Woe to you!... For you load people with burdens hard to bear, and you yourselves do not lift a finger to ease them" (Luke 11:46). Jesus also said to his apostles, "Receive the Holy Spirit. If you forgive the sins of any, they are forgiven them; if you retain the sins of any, they are retained" (John 20:22–23).

## Who Has Authority in Our Lives?

God is the creator, the "author" of our lives. The hope that we will live forever is based on a trust that God is the God of life (cf. Deuteronomy 30:19)
and wants us to live forever (cf. 1 Timothy 2:4). God has the power to sustain our lives. Without God, we cease to exist. Since God is the creator, author, and sustainer of our lives, God has authority in our lives. If you
disagree, just go ahead and try to live forever on your own, without God.

Sin separates us from God, making us unable to live in God's presence. Jesus Christ has the power to forgive our sins and repair our rup-
tured relationship with God, our loving creator. Jesus Christ reveals the
way to God: "I am the way, the truth, and the life" (John 14:6). When we
are baptized in Christ, we receive the power, or grace, of the Holy Spirit
to live our lives in accordance with God's desires, that is, in ways that
make us and others happy and healthy and holy and free.

The Catholic vision of human existence is based on the hope that
deep down, intrinsically, people are made in a way that makes them
want to choose and do the right thing. The strength of this vision is the
belief that human persons are intrinsically good. When we choose and
do evil, we are acting against our own best interests, we are denying our
own best selves. In Lonergan's method, when we act according to the
norms inherently revealed in the ways our hearts and minds function,
we inevitably discern and choose the good, the who and what we authentically are and desire to be. God has made us in such a way that we
naturally tend to orient ourselves toward our divine destination. Power
and authority in the church should foster cooperation with cultural realities that lead to and are congruent with our divine destiny. Authority
ought also denounce and orient us away from that which frustrates our
achieving that for which we are created, union with God. God, our creator and destiny, therefore has ultimate authority over our lives. St. Ignatius says it simply: "Human beings are created to praise, reverence,
and serve God our Lord, and by means of doing this, to save their souls.
The other things on the face of the earth are created for human beings,
to help them in the pursuit of the end for which they were created"
(*Spiritual Exercises of St. Ignatius*, #23, trans. George Ganss, SJ).

We ought to grant authority to that which helps us attain our goal:
union with God and our loved ones for all eternity. God calls us to do only
what is good for us and others. God invites us to live and graces us with

the power of the Holy Spirit to give us eternal life. God demands only that we choose and live in a manner that is coherent with the facts concerning the ultimate purpose and meaning of our lives. God's "demands" are not the impositions of a megalomaniacal tyrant. God's "demands" are divine invitations to live our lives according to the dictates of reality. I can eat fruits and vegetables or junk food and gallons of soda. One diet will make me slim and trim, the other will make me fat and ill. The authority of the healthy diet is evident in the way it fits the ways my body functions. How am I to know which authority to follow? In the same way that I will follow the dictates of an expert fly fisherman if I want to catch a rainbow trout, I ought to follow the advice of the expert on life, life's author and arbiter, if I want to attain eternal life. Note, as John's Gospel makes clear, that eternal life doesn't start at death; it starts at baptism. We are already living eternally now.

> *"Note, as John's Gospel makes clear, that eternal life doesn't start at death; it starts at baptism. We are already living eternally now."*

The question for us becomes what group, community, tradition, and/or institution can aid me/us in our quest to listen for, hear, and heed the invitations and instructions of God? There are innumerable voices and powers clamoring for our attention and allegiance. Which ones really direct us toward the fullness of life and life eternal? For contemporary Catholics, our culture offers a smorgasbord of spiritualities from which to choose. Why should someone choose the Catholic way of life over any of the other offerings?

The Catholic faith, despite all too numerous failures, creates an institutional response to the initiative of God that demonstrates its validity in lives of service that make for progress on both personal and communal levels. The thousands of schools, hospitals, shelters, parishes, soup kitchens, and universities supported by the Catholic Church are an essential part of the lived faith of Catholics. For Catholicism, the Body of Christ is not some amorphous, idealistic concept. The Body of Christ is as real as the flesh and blood and bone of my neighbor in need. In the words of one of my Jesuit theology professors, "If you want to really see Jesus, the next time you're at Mass or in class or at the soup kitchen, look at the person next to you. There he is!" The plethora of non-institutionalized "spiritualities" available may nurture a personal relationship with the divine, and may truly foster a real connection with one's own inner self wherein the mercy and love of God are revealed. As St. Ignatius says about spiritual tools and methods, "If it helps, use it." Still, esoteric methods of the new spiritualities, from the enneagram to aromatherapy to conversations with one's inner child, are ultimately fruitless if they do not encourage us to form organizations and create and maintain social structures that make for life and freedom for all our brothers and sisters on this planet.

Many Catholics dabble in such "surface" spiritualities because they find the Catholic Church unsatisfactory. Non-practicing Catholics have told me, "The Catholic Church isn't spiritual," which usually means they have never heard of the Trappists, John of the Cross, Teresa of Avila, Ignatius of Loyola, or the many other mystical/spiritual traditions in our church (e.g., Benedictine, Augustinian, and the ubiquitous Franciscans). Or they fail to appreciate that spiritualities in the Catholic tradition aim to transform us into agents of the kingdom of God and don't necessarily form us according to the values and mores of our self-esteem-affirming twenty-first-century cultural world. Prayer and fasting may help one lose weight, but that is not the primary aim of prayer and fasting. Even those folks who dabble in "surface" spiritualities often confess that "spiritual" is more attractive for the ephemeral promise of self-improvement ("Meditating helps me be more calm and centered." "Yoga gives me a tight butt"). Catholicism doesn't simply offer a spiritualized means to personal well-being. The practices of the Catholic faith result in a community's and communities' living life to the fullest. In community the Catholic individual relates to self, others, and God in joyful praise and service and love.

The great attraction of various non-institutionalized spiritualities is the seeming freedom from authority they intimate. Somehow one will be able to contact the mystery of existence without the messy and mundane of the human condition and its inherent need for institutions. For a few unique persons, such individual paths are the way God calls and leads. Yet, in the Catholic tradition, even unique saints and mystics attest to the strength and direction afforded them by the tried and tested truths of the faith and methods of prayer that guide them on their journey. On the other hand, un-tethered and un-rooted surface spiritualists seek blindly for the divine, and too often, after all their explorations, end up right where they started, locked into self with little lasting experience of transcendence. Authentic spiritual practices (e.g., anything from the rosary

to vision quests to yoga) rarely lead to true transformation when practiced a few months and then dropped for a new "discipline." The depths
of the spiritual life are usually opened up only after years of arduous fi-
delity. Authority in spiritual practices is demonstrated by the service
given and freedom attained by the spiritualities' practitioners. Paradoxi-
cally, the very freedom sought is often found in traditional Catholic spiritualities. Ignatian spirituality is neatly summed up by its description as
a program that "frees us from, frees us for, frees us to be with."

## Sacraments Confer Authority

The freedom so desired by spiritual seekers is already there in sacraments rightly understood and practiced. Sacraments facilitate freedom
and call us to continual conversion. By practicing the faith and celebrating the sacraments, most centrally the Eucharist, and in achieving the
freedom to be who and what we truly desire to be, we actually become
who and what God wants us to be. In being who and what the sacraments sign that we are, we become, through the grace of God, authentic persons. Both facilitated by and recognized in and through
sacraments, such authenticity attests to the action of God in our lives
and thus confers authority. While eloquently articulating the sacramental principle that everything in creation is capable of communicating
the presence and action of the mystery of God, Richard McBrien defines sacraments on both general and specific levels as, generally, "any
visible sign of God's invisible presence. Specifically, a sign through
which the church manifests its faith and communicates the saving reality of [the grace] of God which is present in the church and in the signs
themselves" (McBrien 1981:731, 1255).

As opposed to discrete realities that can exist on their own, sacraments are relational realities. Sacraments exist in the relationships between persons, the community called church,
and God. The saving, loving presence and love
of God (i.e., grace) continues and contours a
person's life to the degree that he or she is authentically appropriating and lovingly living
the grace conferred and recognized by the
community's celebration of the sacraments.

> Sacraments are "those
> actions that achieve in
> human hearts and lives what
> they signify to human
> minds."
>
> —Brian Daley, SJ

Matrimony is one sacrament where this ongoing authenticity and authority of the sacraments is most clearly appreciated and understood. Two people are joined together in Christ by their marriage vows. Their marriage is recognized by all who know them. They are recognized by all as the parents of their children. The authority they enjoy and for which they are responsible as husband and wife, and as parents, is mediated by their living out their marriage vows daily. To the degree that they authentically love one another and their children, the marriage deepens the expression of Christ among us. To the degree that they fail to love and serve one another as they vowed to do, the marriage becomes less capable of expressing the presence of God. As any married couple will tell you, some days are better than others at revealing to all the love of God that penetrates and permeates their relationship as husband and wife. But, when their love does shine through, one has to be deaf and blind to be unaware of what is happening.

Baptism is what makes a person a Christian, and baptism in the Catholic Church makes one a Catholic Christian. One's dignity as a daughter or son of God, in the Catholic tradition, comes from being created by God and baptized into Christ Jesus. The authority one has as a baptized person is evident to the degree that one is authentically practicing the Catholic faith. That baptismal grace gets lived out in relationship to the church, a multi-faceted reality. The church is the people of God, the Body of Christ, and the eucharistic community. The celebration of the Eucharist centers and directs the desires and communal needs of the Catholic community. In praying for "truth and life...holiness and grace...justice, love, and peace" (Preface for the Feast of Christ the King), the Catholic community pledges to serve in ways that make those desired realities operative in the lived practices of our societies and cultures. The way the desired justice and peace and love become real and "take on flesh" is in and through the practices of people, in and through the institutions that make up the daily patterns of our lives.

The church also, like all things human and enduring, is an institution. Sacraments cannot function on an exclusively personal plane. Sacraments, by their nature as signs, are communal, that is, they are community realities that necessitate authoritative articulation of how and what they are. To achieve their goals, or that which they signify, sacraments must go beyond the merely personal and actually connect persons to community and to God. When Catholics claim that "Mass is boring," the root of their dissatisfaction is that their experience of the Mass is not connecting them to the transcendent reality of God rooted in community. The antidote lies both in making the Mass relevant (e.g., through homilies that are intelligible and connected to the realities of people's lives) and in getting Catholics interested in the God of love and life who calls them to mission in and through the church into which they were baptized.

## Institutional Authority

We are made by God, for God, unto God. Atheists and agnostics say that we cannot know if we are made by God. These non-believers state that since they and many others do not believe in God, believers cannot claim to orient society and institutions according to beliefs in God. But atheists and agnostics must recognize that, according to their views, our institutions have to be constructed on their belief that there is no God. It is inescapable. Meaning and community are carried in institutions, and institutions are going to be based on some beliefs of some groups about something. The question is this: If God exists, how could we not measure our lives and institutions on how well they approximate what we believe God desires for and from us?

The argument against measuring institutions on God's designs is that throughout history there have been many battles waged and blood shed over whose "god" will be the arbiter. I've often heard the old complaint, "Religions have caused a lot of wars, so I'm not going to adhere to any religion." Yet, just because there have been wars fought by democracies, we have not jettisoned democratic forms of government. Just because corporations have acted illegally and hurt people, we have not gotten rid of corporations. In the same way, just because some supposed adherents of religions have beaten and killed others in the name of their "god" does not mean religion itself ought to be jettisoned. If anything, such aberrations mean we need stronger institutional religions that can actually convert us and see to it that we live according to the great commandment to love God and love our neighbor as ourself (Luke 10:27).

The antidote to bad religion is not "no religion" or "whatever" religion. The antidote to bad religion is good religion, religion that leads to life and freedom. Individualistic spiritualities may succor personal life quests, but do much less than vibrant, authentic, organized religious institutions to fashion a just and lasting social order. Without such institutional religious powers, we (our families and schools) are left at the mercies of the ever more globalized market economy, and the whims of various "Jihads" and "McWorlds."

*"The antidote to bad religion is not 'no religion' or 'whatever' religion. The antidote to bad religion is good religion, religion that leads to life and freedom. Individualistic spiritualities may succor personal life quests, but do much less than vibrant, authentic, organized religious institutions to fashion a just and lasting social order."*

Most important, any effort to raise one's religion's values, ideals, and practices up as influential cultural influences in society must do so in ways that respect all others persons' human rights. Paramount is transformative dialogue among adherents of various religions, dialogue in which we are willing to be "transformed into a communion in which we do not remain what we were" (Gadamer 1991:378). In the decrees on ecumenism and on relationships with non-Christian religions (*Unitatis Redintegratio* and *Nostra Aetate*), Vatican II clearly called for all Catholics to respect and work with believers of other religions. While celebrating clearly and comfortably who and what we are as Catholics, we can engage in dialogue and prayer with those who seek God in other traditions (Buddhist, Hindu, Muslim). All the religions that have endured have at their core a message of love and reconciliation of all with God. And all religions call on humans to love one another. Despite impostors and charlatans who misappropriate and manipulate the meanings and messages of scriptures, those who through the ages have sincerely sought God have learned that a religion cannot be imposed on anyone. One who forces someone else to believe is living unauthentically. Persons must come to God freely and without being coerced in any way, shape, or form.

In today's world it is more necessary than ever to assert the simple truth that any god who demands human sacrifice is not a God worth worshiping. René Girard's seminal work reveals the power of the story of Jesus, the gospel that reverses all the cultural constructions based on dividing people into opposed camps of "us" versus "them," and the development of gods who sanction our being "us" by standing in opposition to, and even killing, "them." Jesus is the God who commands us to love our enemies, the God who dies for us rather than having us make someone else die in order to honor a supposed god (Girard 1985).

### Institutions as Carriers of Authority and Meaning

Some rebel against or are repelled by the idea that we are made by God and for God. The rugged individualism that runs deep in American culture makes us wary of depending on anyone else. Robert Bellah in *The Good Society* has shown how our deeply ingrained individualism is harming us. What Bellah and his co-authors recognize is that the complex world in which we live necessitates institutional responses to the problems that affect us corporately and individually. And one question that confronts us all, both believer and non-believer, is the relationship with religious authority in our lives and institutions. Even those who want to exile God and religious institutions from the public square have to provide cogent arguments supporting their position. As in so many instances, the answer to the question is revealed in what is more authentic, and thus, what is more truly human.

Institutions are inescapable. Institutions and institutional authority are needed in order to form human community. The social structure of society is "the framework of society, consisting of the social positions, networks of relationships, and institutions that hold a society together and shape people's opportunities and experiences" (Gelles and Levine, 1999:667). The institutional configuration of society makes possible our living and controls and constrains our lives in many ways. Look at the institution of government. One of the functions of government is to decide where roads will run. Without roads, there is nowhere to drive the car. Given the increase in traffic, someone or some group in government is going to have to decide where the roads will go, through your backyard or mine. Or consider a more important issue: abortion. The government decides if abortion will be legal. Although the government in the United States forces no one to have an abortion, the Roe v. Wade decision of 1973 means that I live in a society that has allowed the destruction of some 47,365,629 million unborn children since 1973 (<www.priestforlife.org>, accessed February 2007).

"Institutions are not only constraining, they are also enabling. They are the substantial forms through which we understand our own identity and the identity of others as we seek cooperatively to achieve a decent society" (Bellah 1991:12). Institutions are inescapable, unless you are ready to go out to Montana and live in a cabin by yourself. The principal institutions of family, education, religion, politics, and the economy, and the umbrella institution, mass media, are facts of our existence. It is no more possible to dismiss an understanding of these institutions than it would be to ignore chemistry, biology, and physics for a scientific understanding of our world and our place in it. And to live one's faith necessarily means articulating an understanding of religion's relationship to these institutions.

> Institutions are patterns of social activity that give shape to collective and individual experience.... They shape character by assigning responsibility, demanding accountability, and providing the standards in terms of which each person recognizes the excellence of his or her achievements. Each individual's possibilities depend on the opportunities opened up within the institutional contexts to which that person has access. (Bellah 1991:40)

Institutions are human constructions. Institutions can be as good, or as evil, as the human beings who make them. But individuals are often seriously compromised by the dictates of institutions. There were woefully few individual Germans who stood up and refused to cooperate with Hitler's regime (cf. Zahn 1986). There are hardly any Americans who refrain from driving or riding in cars, even though we now know the damage being done to the planet by fossil fuel emissions. Further, since the power of institutions is cumulative, the good they do can be much more than the sum of individuals' personal goodness, and the evil done by institutions, unfortunately, can be much more than the sum of evil done by the institutions' members. Institutions can become corrupt, but such corruption can be challenged and converted (cf. Bellah 1991:41).

Bellah argues that the problems facing us today are institutional and require institutional responses. Our institutions too often fail to call us to be our best selves, and too often we accept inept and inert institutions passively, instead of striving to call the persons involved in such institutions to respond authentically. It has too often happened that,

---

1,400:
Estimated number of U.S. college students who die from alcohol related accidents each year.

70,000:
Number of sex assaults and date rapes attributed to campus drinking.

(*Time* Magazine 4/22/02, p. 18)

"in the case of dysfunctional institutions, we have simply tried to escape them, and have allowed them to fall apart, rather than reform and revitalize them" (Bellah 1991:50). Drunk driving in the United States is still a practice that kills thousands. In Australia, the police can stop all vehicles at any time and administer a breath test. "Down Under," a place where "blokes" (guys) and "sheilas" (gals) like to have a good time well stimulated by alcohol, they do not outlaw "drunk driving"; they simply do not allow "drink driving." You drink and drive down under and you're in big trouble. No "No Worries, Mate!" for those who put lives at risk by driving under the influence. One institutional response on the personal level in Australia is that for virtually all social gatherings involving alcohol, there are designated drivers. In the United States, institutionally, we have not handled the problem of alcohol and automobiles as well as the Aussies have. According to MADD (Mothers Against Drunk Driving), 16,885 people died in 2005 in the United States as a result of drunk driving, which was the cause of 39 percent of all traffic fatalities (<www.madd.org>, accessed January 2007). Our institutional practices are not strong enough to stop significant numbers of people from driving while impaired. The way Australia handles the problem makes people more free to drive safe from drunk drivers.

Freedom and justice are possible only to the degree that the institutional framework of society sustains and support them. Bellah notes that freedom and justice are intricately connected to the defining and establishment of the common good (Bellah 1991:245). The common good is an idea intrinsically connected to the practice of authority in the Catholic Church. Authority, from a Catholic perspective, recognizes the inherent relationality permeating all of human existence. We ought to cooperate with the good (i.e., that which makes for progress); we ought to resist that which colludes with evil (i.e., that which causes decline). Authorities are those powers and people that can rightly articulate and guide us as we discern between good and evil. The good is demonstrated by the freedom and peace and love emerging in the lives of folks living in a social structure and institutions in that structure. Evil is evident in the enslavement of persons, and in the strife and the apathy and hate present in the lives of people subject to unjust and unloving social structures and institutions.

In the Catholic Church, authority resides ultimately with God. What is to be done, and how it is to be done, is judged by how attentively, intelligently, reasonably, and responsibly the practices and pastoral choices of church leaders authentically express the living out of the gospel of Jesus Christ. Popes, bishops, priests, and laity are all equal as baptized members of the community. The roles that have greater authority in the church are based on the service inherent in the carrying out of Christ's mission: "The Son of Man came not to be served but to serve" (Matthew 20:28). Authority in the church is subject to evaluation according to how well the authorities actually serve the people of God. Authority is difficult because differing groups in the church desire different things. Lonergan's analysis of authority can help us move beyond the "conservative" versus "liberal" stalemate the church faces as we begin the third millennium.

## Longergan's Dialectic of Authority

Power is the ability to make people do something. Authority is the right and legitimate use of power. Lonergan succinctly states that "Authority is legitimate power.... The source of power is cooperation." As we leave the world of childhood, the world of immediacy, we move into the world of adulthood, "a world mediated by meaning and motivated by values." In the world mediated by meaning, "power resides in the world of authority" (Lonergan 1985:5).

We experience the truth of our reliance on authority's word every day. The advertisement "When E. F. Hutton speaks, people listen" was built on the principle that the world, the real world, operates on the word of authority. From the trivial "Yes, Sir, the train will be here at 9:10 AM," to the serious, "Bill, I'm sorry. The cancer has spread and I really recommend that you have surgery," we depend on others' words being true, and they depend on our words being true. To the degree that our words are true, we progress. To the degree that our words are false, we decline. To the degree that we can depend on the veracity and capability of our authorities, we progress. To the degree that we cannot have faith and trust in the veracity and capability of our authorities, we decline.

Lonergan distinguishes between authority and authorities. The authorities are those who hold the positions and offices, but it is the institutions themselves, not the individual temporary authorities, that are invested with authority. "Authority belongs to the community that has a common field of experience, common and complementary ways of understanding, common judgments and common aims. It is the community that is the carrier of a common world mediated by meaning and motivated by values. It is the validity of those meanings and values that gives authority its aura and prestige" (Lonergan 1985:7).

Lonergan schematizes what he calls the dialectic of authority. Meanings and values can be authentic or unauthentic, or situated somewhere along a continuum between the two poles. Meanings and values are authentic to the degree that they result from faithful adherence to the transcendental precepts: Be Attentive; Be Intelligent; Be Reasonable; Be Responsible; Be Loving. Meanings and values are unauthentic to the degree that they are "the product of cumulative inattention, obtuseness, unreasonableness, irresponsibility" (Lonergan 1985:7). "Authenticity makes power legitimate.... Unauthenticity leaves power naked. It reveals power as mere power. Similarly, authenticity legitimates authorities, and unauthenticity destroys their authority and reveals them as merely powerful" (Lonergan 1985:7–8).

Lonergan acknowledges how complicated the authentication of authority actually is. Authenticity and its opposite are found in three groups: (1) in the community itself, (2) in the community's authorities, and (3) in those persons subject to the authorities. Authenticity and unauthenticity, truth and falsehood, right and wrong, injustice and justice, freedom and slavery, peace and strife, are "ever precarious" (Lonergan 1985:8). Communities, authorities and subjects enjoy truth and right and justice and freedom and peace to the degree that they faithfully follow the transcendental precepts. To the degree that they do not follow the precepts written in the very functioning of our better selves, communities and persons in them suffer falsehood, wrong, injustice, slavery, and strife.

To further complicate matters, one of the three groups may be unauthentic and jeopardize the authenticity of the other two. The authorities may authentically call the members of the community to justice and truth and the members may refuse to heed the call. On the other hand, the community's members may authentically appropriate the reading of the tradition articulated by unauthentic authorities. Leadership by unauthentic authorities can lead to the "authentic" appropriation of a bastardized tradition, a process that may infect and infest institutional structures and practices and, like a virus in a computer, replicate and perpetuate itself, infecting and destroying the entire structure from within.

How does one—and one's community—know if the appropriation of the tradition is authentic or not? "Beware of false prophets.... You will know them by their fruits" (Matthew 7:15-1616). The proof of sustained authenticity is progress. The evidence of unauthenticity is decline. Do the blind see? Do the lame walk? Are lepers cleansed? Do the deaf hear? Are the dead raised? Is the good news proclaimed to the poor? (cf. Matthew 11:5). If so, you are in an authentic community. Are these images too biblical for the twenty-first century? Update them. Is the community contributing to the betterment of people? Are small children and the elderly who are too weak to care for themselves provided for and treated well? Are the ignorant educated? Are institutions of medical care run well, and do all in the community have access to health care? Do those enslaved, lost, and made spiritually ill in a consumer society hear a word of freedom and release? Are the addicted and depressed restored to health? Are the powerful called to care for the poor and help the poor do for themselves? Are we moving away from war and the production of weapons of war and toward peace? If so, we are in an authentic community. Unauthenticity is announced by the squabbling that dissipates apostolic energies, by the sniping and backbiting that sap people's joy, by the destruction of organizations and institutions that have provided services to people in need. To appeal to authentic people is easy. Authentic folks know what is good and right and just, and they do it. To appeal to unauthentic people is useless, because the very challenging of the situation produced by the irrational and irresponsible choices of the unauthentic group, and/or their authorities, resists rational analysis. To simply tell the sinful and the stupid that they are sinful and stupid does little to transform the situation, for the sinful and the stupid rarely recognize the objective reality of their predicament. And since we all, to some degree, share in the sinfulness and stupidity of being human, no matter how graced and holy we may be, we must strive to remove the wooden beams from our own eyes before attempting to extract the splinters from the eyes of our sisters and brothers (Matthew 7:3).

Lonergan's solution to the problem of ongoing decline is self-sacrificing love. Such a solution is neither simple nor facile. Such a solution is neither short-term nor painless. Yet such a solution, carefully discerned and gently and lovingly implemented, is the only way to move us, personally and institutionally, into the realm of the reign of God.

> However, beyond progress and decline there is redemption. Its principle is self-sacrificing love. To fall in love is to go beyond attention, intelligence, reasonableness and responsibility. It is to set up a new principle.... In the measure that the community

becomes a community of love and so capable of making great sacrifices, in that measure it can wipe out the grievances and wipe out the objective absurdities that its unauthenticity has brought about. (Lonergan 1985:10)

### Delicate Discernment

The greatest challenge facing the Catholic Church in the United States at the start of the twenty-first century is this delicate discernment regarding which groups and authorities are authentic and which are unauthentic, and to what degree such groups are so. Even more difficult is the keeping of authentic persons and authorities in the church when unauthentic groups and abusive authorities threaten to wear down and marginalize the authentic among us.

How can we make the judgment that some authorities and groups in the church are authentic and are to be cooperated with, and others are to be avoided and not supported? Pay attention to what is going on. Determine which authorities and what groups are authentically living out the fullness of the gospel and the Catholic tradition. Both conservatives and liberals are notorious for picking and choosing certain aspects of Catholicism, while ignoring other central practices of the faith. Those who go ballistic when the altar rails are removed too often seem to have never heard of the Church's social teaching and, when they do hear of it, rail against the teachings of the popes and bishops, condemning the ideas and principles as "socialism" or "communism" (as if capitalism were the eleventh commandment). Liberal Catholics, who thought Pope John Paul II was "out of touch," love to champion causes from AIDS to liberation theology in Zambia, but rarely want to take on the responsibility for serving on the parish council or teaching the little children's CCD classes. One of the most authentic Catholics of this past century, Dorothy Day, was her typically prophetic and challenging self when she said, "In matters of social justice, I get as far to the left as I can. In matters of theology, I get as far to the right as I can." A fair and accurate reading of John Paul II would have to admit that he did much the same.

> "...the Christian of the future will be a mystic or he will not exist at all, if by mysticism we mean, not singular parapsychological phenomena, but a genuine experience of God emerging from the very heart of existence. This statement is very true and its truth and importance will become still clearer in the spirituality of the future."
>
> —Karl Rahner
> (cited in Cozzens 2002:191)

In looking for which groups are authentically living out the fullness of the faith, look at how they live out the liturgy, how they put their prayer into practice, how seriously they are involved with the church on an institutional level, and whether they, if charged with being Catholic, would be in serious danger of a quick conviction. It is hard to claim that one is a Philadelphia Eagles fan if one never follows "Da Iggles" on TV or goes to the games. It is just as difficult to convince anyone that one is Catholic if one never has much of a long-term connection to a parish or Catholic community. The daily and weekly practices of one's life mark one as a Catholic. Or those daily and weekly practices evidence that one is more committed to other organizations' meanings and values.

What marks authentic authorities? Attentiveness, intelligence, reasonableness, love, and the willingness to take responsibility are evidence of the authentic use of legitimate power. The bishops and pastors and lay leaders who lead by example, who struggle to persuade the faithful rather than browbeat believers, who work with, rather than over and against, pastors and parishioners, who strive to articulate the faith and preach the Word in a way that both consoles and comforts while also challenging and confronting, will find flocks healthy and vibrant in their dioceses and parishes. Authorities who exemplify the joke about "liturgists as terrorists" will see people resentful, sullen, and non-participative.

According to Lonergan, the true is what we know as the result of the authentic implementation of the transcendental method. The known is Being (i.e., reality), and the "what" that is known is true insofar as the knower and the knowing community authentically follow the transcendental method. "How do I know if the cultural standards that ground my choices are truly objective standards: In other words, what we are looking for is a transcultrual norm or standard that is independent of specific cultural norms but that is applicable to any and all cultures" (Flanagan 1997:206). According to Lonergan, the "transcultural norm or standard" we seek is the transcendental method itself. And the revolutionary result of Lonergan's work is that the faithful practice of the transcendental method yields a world wherein "ethics goes beyond and subsumes metaphysics" (Flanagan 1997:232). In other words, according to Lonergan, knowing who and what we are and how our minds and hearts function (cognitional structure) re-

"When power meets power there is conflict. When power meets vulnerability there is oppression. When vulnerability meets vulnerability there emerges the communion of intimacy."

—Pat O'Sullivan, SJ

veals reality, what really is (metaphysics), and further reveals ethics, what we ought to do and be. Authority in the church will reside in, and be respected by, those who are authentically knowers and doers of the truth.

## Conclusion

Power and authority in the church must be placed at the service of transforming our world, especially in the areas of gender and race relations and in matters of economic injustice. In our twenty-first-century world, authority in the church will prove its worth to the degree that decent and loving communities form and influence the cultural practices of people in our social world. The failure of bishops to deal with pedophile priests shows what happens when authorities fail. Lawsuits cost large sums and the teaching of the church across the board becomes suspect. Beyond the present crisis caused by clergy scandals is the problem of Catholics too weakly and ineffectually practicing our faith and our church's social teachings. The failure of believers to address issues of injustice costs much in broken lives and suffering communities. Our faith calls and leads us to be the healing presence of Christ in the world. We are the Body of Christ. As St. Teresa of Avila poetically said,

> Christ has no body now on earth but yours,
>     no feet but yours, no hands but yours.
> Yours are the eyes through which the compassion of Christ
>     is to look out on a hurting world.
> Yours are the feet with which he is to go about doing good.
> Yours are the hands with which he is to bless all now.

God doesn't come at us with overwhelming power forcing us to be or act in certain ways. God calls us to a communion of intimacy.

PRACTICES TO AMELIORATE AUTHORITY AND POWER RELATIONS

1. Read Lonergan's short article, "The Dialectic of Authority" (Lonergan 1985).

2. Form real parish councils. Every pastor should create and coordinate a parish council whose members share power and authority with him. Any pastor who fails to do so should find many empty envelopes in the collection basket explaining that contributions will be forthcoming when the parish follows canon law concerning parish councils.

3. Bishops should insist that all parishes and all diocesan offices and schools follow normal accounting procedures and undergo financial auditing by accredited agencies.

4. Lay people should be given a much greater role in the articulation of church law and practices.

5. All of us would do well to prayerfully examine our roles in the creating and sustaining of polarization in the church. The existence of "liberal" and "conservative" camps has weakened the church's ability to be an effective agent of transformation in our world. The need for committed Catholics to work together is crucial. We risk losing another generation if we so not stop the undercutting of efforts of people of good will reaching out to youth (cf. Hoge et al. 2001).

6. Develop and implement pastoral initiatives to reach those people who describe themselves as "spiritual but not religious." Willingness to engage in dialogue with those of other faiths and of no faith will do much to make our own faith stance more credible.

7. The need for dialogue is paramount. More than anything else, true and open dialogue will move us forward. The more transparency and openness in all our church endeavors, the more authentic and true a community of disciples and leaven for the world we will be.

# 5
# Equality Matters
## Catholicism as the Practice of Just Gender and Race Relations

*"As many of you as were baptized into Christ have clothed yourselves with Christ. There is no longer Jew or Greek, there is no longer slave or free, there is no longer male and female; for all of you are one in Christ Jesus."*
　　—Galatians 3:27–28

## Gender Relations

Catholicism is a way of understanding one's life as involved in great transformations, transformation of oneself unto God, and one's community and society in the light of the kingdom of God. In two cultural areas, great transformations have occurred in the past half century, transformations little imagined in 1950. Relationships between men and women and relationships between various ethnic and racial groupings in the United States have changed radically in the past fifty years, maybe more than they did during the previous two centuries. Practicing Catholicism is a way of understanding these changes, and then acting to construct further advances. The intelligent practice of Catholicism can truly fashion communities, society, and a global village in ways that make a world of justice and peace, a world wherein all can enjoy real equality regardless of sex, race, ethnicity, or creed. To do so approximates more and more the kingdom of God where we all will live transformed in the God who is "all in all" (1 Corinthians 15:28). To the degree that our practice of religion and our personal lives maintain forms of gender and racial inequality, we frustrate the designs of God's reign.

### Family Relationships

Radical changes have occurred in family structure in recent decades. In October 2006, the *New York Times*, citing the census bureau's American Community Survey, reported that only 49.7 percent of U.S. households consisted of married couples, down from 76 percent in 1957. Twenty-five percent of households were comprised of one person living alone. (Roberts 2006b). It is a difficult for students in an Introduction to Sociology class to define what a family is. The old 1950s definition of Dad going to work and Mom staying home to care for the kids fits less than 10 percent of American families.

Despite such radical changes in family structure, whenever I meet an old friend whom I haven't seen for a few months, almost immediately I will ask, or they will volunteer, information about their spouse and kids. Most people spend a great deal of their conscious energy thinking about, worrying about, wondering about how to get along with their wife/husband and children. Cell phones have astronomically increased the number of moments people are in touch. For most people, parents, siblings, and children are of prime importance. TV shows like *Friends* and *Will & Grace* present a skewed image of American life. Even HBO's *The Sopranos* and *Six Feet Under*, as uncharacteristic of real life as any TV shows, present people mainly preoccupied with familial relationships. On spring evenings many more dads are at Little League games than hitting the bars and strip clubs. Mothers spend years of their lives preoccupied with the care and well-being of their children, and continue to care for them well into their adult years. A mom is always and forever a mom. Children desperately want warm and loving relations with their parents.

Our relationship with God is named by Jesus as one of child to parent. God is "our" Father. This does not mean that God is like "my" father or "your" father, a charge a distorted version of "pop" psychology sometimes uses to discredit and belittle religion. God is a parent who cares about us all. What God as "Father" meant was simpler when we were clear about the cultural meanings and role of "father." We are not so clear anymore.

This came home to me in the mid-1980s. I had just returned from three years in Chile. I was met at the airport in Philadelphia by my brother and my then four-month-old nephew. I was a bit surprised when I learned that my brother was changing his son's diapers. I doubt it had ever crossed my father's mind to change one of our diapers. But a quiet revolution occurred at the end of the twentieth century in the United States: men discovered they could clean and cover their children's little butts. A few months later, when we were at a family meal, the topic of men changing diapers came up. One guy there announced he was never going to change diapers. Suddenly there was silence; all conversation stopped. My brother looked across the table at him and said, "Yo, Bob, this is the 1980s." It was then that I knew things were changing. As meanings and roles of what it is to be a man, of what it is to be a woman, continue to develop and change, our cultural worlds will be transformed. Gender relations are the basis of any family and of any human community. The church is no exception.

> *"Gender relations are the basis of any family and of any human community. The church is no exception."*

### Gender Issues

*Sex is biological*, and sex differences are rather absolute and obvious, although there is a small percentage of people whose bodies are not self-evidently male or female. But for most, sex is a matter of the XX or XY chromosomes. *Gender is cultural.* Gender has to do with the ways society and culture interact to assign assumptions, meanings, roles, and status to biological females and biological males. Sex is genetically determined, while gender is socially constructed. Women can give birth and men cannot (a sex difference), although both can and should participate in the raising and nurturing of children (a gender, i.e., cultural, practice socially constructed).

Social constructions, agreed upon ways of doing things (i.e., gender, not biology) are what determine much of our lives as women and men. Even as babies, boys are handled more roughly than girls. Boys and girls "know" which toys they are to play with and rigidly enforce the rules. A boy walking into second grade with his Barbie would be mercilessly teased. A high school girl in playing football is considered the exception rather than the rule. Women must decide if they will take their husband's surname after marriage; men may have to decide if they will hyphenate their name, but no man that I know of has taken his wife's name and erased his own. John Gray's "Men are from Mars, Women are from

Venus" series of marriage and relationship manuals are predicated on the idea that males and females are socialized into two different cultures, and if you want to understand your spouse, you have to understand and appreciate the practices and values of the other's culture. Although challenged by more rigorous researchers as being misleading and simplistic (cf. Miller et al. 2007), ideas like Gray's run deep in American culture. The "fact" that there exist cultural differences between men and women is accepted and assumed by many. Still, this "fact" is not as hard and fast as many assume.

All the supposedly obvious differences between men and women are culturally variable and change over time. In sub-Saharan Africa, women do most of the physical labor for the family, such as hauling wood and water. The idea that women are fragile, delicate creatures simply does not compute there. In Iran, women are expected to be cool and logical; men are expected to be emotional. In Russia, most doctors are women (Gelles and Levine 1999:364). Among a tribe in the Philippines, the Agta, women hunt. Some researchers have also questioned males' monopoly on violence. When verbal abuse and competitiveness are measured as indicators of violent behavior, women can rank right up there with the men, and girls can be very mean to other little girls, causing much pain (Renzetti and Curran 1998:256; Simmons 2002). In the United States, the phenomenal success of the women's soccer team in the 1999 World Cup, and the caliber of play in the Women's National Basketball Association, have disproven the idea that women are not "real" athletes.

In January 2007, Mothers Work Inc., a Philadelphia company selling maternity clothes, paid $375,000 to settle a discrimination lawsuit. A Motherhood Maternity store in Florida refused to hire pregnant women, and then fired an assistant manager who blew the whistle on the practice.

(*Philadelphia Inquirer,* January 13, 2007)

Gender issues are constantly being questioned, re-evaluated, and re-negotiated today. We affirm, challenge, or change the "way things are." Who takes whose name at the wedding (how about a coin flip)? Who pays for the date? Whose career takes precedence in a marriage? Who cleans the bathroom, does the shopping, cooks, and cleans up? All these mundane activities, once so ironclad and clear, are constantly up for negotiation in contemporary households.

Gender practices are deeply ingrained and rarely questioned in our day-to-day lives. But such practices do affect us unequally. It was an almost universal phenomenon in the late 1980s and early 1990s as remotes became common equipment with TVs: men controlled the clicker and incessantly surfed from station to station. Women seemed to want to stay with one show at a time. I wondered if this behavior had roots in our hunter-gatherer past: men are hunting through the channels; women like to remain near the "fire" of one station. Such gender differences may not matter, but other differences do. How else explain studies demonstrating that daughters, much more often than sons, must care for an aging and infirm parent?

Some differences are literally life threatening. What do you say to your eighteen-year-old daughter as she prepares for college about the fact that one out of every four women is a victim of rape or attempted rape while in college, and that first-year female students are the most likely to suffer sexual assault, physical abuse, and emotional abuse (<http://oneinfourusa.org>)?

The ingraining of gender practices starts very early. I was once at a big family wedding. The youngest daughter of a family of ten was to be wed (or is that way of saying it too passive? Is "She was getting married" better phraseology?). The mother of the bride had died a few years earlier. The bride's seven sisters did mega-preparations for the event. At the rehearsal party, they read poems they had written for their sister, and presented her and the groom with gag gifts. The wedding Mass and party were wonderful, with the sisters doing readings and overseeing all that goes into greeting guests and receiving gifts. The bride's father was passing out a humorous business card that read, "I'm the father of the bride. If anyone with a bill in his hand is looking for me, tell him I've left the premises." The sisters' various husbands did a bit of watching over their various sons and daughters, nieces and nephews, but the sisters did the lion's (lioness's?) share of baby/child tending. The next day, a Sunday, the sisters were planning a brunch for everyone in the family. I was invited and arrived at about 1:15 PM. There were the guys, the various husbands and boyfriends of the sisters. They were all sitting around, sipping beer and watching the Eagles vs. Giants football game on the TV. When one of the kids would get rambunctious, a guy would yell for his wife, who'd swoop in from the kitchen to handle the child. The little boys were running in and out of the house, whooping it up. The sisters were all in the kitchen, making eggs and bacon, cutting fruit, toasting bagels, preparing juices and coffees. And I noticed the little girls, off in a corner, carefully folding plastic knives and forks in paper napkins and tying ribbons on the rolls of utensils. I asked myself: How do we guys do it? How do we get the women to do all the work? And I saw it right there. It starts young, with little girls working as the little boys are running around yelling and playing. Dad might have once paid for it all, while women did the work. But now that women are often prime earners also, why don't things on the home front change?

Despite the changes in diapering procedures, there is still a great deal of sexism in our societies and cultures. Sexism is the ingrained belief that one sex is better than the other, and has the right to dominate the other sex. Sexism is contrary to the gospel. It's a sinful set of practices that demean women and dehumanize men. There may be a lot of SNAGs (Sensitive New Age Guys) out there, but there is still a lot of covert, and even overt, sexism evidenced in our daily lives. Women suffer the effects of sexism, and men do also. Men's alcoholism, suicide, mental illness, and incarceration rates far exceed those of women.

> "Sexism is contrary to the gospel. It's a sinful set of practices that demean women and dehumanize men."

Men's health in general lags behind that of women, and women live seven years longer than men (Robertson 1989:227-229). Obviously, a great deal of progress has been made in recent decades, but much societal transformation is needed for gender equality to become daily lived reality. Even where the law orders gender equity, we are a long way from making it a reality.

### Jesus' Relationship with Women

The position of women differs from culture to culture, and from era to era. Our model as Catholics is Jesus. How did he treat women? The gospels are filled with examples of Jesus breaking the cultural taboos of his day, dealing with women on an equitable basis. For the men of Jesus' time and culture, women and children were property, things a man owned. Patriarchy was the unquestioned cultural norm of the day, and breaking the canons of the patriarchal family code was unthinkable. To be without family was to be a non-person. Women, slaves, even sons and daughters of the patriarch had little choice but to do what men told them to do.

In the gospels, we see Jesus challenging the gender roles of his times. He speaks to the woman at the well, which surprises his disciples (John 4:27). For Jesus to be speaking to a woman in public was as strange in his culture and time as it would be for a man today to engage a woman in conversation in the ladies' room (cf. Pilch 1995:55–56; 2002:2). Jesus not only engages women in conversation, he travels with women, and some of them foot the bill (Luke 8:1–3). He allows himself to be touched by a "sinful" woman (Luke 7:36 ff.). He refuses to allow the stoning of the woman caught in adultery (John 8:1–11). Women are present at the cross (and some add, "the guys weren't." But, remember, the disciples would have been nailed up there with him if they had shown their faces—and one noted scripture scholar even has a provocative argument that the beloved disciple in John's Gospel is female [Schneiders 1999:220]).

Jesus models for us the ways in which all persons, men and women included, are to be treated equitably in the kingdom of God. In the early years of the church, Paul would write to the Galatians: "There is no longer Jew or Greek, there is no longer slave or free, there is no longer male and female; for all of you are one in Christ Jesus" (Galatians 3:28).

And even Paul's injunction that wives obey their husbands, which sounds sexist to twenty-first-century ears, was quite revolutionary in Paul's time. Immediately after the teaching that wives should be subject to their husbands, he orders men, "Husbands, love your wives" (see Ephesians 5:21–33). Three times in the passage he tells men to love their wives. This was radical advice in a society were many men didn't consider their wives as valuable as their cattle. Both injunctions are preceded by the instruction to all that we be "subject to one another out of reverence for Christ." It is a challenge to the church to always and in all ways keep Christ's egalitarian vision rooted in love as our goal. Equitable practices and standards between various groups are not an option; they are mandated by the logic of God's kingdom. And the challenge goes on as we continue through the centuries. Certainly as a community called church, we must practice equality in matters of ministry.

Mild chaos swirls around me as I teach the first grade at Holy Name School in North Camden, New Jersey. Getting half an hour of class time gives me a chance to spit against the forest fire burning at the self-esteem of our inner city, mostly Latino kids. Today I'm trying to instill in our munchkins the idea that they can be anything they want to be. I start by going around the room and asking, "What do you want to be?" "I want to be a doctor!" "I want to be a teacher!" "I want to be a cop." Little hands and arms are waving enthusiastically, each child eager to blurt out her or his dream. Gabriella, curly haired, bright eyed, with a silly putty smile made more comical by the missing front teeth, is almost jumping out of her chair. "Gabby, what do you want to be?" Six-year old Gabriella proudly announces "I'm going to be a priest!" Sr. Dorothy Crowley, SSJ, amused, gives me a raised eyebrow look communicating, "Buddy, you got yourself into this. Good luck." The six-year-olds sense something askew, but they're not sure what it is. I ask, "Gabby, why do you want to be a priest?" "Because they're nice to people, they sing, and they make everybody laugh." Gabriella is certainly capable of doing that. Will she ever get the chance?

The question of women's ordination in the Catholic Church is a cultural question some unwisely try to treat theologically. There are those who say the theological discussion on women's ordination is finished. But the anthropological discussion cannot be denied. The effects of the attempt to impose silence about this issue makes Catholics trying to live a vibrant and freeing faith in contemporary society seem to be mindless monads, unable to respond to people who ask why the church refuses to ordain women. Anthropologically and sociologically, this closing of the theological discussion has to be examined. To argue that women cannot be ordained priests because only men were present at the Last Supper ignores the text of scripture. The Gospel of Mark (on which the narratives of both Luke and Matthew are based) says Jesus was at table with the twelve. It does not say only the twelve. It does not say women were not there. It does not say that, since no women are mentioned, women may never, ever be ordained. Actually, to use the Last Supper as a text for ordination is problematic on another score. One could question whether the twelve were actually "ordained" at that point. Mission and ministry are better seen conferred in the resurrection narratives (cf. Matthew 28:18–20; Mark 16:15–20; Luke 24:47–48). John's Gospel, the most mature of the four, has no Last Supper scene at all. And surely women were present at the multiplication of the loaves (John 6:1–14), and the multiplication of the loaves is the only miracle recorded in all four gospels. Whether or not women can be ordained is not going to be definitively answered by appeals to sacred writings compiled in cultures and times wherein women's

> "What do we do when a church proclaims the equality of women but builds itself on structures that assure their inequality?...Men who do not take the women's issue seriously cannot possibly be disciples."
>
> — Joan Chittister, OSB
> (Sojourners
> January/February 2002)

roles were categorically different from the way they are today. To do so would be as crazy as to advocate the reinstitution of slavery because the Bible says it's acceptable. The 1976 Pontifical Biblical Commission realized that the New Testament does not provide an answer to the question of whether the church can ordain women (Schneiders 1999:95).

Cultural issues are historical, and to deal with such issues the church will have to appeal to transcultural and transhistorical method, the method based on the norm of authenticity. The question for Catholics in the twenty-first century is not, "Did Jesus ordain women?" The question ought to be, "Is Jesus Christ calling women to serve as ordained priests?" Canon law states that all the baptized, male and female, are to be free from coercion in choosing their vocation (canon 219). Does the refusal to test a woman's vocation to ordained ministry, de facto, constitute coercion? The indication that women ought to be ordained is in the discerned judgment that the church will progress rather than decline if women are ordained. The indication that the exclusion of women from the ordained priesthood is unauthentic is the continual decline of the church's vitality and the inability of the church to fulfill its mission, especially the mission to be a eucharistic community. The church is not ordaining women, and the church is also ordaining fewer and fewer men. Maybe the two social facts are related. Men who are taught by women, work with women in business, and live lives wherein women are considered equals, may be dissuaded from considering a vocation and way of life that structurally excludes women. Another thought experiment: reverse the situation. Would men join a church in which men were denied ordination and only women could image God in the church's sacred rites? How many men would donate money to such a church, or urge their daughters to seek ordination in such a church, especially if celibacy were a requirement for ordained ministry? Sociologically we know that mothers and the nuns who taught eighth grade used to be the biggest recruiters for the priesthood. Ordinations have plummeted as mothers no longer support their sons' vocations, and eighth-grade boys no longer have nuns teaching them in grade school.

The real indication that the ordination of women is more authentic will be revealed in the prayerful and holy desires of faithful, converting Catholics. Yet, in talking with women, especially younger women of college age, I discover that the vast majority find the fact that women cannot be ordained somewhat irritating, but aren't really angry about it. Women are more frustrated, angered, and upset by economic injustice.

### Economic Discrimination against Women

It's a fact, and a not very hidden fact, that women, on average, earn less than men in comparable jobs. Women lag far behind men in terms of median income and earn only seventy cents in comparison to every dollar men get (Thompson and Hickey 2005:321). There exists a "glass ceiling" women bump into on their way to the top. Only 2 percent of the most highly paid employees at Fortune 500 companies are women. Women administrators only get 68 percent of what men earn. In the corporate world, women VPs are paid only 42 percent of what their male counterparts take home (Gelles and Levine 1999:370).

The U.S. Family and Medical Leave Act of 1993 (up to twelve weeks of unpaid leave for family and medical emergencies) finally was passed. Still, of all industrialized countries, only New Zealand and the United States do not have laws requiring employers to provide time off, with pay, to new parents (cf. Gelles and Levine 1999:371). And in our homes, inequality in the family persists. "The second shift" (women carrying the burden of most of the housework even though they also work outside the home), girls having less money spent on their education than their brothers, the persistence of wanting a boy child: all these are expressions of a sexist society. It took a long time for women like Condoleezza Rice, Hillary Clinton, and Nancy Pelosi to emerge as political powers. In the United States, women were not allowed to vote until 1920. In the first 222 years of the republic, 1,843 senators were elected. Only 23 were women. In Congress, out of 9,643 representatives, only 190 have been women (Goodman 1998:11a). All forty-three presidents have been men, and only one vice presidential candidate, Geraldine Ferraro, was a woman. Things are now moving in a more equitable direction. In 2007, the House of Representatives has seventy-one women, and sixteen women are now senators. Nine state governors are women (C. Lewis 2007).

### Sexism and Violence against Women

One afternoon in 1989, in Glen Ridge, New Jersey, several boys—large boys, football players mostly—led a young girl—a mentally challenged girl, a girl whom they had known most of their lives—into a neighborhood basement rec room. They proceeded to rape her with a baseball bat. This crime is scarier than the *Lord of the Flies*, for this heinous act was perpetrated in a supposedly "normal" suburban environment. It is scarier still because this supposedly normal suburban world was rife with acceptance of sexist behavior. Bernard Lefkowitz's *Our Guys* chronicles and describes the culture that produced the young men who raped Leslie. The Jocks' style and culture ran the high school in Glen Ridge. The rape of Leslie was committed in a specific cultural milieu, a context of sex as a right, a place were the message was that boys could do whatever they wanted to girls, and to anyone else. The Jocks labeled girls who performed oral sex on them "Hoovers" and "Seals." "They would often refer to girls who were available as 'animals'" (Lefkowitz 1997:127). At the trial, after twelve days of deliberation, the jury convicted three of the young men. They were now convicted rapists. The judge let them out on bail until sentencing. They could have gotten forty years. The judge gave them fifteen years maximum, in "a young adult offenders" institution with an "indeterminate minimum" term of imprisonment. The sentence was essentially a slap on the wrist. One *New York Times* reporter on an elevator outside the courtroom was overheard saying, "I thought the judge was going to send them a message....I guess he did: 'If you're white it's all right'" (Lefkowitz 1997:419).

Sexism, racism, and issues of class work together in an unholy trinity in our times and culture to dehumanize and falsely bolster men, functioning as a perverted basis for their self-esteem. The whole eruption in 2006 around the Duke lacrosse team being accused of raping an African American dancer they had hired for a private party indicates how confused our culture is on the relationships between race, sex, and class. Even though the rape charges against the lacrosse players were eventually dropped, the incident focused attention on the dynamics coursing through young adults' lives. Saddest of all are the young women at Duke who so ingratiate themselves with the players on campus. A few weeks after the allegations, a *Rolling Stone* reporter visited Duke and graphically described the out-of-control sexist college culture (Reitman 2006). The young women at Duke service young men they wouldn't look at twice in the real world, just because they happen to be lacrosse players or a frat boys. Why? Because they are immersed in a sexist culture, a culture that the best and brightest of our nation's young women accept. Tom Wolfe's novel *I Am Charlotte Simmons* is a

> Sexism takes a lethal toll worldwide as the practice of sex selective abortion decimates the female population. Studies show that more than 100,000,000 women are missing.
>
> (Brym and Lie 2007:588)

searing indictment of the racist and sexist scene on most college campuses in the United States today. "One Duke woman, who confessed to having sex with a popular guy in order not to lose him said, wistfully, 'I have done things that are completely inconsistent with the type of person I am, and what I value'" (Whitehead 2006). A faith that frees must offer people, especially young adults, the challenge and means to achieve gender equity across the board, in all the relationships of their lives.

We cannot stop at challenging sexism. Many have observed that the greatest beneficiaries of the civil rights movement of the 1950s and 1960s were white women. Affirmative action has made a world wherein women now are showing that they are not only men's equal, but their betters (Kindlon 2006). Although there is a long way to go before we can truly claim gender equity (and in the underdeveloped world that's a long, long way), great strides have been made, and real transformation on many levels has been achieved. But in the area of race relations, progress has stalled.

## Race Relations

Racism consists of (1) the belief that one race is inferior to another, and (2) the societal practices, both public and private, that structure society according to racist assumptions. Racism, sexism, and class inequality function together in a sinful triad to perpetuate patterns of discrimination and hatred. The world and our country have a long way to go before we can assert that racism no longer pollutes our social ecology. Organizers of the 2006 World Cup needed to enact a concerted campaign against racism. In an article reporting on how affluent African Americans in the United States cannot find women to help them with child care, one nanny referred to the black child being cared for by another nanny as a "monkey" (Kantor 2006). In January 2007, Charles T. Tyson, the first black mayor of South Harrison, New Jersey, received racist death threats (Jones 2007). Years ago, Billie Holiday sang of "Strange Fruit," but the horrific history of lynching in the United States is not a thing of the past (cf. Marsh 1997).

Today, there are over 750 racist and neo-Nazi groups in this country.

(cf. Southern Poverty Law Center 2007).

In June 1998, James Byrd, a forty-nine-year-old African American man living in Jasper, Texas, was savagely beaten by three white men, chained by his neck to a pickup truck, and dragged over country roads until he was decapitated. Two of the perpetrators were sentenced to death. Martin McLaughlin (1998) argues that the conditions of social and economic deprivation in Jasper contributed to the crime. Then governor George W. Bush refused to visit Jasper to attend a ceremony held by those outraged at the lynching. McLaughlin notes that high school dropouts (2,816) vastly exceed college graduates (1,649) in a town of 8,400. Jasper's median income is $20,451, and one-fifth of the population of the town lives in poverty. McLaughlin argues that these conditions breed the overt and virulent racism that is growing in the United States at an alarming rate. Robert Brym and John Lie reveal that Byrd's murderers were white supremacists who expressed no remorse for their crime. In 2003, there were 7,489 hate crimes reported in the United States (Brym and Lie 2007:301).

In order to make a world in which justice and peace can flourish, we must eradicate racism from our hearts and minds and institutional practices. The former archbishop of Philadelphia challenged us to do just that. Cardinal Bevilacqua's 1998 pastoral letter "Healing Racism through Faith and Truth" strongly states that racism is a sin: "Racism is a moral disease and it is contagious. No one is born a racist. Carriers infect others in countless ways through words and attitudes, deeds and omissions. Yet, one thing is certain—the disease of racism can and must be eradicated.... In short, racism and Christian life are incompatible." Cardinal Bevilacqua honestly recognizes the existence of racism within the Catholic Church and calls on us to ask God's pardon. He rightly teaches that racism threatens our eternal salvation. "Jesus is clear that this is a matter of holiness and a matter of salvation. Our attitudes and actions towards others enter the mystery of our communion with God. Racism is a sin that weakens and diminishes this sacred union...." Cardinal Bevilacqua asserts that if this teaching of our faith is to have a real impact on our lives, we must engage our minds and hearts and grapple with the problem. "Racism has been condemned as a sin many times.... For the truth to have an impact on us, for it to really set us free, it must become our truth. It must be operative within us. It must penetrate and ignite our minds and hearts" (Bevilacqua 1998).

Racism can divorce us from God. Imagine a racist approaching Heaven. All his life he has hated African American people. All his life he has not wanted to live near, or be associated with, persons of darker skin tone. As he looks into Heaven, he sees numerous African American people. The racist will not be thrown out of eternal bliss. It is simply that, as the racist realizes that Heaven means accepting persons of all kinds, nationalities, and creeds, he will never want to enter. And that will be Hell.

### There Is No Such Thing as Race

In my introductory sociology classes, I'll take a day where I'll call everyone in the room up to the front, one by one. Each of the fifty to sixty students comes up individually. I look them in the eye, glance at their left ear lobe, and tell them to sit on the right or left side of the class. In three or four minutes, about 85 percent of the students are sitting on my left and 15 percent are on my right. I then announce that there is an obvious genetic difference between the two groups. Immediately someone says it has something to do with ears, or earrings. I admit that the looking at the earlobe is a dodge. It has nothing to do with the classification. It takes a few minutes and several guesses, but soon they are stumped. Usually, they cannot see any difference between the two groups. Eventually, I have those on my right stand up. The difference is startlingly immediate. Everyone on the right is taller than I am. Everyone on the left is shorter. I then go on to make the point that we could equate "shortness" with undesirable characteristics: short people are lazy, dumb, unmotivated, and so on. Tall people are talented, and good, and hardworking. Tall people, like physically attractive people, have an advantage in life. Usually the taller candidate wins an election (remember that Al Gore won the popular vote in 2000 over George W. Bush and many claim Kerry actually won Ohio in 2004 [Kennedy 2006; Freeman and Bleifuss 2006]). These assertions immediately cause an uproar among the "shorts," and terrifyingly quick agreement among the "talls." As the exercise spins out, the students begin to see that arbitrary social constructions like height are no different from the racial classifications to which we are all so accustomed. Often a sharp, perceptive student will note that the exercise is flawed. "The blacks are the minority in the United States," he or she will say. I reply, "Yes, but the exercise mirrors not the United States but the world. The globe is roughly 30 percent Caucasian, 70 percent people of color." "Tall people" should watch out. They are outnumbered!

What is so sad about racist attitudes and actions is that there truly is no biological basis to the delineation of "races" based on skin color.

The concept of "race" is a social construct, not a biological truth. Just as the "short" and "tall" exercise is based on a completely arbitrary norm, my height, so too classifying "races" according to skin color is quite arbitrary.

> Skin color is subject to great variation and is produced mainly by two factors: distribution of blood vessels and amount of melanin found in a given area of the skin. Exposure to the sunlight increases the amount of melanin in the skin and hence, the skin darkens. It is now known that the melanin acts to protect the skin against damaging ultraviolet solar radiation. Since the highest concentration of dark skinned people tends to be found in the tropical regions of the world, it appears that natural selection has favored heavily pigmented skin as protection against strong solar radiation of equatorial latitudes. Similarly, people living in northern latitudes tend to have lightly pigmented skin; this lack of pigmentation is advantageous, for it seems to enable the weak ultraviolet radiation of northern latitudes to penetrate the skin and stimulate formation of Vitamin D. (Haviland 1982:157–58)

Before Vitamin D fortified milk was widely available, those lacking sufficient Vitamin D were liable to contract rickets. Skin color, which originally was simply the body's way of adapting to changing environmental conditions, is not a significant biological difference between persons.

We all have the same red blood in our veins. We could just as easily sort people according to weight, or eye color, or ear size. In the past, we grouped people according to their place of origin (e.g., Irish and Italians) and religion. These arbitrary categorizations have too often hurt, and sometimes punished, innocent people. But, since our society does imbue skin color with all sorts of meaning, racial constructs and classifications harm some people and help others.

### Demographics, Inequality, and Religion

The United States is radically changing. Many whites do not realize that this country today is some 35 percent "non-white." Some demographers predict that over the course of the twenty-first century this percentage will rise dramatically.

U.S. POPULATION BY "RACE" THROUGH THE TWENTY-FIRST CENTURY

|          | 2025  | 2050  | 2100 |
|----------|-------|-------|------|
| White    | 60.1% | 52.7% | 40%  |
| Hispanic | 16.2% | 21.1% | 33%  |
| Black    | 13.5% | 15.0% | 13%  |
| Asian    | 07.5% | 10.1% | 14%  |

(Hess et al. 1996:260; Schaefer 2001a:3; Schaefer 2007:252)

Inequality can be measured in many ways, but wealth (i.e., assets) and income levels are prime indicators of one's position in society. In terms of wealth, races are not equal in the United States. As a result of 244 years of slavery and decades of Jim Crow segregation laws enacted following the Civil War, African Americans have never consistently been able to play on a level playing field. In 2000, the median net worth of whites was $79,400, while that of African Americans was $7,500. Excluding home equity, the median net worth of white households was $22,566; that of African Americans was $1,166 (Domhoff 2006).

In terms of income too, races are not equal. Even though African Americans and Latinos have experienced significant increase in their shares of income, equality with whites is still a long way off.

MEDIAN HOUSEHOLD INCOME 2005

| U.S. Median Household Income | $46,326 |
|---|---|
| Asians/Pacific Islanders | $61,094 |
| Whites | $50,784 |
| Hispanics | $35,967 |
| Native American | $33,627 |
| Blacks | $30,858 |

(August 26, 2006 Press Release <www.census.gov>)

According to the Census Bureau, in 2005, with the poverty line set at $15,577 for a family of three and $19,971 for a family of four, 12.6 percent of people in the United States were poor (up from 11.3 percent in 2000). Almost 25 percent of African Americans, 22 percent of Hispanics, and 8 percent of whites live in poverty in this country (<www.census.org>).

The implication of all these facts is clear. Either we will learn to handle our cultural and "racial" differences, or the first half of the twenty-first century will be volatile, and likely violent. Our Christian faith should inspire us to learn about and overcome racism, prejudice, and discrimination. The gospel requires this.

African Americans in this country have traditionally been strengthened and empowered by the force of the gospel operating in small churches throughout the country. Abolition in the 1800s and the civil rights movement of the twentieth century were rooted in the experience and culture of small African American congregations. The ecclesial style of these Christian communities was centered on the preaching of the Word and on the personality and charisma of the local pastor. Martin Luther King, Jr., was the greatest exemplar of this. The problem in linking mostly white, Catholic communities and largely Protestant African American congregations lies in the different ecclesial styles of the churches. Where the sacramental emphasis of the Catholic Church was a religious style that helped shepherd huddled masses of Eastern European ethnic communities out of the ghettos and slums of New York and Chicago into the American mainstream, African American emphasis on the Word and its inherent power to liberate formed the basis of the African American movement, often in the face of the threat of the insane hatred of entrenched racists and racist institutions. And, it must be admitted, on the whole, as an institution, the Catholic Church in the United States was not in the forefront of any efforts to ameliorate racial relations in this country. Despite a few notable exceptions (e.g., John LaFarge, SJ), Catholics were not known for linking love of Christ with love of African American brethren.

To dedicate ourselves to struggle against racism and its practices, in our hearts and minds, in our homes, in our parishes, in our businesses and in our world, is a conversion to be prayed for, not only to benefit our African American brothers and sisters, but also to make us all more the followers of Christ, to form us all as the disciples we are called to be. The Lord who told us the parable of the Good Samaritan (Luke 10:29–37) is not interested in our bolstering the ideologies and insanities of racists and racism.

> "Shaq is rich. The white man who signs his check is wealthy."
> —Chris Rock, HBO Special

## Institutional vs. Personal Racism

St. Joseph's, the Jesuit university where I have taught during the past ten years, is a lovely college campus. Majestic, ivy-covered buildings stretch for several miles alongside one of Philadelphia's main arteries, City Avenue. The four-lane road is Route 1, which was the East Coast's Route 95 before the interstate highway system was built. City Avenue also is the dividing line between largely African American West Philadelphia and the mostly white suburb of Lower Merion. St. Joe's has a predominantly white student body and faculty. Despite efforts to attract African Americans as students and faculty, despite efforts on the part of the university's Office of Multicultural Life to educate people and to ameliorate race relations on campus and relations between the university and the neighboring community, despite student rallies to end racism, despite campus-wide efforts to appreciate and celebrate diversity, St. Joe's remains a quite monolithic place. Why? These efforts have been sincere and extensive. Virtually all faculty and staff would attest to their openness to "people of color." There would be no toleration of overt racists on campus. But, if you walk around the campus, you have to admit what a Latina friend of mine pointed out on her first visit to this Catholic Jesuit university where I teach. "This place looks like a plantation." She is right. Virtually all the janitorial and food service staff are African American. Virtually 95 percent of the faculty and students and staff serviced by those African Americans are "white."

Saint Joseph's did not choose to be institutionally racist, but the reality is there to see. Blacks and whites read the reality very differently. Whites see a nice college campus on City Avenue. Blacks see a fortress separating the West Philly ghetto from the lily-white Montgomery County suburbs. Whites see a Jesuit institution dedicated to the fostering of faith and the promotion of justice. Blacks see a "Catholic" school where very few faces are brown or even tan. Whites don't often ask themselves if St. Joseph's is a racist environment. After all, there are crucifixes on classroom walls, and I've never heard of a Confederate flag in a dorm room. But, in survey after survey, we hear that people of color feel uncomfortable at places like St. Joe's. When my white students voice incredulity at this, I ask them if they would feel comfortable at Howard University in Washington, or at Morehouse or

According to a *New York Times* report, a seven-year study reveals Nissan systematically charged blacks more than whites for car loans, regardless of their credit histories.

(*New York Times,* July 4, 2001)

Spelman in Atlanta. After explaining what these schools are and have been, they see my point.

Chicago journalist Clarence Page writes that racism is less a personal belief than a public practice. "Racism is the rational result of a racially imbalanced society" (Page 1996:77). Freedom is not free, or easy, for African Americans or for whites. Page challenges whites to become anti-racist as he challenges blacks to survive racism. According to Page, racism cannot complete its dirty, deadly work unless non-whites serve as its accessories, which they do when they internalize the second-class and helpless image others try to project on them (Page 1996:94). Self-love means tough love. Blacks must own up to and accept responsibility for their actions and their lives. "We African American too often flatter white racism unnecessarily by exaggerating the power it holds over our lives" (Page 1996:96). But, most important, Page sagely argues, "the work of rebuilding race relations is not for black people to do alone. Americans of all colors are PLWRs—People Living with Racism" (Page 1996:98).

### The Presence of Latinos

Today the Catholic Church in the United States is 33 to 40 percent Latino. This fact comes as a surprise to many Catholics, who know only their largely white parishes in the suburbs. The challenges and opportunities afforded our church by the increasing numbers of Hispanics are manifold. Our local churches are stretched and called to grow culturally by the increasing numbers of Latinos joining us. Such cultural pluralism is enriching and requires careful attention on the part of non-Latinos to understand the permutations and differences among Spanish speaking Catholics: Puerto Ricans are not Mexicans, and Mexicans are not Chileans. We are a multicultural church on many levels, and the more we pay attention to the fact that we are European Americans, Mexicans, Vietnamese, Native Americans, and so on, the more we will appreciate the gift so many cultures are to the Body of Christ and the building up of the kingdom of God.

A full treatment of the multicultural nature of the church in the United States today would be another book. I can do no more than simply touch on these topics here before moving on to what affects us all, no matter what our ethnic background. Nevertheless, the challenge of the church to call Latinos to resist racist attitudes and actions against blacks with whom they often find themselves in economic and residential comtpetition is real and critical. A visit to the Catholic bishops' website Justice for Immigrants (JFI 2007) would help us all to better understand our church's challenge.

## The Discipleship of Equals

Those persons converted to Jesus Christ, his reality the root of their hearts and minds, and his power operating in their choices and lives, will form Christian communities (i.e., churches and parishes) called by God to tackle the social problems of the day. Sexism and racism are two prime problems diminishing the life opportunities of millions of our brothers and sisters. Cardinal Avery Dulles, SJ, has called the church a community of disciples. The community of disciples who practice Catholicism are people converted to Jesus' kingdom vision. Such conversion is lived out in the construction of a world where all are treated as equals, brothers and sisters in the same Lord, children of the same God.

That equality has to begin in our homes, with men and women being equal partners in the construction and living of family life. That equality has to extend to the workplace, with everyone receiving equal pay for equal work. Women have as much right to and need for a just salary as do men. That equality has to reach across the problem of the twentieth century, the issue of the color line, and make differences of skin tone no more significant than differences in height, eye color, or blood type.

To be a Catholic is to be a person dedicated to the eradication of sexism and racism in our hearts, our homes, and our land. And, let's face it, we cannot call for an end to sexism and racism in society if we are unwilling to eradicate such sins from within our own church. It would betray the Lord who boldly walked with women (cf. Luke 8:1–3) if our institutional church were to become a bastion of sexism in a society that was gradually diminishing sexist policies and practices. And it would betray the Lord whose one commandment was love (cf. John 15:12) if we as Christians were to put limits on that love.

The truth of the matter is that seeds of sexism and racism are rooted in class differences. The hatreds that spawn the erection and maintenance of gender and racial hierarchies are in reality economic facts of injustice and inequality. We will not eradicate racism and sexism until we tackle the prime source of inequality: economic injustice.

There is no entry for sexism or racism in the index of the Catholic Catechism.

PRACTICES TO AMELIORATE GENDER AND RACE RELATIONS

1. Read up on the topics: David Halberstam's *The Children*; Tylor Branch's trilogy on the civil rights movement; the New York Times books *Class Matters* and *How Race Is Lived in America*; Cornel West's *Race Matters*; Susan Faludi's *Backlash*; James Carrol *Constantine's Sword*.

2. Every year, get to know someone of another race and talk to that person about race. Every year, have a serious conversation with a member of the opposite sex who really differs from you on the issue of gender relations.

3. Monitor your elected representatives on the local, state, and national level in terms of what they are doing about issues of race and gender.

4. Go to a church in which the congregation is predominantly of a race that differs from your own.

5. Do an examination of consciousness: How often does racism matter to you and your community?

6. Do an examination of consciousness: How often does sexism matter to you and your community?

7. Read a novel (e.g., *Native Son*, *Beloved*) or see a movie (e.g., *Crash*, *North Country*) that deals with matters of racism and sexism. Discuss the novel or film with friends and neighbors.

# 6
# Money Matters
## *Catholicism as the Practice of Economic Social Justice*

*"For the love of money is a root of all kinds of evil, and in their eagerness to be rich some have wandered away from the faith and pierced themselves with many pains."*
—*1 Timothy 6:10*

"Do you believe in capitalism?" I ask my students at Saint Joseph's. They stare at me as if I have three heads. Capitalism is self-evident in their lives. To question the tenets of capitalism is unthinkable. When I point out that a lot of things "demanded" do not get "supplied" (e.g., world peace, universal health care, free college tuition), their faith in the law of supply and demand is not diminished. When I point out capitalism's gross inequities and distortion of values (e.g., teachers' salaries vs. baseball players' earnings), students do not question the rules of the game of wages. Then I ask, "Do you believe in God?" The students accept this as a normal question. Suffering, unanswered prayers, and lack of empirical evidence for God's existence have led them to question the faith. I then try and teach them that for most of human history, belief in God was as real and as powerful as their belief in, and acceptance of, capitalism. Why do we so easily accept the revelations of capitalism, while doubting God?

As an undergraduate at Lafayette College in Easton, Pennsylvania, I was taught that economics is the study of the distribution of scarce resources among alternative uses, the distribution of finite goods among infinite wants and desires. The cultural question is who gets to decide who gets what, and on what basis are those choices made? What kinds of persons are doing the choosing? Are they converted persons, persons who want the best for all involved? Are they persons who truly desire a world of justice wherein all get what they need and deserve? And is the system in which they operate fostering the choosing of what makes us happy, healthy, holy, and free? Or is the economic system furthering only the aims of profit, the desires of the stockholders, and the needs of corporations? (cf. Korten 2001). There are over one billion people on earth who call themselves Catholic. What a world it would be if all Catholics, roughly one sixth of our planet's population, all became economic choosers according to the norms inherent in the functioning of our own minds and hearts, the norms articulated in Jesus' preaching of the kingdom of God.

Ultimately, it's a question of what kind of world we want. Do we want our world to resemble the *Titanic* or *Noah's Ark*? When I was a little kid, we learned a song at YMCA day camp.

> Oh, they built the ship Titanic to sail the ocean blue
> And they said it was a ship that the water'd never go through.
> But the Lord's almighty hand said that ship would never land.
> It was sad when that great ship went down.

But, as little kids, we were not taught this verse:

> Oh the ship was full of sin and the sides about to burst
> When the Captain cried, "Women and children first!"
> But they kept the poor below where they'd be the first to go.
> It was sad when that great ship went down.

There were 2,207 passengers and crew on board. With 1,178 seats in lifeboats, only 1,029 had to swim. But more than 1,500 people lost their lives. Sixty percent of wealthy first-deck passengers were saved. Thirty-six percent of second-deck passengers were saved. Twenty-four percent of lower deck or "steerage" passengers were saved. Ninety-seven percent of the women and children in first class were saved. Eighty-nine percent of the women and children in second class were saved. Forty-two percent of the women and children in steerage class were saved.

> One of the reasons so many wealthier passengers survived was that access to the lifeboats was from the first and second class decks. The locked doors and other barriers that kept the third

class passengers from venturing up to the upper decks during the cruise were not removed when disaster struck. In addition there is evidence that little effort was made to save the people in steerage. Some were even forcibly kept down by sailors standing guard. For the passengers on the *Titanic*, social inequality meant more than just differences in the comfort of their accommodations or the quality of food they ate. It literally meant life and death. (W. Hall 1986, cited in Newman 2006:326)

The world of *Noah's Ark* was one in which all who got on board were saved. The world of the *Titanic* was one in which the rich had a much better chance of surviving than did the poor. More and more, our diamond-shaped world of the United States in 1945–1973, with a few poor at the bottom and a few rich at the top and a mass of middle-class people in the middle, is becoming a pyramid, with a very few rich a the top, a few more in the middle class, and more and more spread out at the bottom. The world is becoming increasingly like an inverted champagne glass, with many poor at the bottom and a very few "super" wealthy at the top.

At the dawn of the twenty-first century, we live in a world where the World Bank and the United Nations attest that more than 1.1 billion people live on less than $1 a day and 2.7 billion of our brothers and sisters survive on less than $2 a day (World Bank 2007). *One: The Campaign to Make Poverty History* reveals that AIDS and/or extreme poverty kills a child every three seconds. Clean water is just a figment of the imagination for more than 1 billion people.

In the United States in 2005, 37 million Americans were poor (1.1 million more people than in 2003); 13.2 million children (17.6 percent of children in America) are living in poverty and 7.7 million U.S. families (9.9 percent of families in America) are recognized as poor (U.S. Census 2006). The U.S. Bishops Campaign for Human Development website notes: "On average, more than one out of every three Americans—37 percent of all people in the

> As Catholics, we are heirs of a long tradition of thought and action on the moral dimensions of economic activity. The life and words of Jesus and the teaching of his Church call us to serve those in need and to work actively for social and economic justice. As a community of believers, we know that our faith is tested by the quality of justice among us, that we can best measure our life together by how the poor and the vulnerable are treated.
>
> —*Economic Justice for All*
> (U.S. Bishops 1986,
> Introduction, #8)

United States—are officially classified as living in poverty at least 2 months out of the year" (USCCB 2006b). In August of 2006, the *New York Times* reported that "...the share of the [U.S.] population now in poverty—12.6 percent—is still higher than at the trough of the last recession, when it was 11.7 percent. And among the poor, 43 percent were living below half the poverty line in 2005—$7,800 for a family of three. *That's the highest percentage of people in 'deep poverty' since the government started keeping track of those numbers in 1975*" (editorial, *New York Times*, August 30, 2006; italics added).

Bill Moyers makes the argument that the social compact of the United States contained in the preamble to the Constitution has been grossly violated. Our schools need $268 billion just to make them physically safe for children to occupy. Our roads and power grid are in horrible shape, and our supposed technological superiority is a facade. The United States is drowning in debt, yet the richest 1 percent will get over $479 billion over the next ten years as a result of President Bush's tax cuts in 2001. Pension plans are in jeopardy, workers' wages are worth less and less, and the concentration of wealth in the hands of the rich has reached Gilded Age proportions. In the past twenty-five years, manufacturing workers' real wages fell 1 percent; real income for the 1 percent at the top of U.S. society rose 135 percent. In 1960 the income gap between the top fifth of the population and the bottom fifth was thirtyfold. Today the top fifth gets seventy-five times what the bottom fifth gets (Moyers 2006). Moyers charges that wealth concentrated among the rich does not benefit the rest of society. Even a robber baron like J. P. Morgan felt those in charge should get only twenty times more than the workers. According to Moyers, the average CEO today grabs 262 times what an average worker gets. Real weekly wages for workers have declined from $332 a week in 1972 to $278 a week in 2004. Moyers quotes a Goldman Sachs report that states: "The most important contributor to higher profit margins over the past five years has been a decline in labor's share of national income" (Moyers 2006). Moyers speaks for those on the other end of the economic ladder.

> So it is that to make ends meet in the face of stagnant or declining incomes, regular Americans have gone deeper and deeper in debt—with credit card debt nearly tripling since 1989. Poor kids are dropping out of high school and college at alarming rates, the middle class and working poor have been hit hard by

a housing squeeze, 45 million or more Americans—eight out of ten of them in working families—are without health insurance. "The strain on working people," says the economist Jeffrey Madrick, "has become significant. Working families and the poor are losing ground under economic pressures that deeply affect household stability, family dynamics, social mobility, political participation, and civic life." The American Dream has had its heart cut out, and is on life support. (Moyers 2006)

Although scholars (e.g., Selznick 1992; A. Wolfe 1989; Singer 2006) and liberal commentators such as Thom Hartmann (2006) have questioned the morality and the justice of these developments, their analysis and arguments fail to persuade large numbers, and U.S. Catholics are little different from their neighbors in their attitudes toward aiding the poor and/or restructuring the social systems of which we are a part.

In order for Lonerganian conversions to develop and take root among Catholics in the United States and beyond, deeply rooted cultural assumptions must be challenged and transformed. Among the ideologies we must confront and reorient are (1) the cultural assumption that corporate capitalism is moral, inevitable, and unchangeable and (2) the cultural assumption that the affluent life is better than living sanely and simply.

## Countering Corporate Capitalism

David Korten, who holds an MBA and PhD from Stanford, calls for transformation of the present economic system. "We must break free of the illusions of the world of money, rediscover spiritual meaning in our lives, and root our economic institutions in place and community so that they are integrally connected to people and life" (Korten 2001:16). Korten argues that a sane and sensible capitalism, a true market economy, has been distorted by the machinations of corporate capitalism. He critiques our economic system, which demands that we work harder and harder for less and less (Korten 2001:47). The free market's ideology, which Korten names the "worship of greed," calls for faith in ever increasing economic growth, markets unfettered and unrestrained by governments, and the applauding of the always expanding and more deeply penetrating processes of globalization (Korten 2001:76). The privatization of all public entities yields only to the infrastructure governments must maintain to ensure public order and property and contract protection. The assumptions on which this free market ideology rests completely contradict Catholic social teaching. Free market ideology assumes that we are motivated primarily, if not exclusively, by self-interest; that whatever provides the most lucrative financial rewards to the company or individual is most beneficial to society; that ever more pressured competition makes more sense (i.e., is "more rational") than learning how to work cooperatively and peacefully. This free market agenda assumes that people are normally greedy, driven by the desire for

> "The assumptions on which ... free market ideology rests completely contradict Catholic social teaching."

ever more acquisitions, and that the pursuit of such drives creates optimal social outcomes (Korten 2001:77). This is the agenda offered by contemporary ideologues whose program appears under various names: "neoclassical, neoliberal, or libertarian economics, market capitalism or market liberalism" (Korten 2001:78). According to Korten, "[Adam] Smith saw corporations, much as he saw governments, as instruments for suppressing the beneficial competitive forces of the market" (Korten 2001:62). For Adam Smith, self-interest did not equal greed, and Smith mentions the famous and often reverently invoked "invisible hand" only once in over one thousand pages! (Korten 2001:81, 83).

Korten goes on to build a magnificent case that corporations now (illegitimately) run the world and insulate themselves from the discipline of the market. Just five hundred corporations control 70 percent of world trade (Korten 2001:126). Citing the work of Sarah Anderson and John Cavanaugh of the Institute for Policy Studies, Corporations.org reports that the top twenty-two economic entities are countries. Numbers twenty-three, twenty-five, and twenty-six are General Motors, Wal Mart, and Exxon Mobil, ranking ahead of countries like Poland, Norway, Indonesia, and Saudi Arabia. Of the world's top one hundred economic entities, only forty-nine are countries. Fifty-one are corporations (Corporations.org 2007). Korten examines this juggernaut of corporate colonization of our lives and calls for transformation and change. He urges citizen groups to form and struggle against corporations' rule over our lives. The antidote to our present predicament is the healing, amelioration, and re-construction of civil society (Korten 2001). Thom Hartmann argues that corporatocracy's free market ideology obscures the fact that "free" markets are a mirage, that in fact markets are creations of governments who set the rules of the game. Since Ronald Reagan's presidency, our government has been making rules in favor of the rich and corporations, rather than protecting the middle class (Hartmann 2006).

Another voice calling for transformation and sanity in our overly corporatized world is one of the globe's most successful venture capitalists, George Soros. He has said that we can have a market economy, but we cannot have a market society. In his call for the reform of global capitalism, he writes: "The relationship between market values and social values is not easy to untangle. The problem is not in establishing that there is a difference between the two; it is in deciding when we should be guided by one and when by the other" (Soros 2000:138). What kind of world do we get when we fail to properly distinguish market and social values? We get a world prophetically dissected and described by one of Catholicism's most insightful twentieth-century voices, Trappist monk Thomas Merton, over a half a century ago.

> It is true that the materialistic society, the so-called culture that has evolved under the tender mercies of capitalism, has produced what seems to be the ultimate limit of this-worldliness. And nowhere, except perhaps in the analogous society of pagan Rome, has there ever been such a flowering of cheap and petty and disgusting lusts and vanities as in the world of capitalism, where there is no evil that is not fostered and encouraged for the sake of making money. We live in a society whose whole policy is to excite every nerve in the human body and keep it at the highest pitch of artificial tension, to strain every human desire to the limit and to create as many new desires and synthetic passions as possible, in order to cater to them with the products of our factories and printing presses and movie studios and all the rest. (Merton 1948:147-148)

## Countering Affluent Lifestyles

Thomas Merton in 1948 already foresaw a world in which a "market-values-alone-capitalism" swamps the spiritual and personal values on which human culture is constructed. Corporate capitalism has given some in the United States a wonderful world, while leaving many in a world of ever increasing stress and struggle for survival. In the last quarter century, this country has increased its GNP by a factor of five. "In 1975, the 5.2 percent of the world's population in the U.S. garnered 12 percent of the world's income and almost 25 percent of the world's wealth. By 1999, the USA, now 4.1 percent of the globe's populace, had increased [its] share to 29 percent of global income and 33 percent of the planet's wealth" (Vitillo 2002:6).

> The prosperity in this country, however, is concentrated among increasingly smaller numbers of people. During the unprecedented economic boom of the late 1980s and 1990s, for example, 47% of the total real income gain found its way into the pockets of the top one percent of income recipients. Forty-two percent of the income gain was enjoyed by 19% of the next highest income earners, and only 12 percent accrued to the bottom 80 percent. (Vitillo 2002:6)

According to a 2006 special report in *The Economist*, Americans are not in revolt over these developments of ever increasing inequality. "The gap between rich and poor is bigger than in any other advanced country, but most people are unconcerned. Whereas Europeans fret about the way the economic pie is divided, Americans want to join the rich, not soak them. Eight out of ten, more than anywhere else, believe that though you may start poor, if you work hard, you can make pots of money. It is a central part of the American Dream." *The Economist* asserts that Americans want more economic growth rather than income redistribution. The productivity of American workers was, to some degree, "raising all boats" until a few years ago. Around 2000, worker wages stalled. "The fruits of productivity gains have been skewed towards the highest earners, and towards companies whose profits have reached record levels as a share of GDP" (*The Economist* 2006).

Even for those benefiting disproportionately from the ever widening gap between the rich and the poor are not ultimately all that well off. Frankly, all this material wealth does not translate into a good life, even for the rich. *Affluenza*, a provocative PBS special and book, argues that wealth and the pursuit of riches is literally killing us and destroying our world. In the United States, we have two shopping centers (46,438) for every high school (22,180) (De Graaf et al. 2005:13). We work many more hours than any nation on earth, yet 90 percent of our workers say they would like to have more time with their families. Forty percent of our lakes and rivers are too polluted for swimming or fishing. We make up less than 5 percent of the planet's population but we produce 25 percent of the globe's greenhouse gas emissions. Our CEOs get 475 times more compensation than our workers, an amount that has increased tenfold since 1980. "Since 1950, we Americans have used up more resources than everyone who ever lived on earth before then" (De Graaf et al. 2005:4).

Here in the "Land of the Free and the Home of the Brave," we spend almost 66 percent of our $11 trillion economy on consumer goods. We blow $200 billion a year on holiday gifts ($850 per person), but 33 percent of us cannot remember what we gave our significant other the year before. Without Santa, we'd lose 25 percent of all retail sales. In terms of what we spend, higher education means less to us ($99 billion a year) than do our shoes, jewelry, and watches ($100 billion). Thirty percent of Americans buy their pets Christmas gifts. Only 11 percent of us choose to give our neighbors presents (De Graaf et al. 2005:13).

Seventy percent of Americans go to a mall weekly, more than attend church. Megamalls are our contemporary cathedrals, symbols of who and what we really are and desire. Americans find six hours a week to go shopping, but only forty minutes to play with the kids (De Graaf et al. 2005:41–42). For 93 percent of American teenage girls, shopping is their favorite activity (De Graaf 2005:13–15). Our ever swelling affluence is evidenced by the palatial size of our houses. In 1950, the average house size was 950 square feet; by 1970, it was 1,350 square feet; and by 2000, it was 2,300 square feet (De Graaf et al. 2005:24). But drive through suburban America between the hours of 7 AM and 6 PM. No one is home. The kids are in day care, and everyone else is out trying to earn enough to pay the mortgage.

Is any of this affluence making us happier? For our 111 million households, we have 204 million registered cars. We have more cars than we have drivers, but clogged roads mean we waste $60 billion a year in lost time and gas while stuck in traffic (De Graaf et al. 2005:33, 36). If you are commuting forty-five minutes, twice a day, that's more than two weeks spent sitting in your car, at a cost of over $6,000 a year to run your car. If you walked to work you could save that money and that time and "rent a house in the South of France" (Kunstler 1998:69–70). And over 50,000 people a year die in auto accidents (Kunstler 1998:68).

All this affluence leads to increasing levels of stress. We now work 160 hours more each year than we did in 1969, and we sleep 20 percent less than we did in 1900. The market world in which we live, filled with 30,000-plus item supermarkets, 2.5 times as many items as 1985, offers everything but what we need to build happy families. Our divorce rate is double that of 1950 (De Graaf et al. 2005:42–48). We pay little attention to the marketers who strive to capture, own, and brand our children. Almost 500,000 children are sexually abused each year, and teen depression and suicide have tripled since the 1960s. We have become a nation of loners, "bowling alone," "cocooning," existing in oxymoronically labeled "gated communities" (De Graaf 2005:57–67). More Americans suffer bankruptcy each year than graduate from college. There are more than a 1,500,000 personal bankruptcies annually, up from 313,000 in 1980 (De Graaf et al. 2005:20).

Worst of all is the erosion of trust that is taking place. As horrible as were the machinations of the Enron and World Com executives in 2002, and the bishop and priest pedophile scandals in the Catholic Church, the daily, neighborhood-level lack of confidence in one another is a much greater long-term threat. Our children cannot roam the streets the way I did as a boy. My mother's oft-repeated injunction, "You kids are driving me crazy. Go outside and play," has become a thing of the past. We have to guard our children from predators, some of whom have even been their priests. And we have to guard ourselves from the lawless among us. The United States now has 2 million people imprisoned, the highest incarceration rate in the world, a rate ten times greater than that of other industrialized countries (De Graaf et al. 2005:87; see USCCB 2000). When Mother Teresa visited the United States, she pronounced it "the poorest place I've ever seen in my life." She was talking about the poverty of spirit, the "poverty of soul," so evident in American lives.

> *"When Mother Teresa visited the United States, she pronounced it 'the poorest place I've ever seen in my life.' She was talking about the poverty of spirit, the 'poverty of soul,' so evident in American lives."*

> When Affluenza infects our communities it starts a vicious cycle. We begin to choose things over people, a choice that disconnects us from community life and causes even more consumption, and more disconnection.... Have we become too distracted to care?... We assume that someone else is taking care of things— we pay them to take care of things so we can concentrate on working and spending. But to our horror, we discover that many service providers, merchandise retailers, and caretakers are not

really taking care of us anymore. It might be more appropriate to say they're *consuming* us. (De Graaf et al. 2005:71)

The Affluenza illness produces a world of "haves" and "have-nots." In 1981, the United States ranked number 13 of 22 industrialized nations in income equality. At the end of the millennium, the United States had the highest levels of income inequality on the list. In 1979, the rich (those earning a million dollars) in the United States gave 7 percent of their income to charity; in 1992 that amount had dropped to less than 4 percent. Of the ten million people who daily go hungry in America, forty percent are children. America's top 20 percent of households earn roughly as much as the bottom 80 percent: that's a "record high rate of inequality" (De Graaf et al. 2005:82–83).

The appropriation of Catholic social teaching can be a powerful antidote to the ills and injustices caused by the machinations of unbridled capitalism: In 1967, Pope Paul VI prophetically addressed the dynamics that Korten and *Affluenza*'s authors describe. If the counsel of Catholic social teaching had been a primary shaper of the cultural assumptions of our economy, rather than the Gospels of Michael Milken and Milton Friedman, how different today's world would be.

> But it is unfortunate that on these new conditions of society a system has been constructed which considers profit as the key motive for economic progress, competition as the supreme law of economics, and private ownership of the means of production as an absolute right that has no limits and carries no social obligations.... One cannot condemn such abuses too strongly by solemnly recalling once again that the economy is at the service of man. But if it is true that a type of capitalism has been the source of excessive suffering, injustice and fratricidal conflicts whose effects still persist, it would be wrong to attribute to industrialization itself evils that belong to the woeful system which accompanied it. On the contrary, one must recognize in all justice the irreplaceable contribution made by organizations of labor and industry to what development has accomplished. (*Populorum Progressio*, #26)

In 1993, a Thai toy factory burned, killing many of the female workers, women who could not afford to purchase the toys they made for affluent kids in other parts of the world.
(De Graaf et al. 2005:81)

## Power and Immortality

Why do we allow such inequality? Why do we accept "the way it is" as "that's just the way it is"? Ernst Becker in *Escape from Evil* argues that for primitive human persons (and for us) economic activity is "sacred to the core" (Becker 1975:26). Social life consists of a constant "dialogue of gift giving and receiving" (Becker 1975:27). Primitive men realized their insecurity, their inability to give life to themselves, alone. They felt the need to recognize and give something to the powers that gave life to them. For primitive men, those powers were invisible (i.e., the gods) and all had equal access to them. Primitive equality ends with the emergence of "personal" property. Social imbalances are the result of personal merit and recognition by others. Primitives who distinguished themselves got what men want most, wives. What in human nature allowed us to go along with inequality? Our own acceptance of unfreedoms. According to Becker, Rousseau was wrong. Man is never free from the bondage he carries within himself. It is a bondage he needs in order to live (Becker 1975:41–43).

People bind themselves to power. Primitives were frank about power. Power is the life pulse that sustains man. Often, for primitives, the dead had the most power (Becker 1975:45). But this is not so strange. Think of inheritance. The power of the dead gets passed on.

The reality of power is often unseen. In primitive times, ritualists and shamans controlled the sources of power via ritual. According to Becker if you want power, you control ritual! In any culture, a prime question is this: Who has the power to mystify? Where do they get it? How do they keep it? In speaking of the sacredness of class distinctions, Becker quotes Norman O. Brown, "All power...is sacred power, because it begins in the hunger for immortality; and it ends in the absolute subjection to people and things which represent immortality power" (Becker 1975:49).

The point of all this is simple. Human persons fashion unfreedom as a bribe for self-perpetuation (Becker 1975:51). We sell our souls to that which we think gives us, or promises to give us, the power to live and the power to achieve immortality. Becker argues that men began to want a visible god to whom they could make their offerings. Israelites wanted freedom from such tyrannical images. The visible idol (Pharaoh) was defeated by the invisible God (Yahweh), and the slaves went free. But all too soon a chiefless tribe desired a king as a visible sign of prosperity (1 Samuel 8:6–22). To accept a visible god inevitably leads to the subjection of oneself to that visible god's agents. One eventually measures one's worth by how much one can pile up for that god and that god's agents. The result is alienation. No longer does ritual itself sustain us, as it did primitive peoples. We now allow family and religious rituals to be absorbed into state rituals (Becker 1975:52–62). And, I would add, now we subject ourselves to corporations' rituals. Super Bowl Sunday is an excuse to watch the advertisements (the Spanish word for ads, *propaganda*, is a more accurate description). Jay Leno's show is a nightly ad for recently released movies.

Early Christianity arose as the primitive world of agriculture was giving way to the era of domination by the state. Becker notes that Otto Rank saw Christianity as the religion of the Son in contradistinction to the patriarchal religions' era of the Father. Christianity places us in relationship with the Lord, not subjection to God. But Christianity failed to provide the universal democratic equality it had promised. The state has dominated ever since. Christianity's alternative was never realized (Becker 1975:70–71). We fail to recognize the heroic nature of our call as Christians and have forgotten the original energy of our religion's charge that we transform our world and achieve immortality as those blessed because we are mindful of the poor (cf. Becker 1975:174).

As various immortality symbol systems were discredited and fell into disuse, money arose as the new immortality principle. It seems to me that money has become for us what water is to fish: it is the ocean in which we swim, that without which we cannot live. Gold, literally sun power, becomes the new symbol of health and immortality. Street level drug dealers in North Camden often displayed garish gold chains as they sold their wares during the crack epidemic of the 1990s. The first mints were set up in temples, and temples were the first banks (think of the meaning of the driving out of the money lenders by Jesus in John 2). Instead of measuring our worth by what gives life, as primitives did, we now measure our worth by how much money we have. Ever since money took over, men and women have not been able to endure economic equality, because we have no faith in truly transcendent, invisible, immortality systems. "Things," not God, now grant immortality. The power to achieve immortality is now believed to lie in accumulated wealth (Becker 1975:87).

> *"It seems to me that money has become for us what water is to fish: it is the ocean in which we swim, that without which we cannot live."*

People now become takers and hoarders of things and wealth, not givers and sharers of the goods of the earth. Go to any ritzy, seaside resort like Avalon, New Jersey, and see the million-dollar homes standing empty forty to fifty weeks of the year. The wealthiest people in the world vie to see who will sit tenuously atop the *Forbes* list of the globe's richest. Suggest that they give it away and you are considered crazy. But that is precisely the counsel of Jesus, and of his followers (e.g., St. Francis of Assisi).

> This is one of the reasons, finally, that primitive Christianity is a real threat to both commercialism and communism, at least when it takes its own message seriously. Primitive Christianity is one of the few ideologies that has kept alive the idea of the invisible dimension of nature and the priority of this dimension for insuring immortality. (Becker 1975:86)

Becker wanted to know how humans can find helpful, life-giving, sustaining myths to satisfy our thirst for answers and meaning in a seemingly meaningless existence. His final conclusion was that we needed a new form of heroism, the heroism of a new sainthood (Becker 1975:163). Such saintly living would reveal our unconscious repressions, the ways in which we hide our true selves from ourselves. Living for sainthood would grant us many graces: self-knowledge, the ability to be in awe of creation, and freedom from fears, especially the fear of death. Really lived religion would help us overcome the tension at the heart of human existence, the fact that we know we are both animal and divine. "Men deny both in order to live tranquilly in the world. Religion overcame this double denial by maintaining that for God everything is possible" (Becker 1975:163). With God, we can overcome even our enslavement to the idolatry of money and wealth.

The old adage goes "Money makes the world go round." The drug dealers in North Camden once commissioned a wall mural in which the word CREAM was prominently displayed. CREAM was an acronym for "Cash Rules Everything Around Me." Too many of us are enslaved in a system wherein money becomes the primary meaning of our existence. Remember the question I mentioned previously: I ask undergrads if they would take "Catholic" off their resume if it would get them a job. The vast majority of students have no trouble with dropping "Catholic." "I can still go to Mass on my own," they argue. I point out the fact that they would not disown their allegiance to the Philadelphia Eagles. What if their bishop asked them to quit a law firm? The answers to such questions reveal who and what really has influence and power in our lives. Too many Catholics would readily give up the practices of our religion, but we'd never give up our jobs. It is not that money in itself is evil. It's the love of money, the depending on money as the measure of our worth, as the foundation of meaning in our lives, that gets us in trouble.

Jesus taught much more about the dangers money poses to our eternal salvation than he did about sexual practices (Luke 6:24, 16:19 ff.). The gospels are full of warnings to those who enjoy great wealth (e.g., Luke 1:53). Culturally, we in the West are, at root, capitalists. The question is, what happens when corporate capitalism and Christianity conflict? Which wins? Jesus or Money? Who or what do we think will save us (i.e., give us eternal life), Jesus or our stockbrokers? Another saying states that, "You can't take it with you." So, with what will we get into Heaven?

## The Church and Economic Justice

The Catholic Church clearly teaches that economic justice is a large part of God's kingdom. "The equal dignity of human persons requires the effort to reduce excessive social and economic inequalities" (*Catechism of the Catholic Church,* #1947). Jesus came to preach good news to the poor (Luke 4:18) and "makes active love toward them [the poor] the condition for entering his kingdom (cf. *Mt* 25:31–46)" (*Catechism of the Catholic Church,* #544). We are called to do justice by Jesus in Luke's Gospel. Jesus said, "blessed are you poor" and "woe to you that are rich" (Lk 6:20, 24). God does not favor those who are economically successful. As a matter of fact, economic success may cause a blindness that threatens our eventual ability to be with God for all eternity. The rich man of Luke 16, "Dives" (Latin for "rich man") is lost not for having simply failed to help Lazarus, the poor beggar at his doorstep. The rich man's great sin was ignoring Lazarus. The lessons of Luke's parable of the rich man and Lazarus are unsettling for the well-off. The rich people of the world will be called to account for failing to appreciate the fact that they are in relationship with the poor of the world (Matthew 25:31-46). This note of warning to the rich sounds throughout scripture. Mary's *Magnificat* sings of what happens when God bursts into our reality. "He has filled the hungry with good things, and sent the rich away empty" (Luke 1:53).

The prophets of the Old Testament thundered and condemned the economic injustices of their times. Isaiah tells us that God is "a God of justice" (Isaiah 30:18) whose servant will bring forth justice to the nations (Isaiah 42:1). Jeremiah sings that God delights in justice (Jeremiah 9:24), and Ezekiel images God as one who feeds the flock with justice (Ezekiel 34:16). Amos thunders that justice must "roll on like a river" (Amos 5:24; NIV) and bitterly condemns the complacent and secure of Zion (Amos 6:1) who have "turned justice into poison" (Amos 6:12). Amos excoriates those who have trampled on the poor (Amos 5:11) and deprived the poor of justice (Amos 5:12). Micah teaches us "to do justice, and to love kindness, and to walk humbly with our God" (Micah 6:8) a text quoted by President Jimmy Carter the day of his inauguration. And where it all started, in the liberation of the slaves from Egypt, we hear God's first words to Moses: "I have observed the misery of my people who are in Egypt; I have heard their cry on account of their taskmasters. Indeed, I know their sufferings, and I have come down to deliver them..." (Exodus 3:7–8). This God of the Old Testament who hears our cries and responds to our suffering demands that justice be done for the poor and powerless, for those who cannot defend themselves.

In 1986, the U.S. Catholic Bishops issued *Economic Justice for All*, a two-hundred-page pastoral "letter" (i.e., small book) instructing the church in the United States on matters concerning the economy. An extraordinarily well thought out and nuanced reflection on what economic justice is and entails in the United States, *Economic Justice for All* garnered praise from academics and those who seriously study the economy and the economy's effects on social and cultural conditions, while drawing ire and fire from conservatives, especially well-known conservative Catholics. The strongest aspect of the bishops' vision has to do with the principles on which economic justice is based and on which economic decisions must be made. These six principles govern (or ought to govern) the economy from a moral standpoint.

> "Central to the Biblical presentation of justice is that the justice of a community is measured by its treatment of the powerless in society, most often described as the widow, the orphan, the poor and the stranger (non-Israelite) in the land. ...What these groups of people have in common is their vulnerability and lack of power. They are often alone and have no protector or advocate. Therefore, it is God who hears their cries (Ps 109:21; 113:7), and the king who is God's anointed is to have special concern for them."
>
> (USCCB 1986, #38)

1. "Every economic decision and institution must be judged [on] whether it protects or undermines the dignity of the human person" (#13).

2. "Human dignity can be realized and protected only in community" (#14).

3. "All people have a right to participate in the economic life of society" (#15).

4. "All members of society have a special obligation to the poor and vulnerable" (#16).

5. "Human rights are the minimum condition for life in community. Human rights include not only civil and political rights, but also economic rights. As Pope John XXIII declared, 'all people have a right to life, food, clothing, shelter, rest, medical care, education, and employment'" (#17).

6. "Society as a whole, acting through public and private institutions, has the moral responsibility to enhance human dignity and protect human rights" (#18).

Decrying poverty in the United States and worldwide, the U.S. bishops argue in *Economic Justice for All* that economic "decisions must be judged in light of what they do *for* the poor, what they do *to* the poor, and what they enable the poor to do *for themselves*" (#24). Gleaned from theology, biblical and church traditions, and social science, the bishops' teaching holds as a fundamental criterion that all economic choices must be "at the service of all people, especially the poor" (#24). Most important, the bishops demand that all get a place at the table. To overcome "marginalization and powerlessness," the bishops say, "basic justice demands the establishment of minimum levels of participation in the life of the human community for all persons," and they add that the most heinous offense is to treat persons as if they are no longer members of the human family (#77).

In 1996, The Catholic bishops of Australia came forth with an even stronger statement. Simply put, these bishops think it is time to eradicate poverty the way we have eliminated other social sins like slavery. In the same way that slavery is no longer legal, anywhere on the globe, we ought to strive to make poverty unallowable. To bolster and ground their argument, the Australian bishops articulate the principles on which their presentation is based.

A NEW BEGINNING:
ERADICATING POVERTY IN OUR WORLD

Values and Principles
*The Australian Catholic Bishops, September 1996*

1. All persons have an essential dignity by virtue of the fact that they are created in the image of God. This dignity is the basis of all rights and responsibilities associated with being human. The purpose of society is the human person.

2. The human person is not to be understood as a self-sufficient individual, separate and independent from others. The human person is social by nature.

3. The principle of subsidiarity.

4. The purpose of the State is to promote the "common good." ... The State is required to intervene actively in society, including the economy, to promote and ensure justice.

5. The principle of participation states that human beings have a right to participate actively in decisions which affect their lives. The emphasis here is on the responsibility arising out of human dignity, to be "subjects" rather than "objects."

6. The principle of the universal purpose of goods states that the goods of the world are meant for all.... [T]he right to private property...is not absolute or unchangeable.

7. Conversion involves ongoing and personal change and social transformation.

8. Genuine human development involves more than an improvement in the material and economic aspects of life. The eradication of poverty will involve more than increases in wealth and income.

9. The biblical understanding of poverty is more sophisticated than that held by many people today. The economic dimension...is simply one part of the reality of poverty.

10. Catholic Social Teaching...has consistently rejected Marxism as an ideology and communism as a form of government and social organization. It has also rejected the excesses of capitalism, as well as some of the philosophical positions underpinning it. Communism does not take enough account of the human person, while capitalism does not take sufficient account of the social nature of the human person.

11. The practical implications of the biblical and Catholic social teachings for the eradication of poverty can be summed up by using a word and a phrase. The word is solidarity and the phrase is preferential option for the poor.

## The United States and Economic Justice

The Australian bishops' views on economic justice are not far from our American political and social traditions. The Declaration of Independence stated the truth that all men are created equal. Lamentably, this equality did not extend to African Americans until after the Civil War of the 1860s and the civil rights movement of the 1960s, but the ideals of justice and equality articulated in 1776 planted the seeds that grew in subsequent centuries, not only in the United States, but eventually around the globe. The preamble to the Constitution clearly states that we form the union to establish justice:

> We the people of the United States, in order to form a more perfect Union, establish Justice, insure domestic Tranquility, provide for the common defense, promote the general Welfare, and secure the Blessings of Liberty to ourselves and to Posterity, do ordain and establish this constitution for the United States of America.

President Franklin D. Roosevelt, in presenting an *Economic Bill of Rights* to Congress in 1944, argued, "We have come to the clear realization of the fact that true individual freedom cannot exist without economic security and independence.... We have accepted...a second Bill of Rights under which a new basis of security and prosperity can be established for all—regardless of station, race or creed." Among these are:

- The right to a useful and remunerative job...
- The right to earn enough to provide adequate food and clothing and recreation...
- The right of every family to a decent home;
- The right to adequate medical care and the opportunity to enjoy good health;
- The right to adequate protection from the economic fears of old age, sickness, accident, and unemployment.
- The right to a good education.

> —Franklin D. Roosevelt (quoted in Sklar 1995:170)

It is difficult to ascertain how we went from the America of the middle 1940s, when Franklin D. Roosevelt was calling for social justice on such a massive scale and movies like *It's a Wonderful Life* were lauding the decent common man, to the "grab all you can get" world of the 1980s and 1990s, with the Reagan and Bush agendas for giving tax breaks to the rich enacted as law, and Gordon Gekko's panegyric to capitalism in *Wall Street* being offered as our creed of greed. It is no wonder that the insanity of *American Beauty* is now trumpeted as the American way of life. Yet, sadly, statistics bear out the ever increasing economic gap and social abyss widening among citizens of the United States of America. The Land of the Free and the Home of the Brave is becoming the land of the "haves" and "have-nots."

> *"The Land of the Free and the Home of the Brave is becoming the land of the 'haves' and 'have-nots.'"*

The United States and world today little resemble places wherein the ideals and vision of the God of the Old and New Testament and of Catholic bishops holds sway. Yet, the good news is that we are at a point where the vision of justice and equality may have a better chance of taking hold than at any time in history. Just think: it has been only in the last twenty-five years or so that we have figured out how to make enough food to feed all the people on the planet. Famines that take place today are due much more to political problems than to production shortfalls. Food production surpasses the wildest dreams of our ancient ancestors, who spent most of their lives wondering whether there would be a fruitful harvest and where their next meal was to come from. Clothing is more plentiful than anyone ever imagined.

I was once on a bus in Bolivia and saw a little kid walking around wearing a Philadelphia Eagles tee-shirt with a logo of hockey sticks. That day I learned where the mistakes at the shirt factory end up. But at least the kid had the shirt. The biblical mandate to clothe the naked has been achieved. Today the top half of the top 1 percent of the population may have 50 percent of the wealth, but in 1900 they had 70 percent. Things have actually been getting better. As we live in our contemporary situation and struggle to make our times more equitable and just, we need to remember how much has already been achieved. Globally, poverty has decreased more in the past five decades than in the previous five centuries (UNDP 1997 in Friedman 2000:350).

The United States is a stratified society. It is amazing that college students know lyrics to thousands of songs, yet virtually none of the students in Introduction to Sociology classes have any idea of the extent and degree of income stratification in the United States. These are not hidden numbers; they can be easily found on the Internet.

The *2007 Statistical Abstract of the United States* reports that in 2004 household income distribution in the USA broke down this way: 15.4 percent had less than $15,000; 12.9 percent had between $15,000 and $24,999; 11.9 percent had between $25,000 and $34,999; 14.8 percent had between $35,000 and $49,999; 18.3 percent had between $50,000 and $74,999; and 15.7 percent had over $100,000 (Table 671).

Aggregate household income broken into quintiles shows even more inequality. The dollar amount for income levels of quintiles are given in constant 2004 dollars:

| % AGGREGATE INCOME | BOTTOM 20% | 2ND QUINTILE | 3RD QUINTILE | 4TH QUINTILE | TOP 20% |
|---|---|---|---|---|---|
| 1980 | 5.3% | 11.6% | 17.6% | 24.4% | 41.1% |
|  |  | >$22,581 | >$38,019 | >$53,848 | >$75,560 |
| 2004 | 4.0% | 9.6% | 15.4% | 23.0 | 47.9% |
|  |  | >$24,780 | >$43,400 | >$65,832 | >$100,000 |

(from Table 678)

In 1980, the top 5 percent of households in the United States had 14.6 percent of aggregate income (such households had upwards of $119,420 annually in 2004 dollars). By 2004, the top 5 percent of households had increased their share to 20.9 percent (such households had upwards of $173,640 annually) (Table 678).

Distribution of wealth is even more unequal. In 2003, the top 20 percent had 84 percent of the wealth, the fourth quintile had 11 percent; the third quintile had 5 percent; and the second and first quintiles split the last 2 percent (Macionis 2007:281).

Charts containing figures like these can be found are in most sociology textbooks, and information about income inequality regularly appears in magazines like *Time* and *Newsweek*. But very few in the United States are aware of just how unequal the distribution of wealth in American society really is.

THE CLASS SYSTEM IN THE UNITED STATES

|  | % of Pop. | Income |  |
|---|---|---|---|
| Capitalist | 01% | $1,000,000 + | Investors, heirs |
| Upper Middle class | 15% | $125,000 + | Professionals (graduate degree) |
| Lower Middle Class | 34% | about $60,000 | Semi-professionals (college degree) |
| Working Class | 30% | about $35,000 | Workers (high school graduate) |
| Working poor | 16% | about $17,000 | Laborers (high school graduate) |
| Underclass | 04% | $16,000 or less | Unemployed (some high school) |

Henslin (2007: 269)

Just 1 percent of the people in the United States are phenomenally rich, garnering more than $1 million annually. Only some 15 percent of Americans enjoy a lifestyle of $80,000 to $100,000+ a year. Some 60 percent of us are somewhere between $30,000 to $60,000 a year. About 25 percent of our brothers and sisters in the States get by on less than $20,000 a year. One challenger at a talk I once gave charged, "Fr. Malloy, this scale is just your Marxist opinion." These are not "liberal statistics," as another heckler once jeered. Go to <www.census.gov>. Click on income. The numbers are there for all to see. Check it out for yourself.

For years I've been running a thought experiment with my classes. How much would it take to eradicate poverty in the United States? To give $10,000 to every poor person would take, in round numbers, $400 billion dollars. I'm not suggesting that we simply hand poor people the money. It needs to be given in the form of vouchers for food, clothing, housing, health care, and education.

Princeton philosopher Peter Singer in *The New York Times Magazine*, makes much the same argument that I am making here (Singer 2006). Using the numbers crunched by economists Emmanuel Saez and Thomas Piketty, Singer notes that 14,400 taxpayers make up the top 0.01 percent in the United States. To keep the numbers simple, let me show how easy it would be to eradicate poverty in this country. Just take a little bit from the top 1 percent, the richest 3 million Americans. Since the "top top,"

"The richest 1 percent of Americans took in 21.8 percent of all recorded income in 2005—double their share in 1980. This means that the 300,000 Americans at the top made almost as much money as the 150 million Americans at the bottom."
—Mortimer B. Zuckerman, Editor-in-Chief, *U.S. News and World Report,* 6/11/07, p. 72

the 0.01 percent (or the 14,400 taxpayers mentioned by Singer), have average annual incomes of over $12.5 million, they would pay proportionately more, as would those in the top 0.1 percent, the 129,600 taxpayers whose income averages $2 million. Taking an average of $135,000 from the top 1 percent would immediately eliminate poverty in the United States. Or the plan could be scaled to the top 1.5 million, or the top 750,000 taxpayers. Even after such redistribution, all those at the top would still have incomes well above those of the vast majority of people on earth (Singer 2006:61).

---

### TO ERADICATE POVERTY IN THE UNITED STATES

To give every single poor person (man woman and child) $10,000 a year:
Redistribute an average of $135,000 from the richest 1 percent.

| 40 million poor people x $10,000 | | = $400 billion |
|---|---|---|
| Options: | | |
| Top 3.0 million taxpayers | x $135,000 | = $405 billion |
| Top 1.5 million taxpayers | x $270,000 | = $405 billion |
| Top 750,000 taxpayers | x $540,000 | = $405 billion |

---

Is eradicating poverty such a crazy, Don Quixotesque, "impossible dream"? Is the lifting of all our brothers and sisters above the poverty line an unattainable ideal? One of the great politicians of the twentieth century did not think so. After experiencing firsthand the poverty of rural Texas as a young schoolteacher, Lyndon B. Johnson went to Washington. Years later, as president, addressing Congress on March 16, 1964, he said, "For the first time in our history, it is possible to conquer poverty." Thus began the war on poverty (P. Johnson 1997:874). We never lost that war. We simply stopped fighting it as Vietnam and then Reaganomics dramatically skewed the mechanisms of wealth distribution toward the desires of powerful elites in the United States. Groups like Sojourners in Washington, DC, have been seriously advocating mobilization to overcome poverty for years and have stepped up their efforts since the dawn of the new millennium. In May of 2000 they were inviting folks to sign a "Covenant to Overcome Poverty," and in May of 2002 they convoked a symposium on the matter in Washington, DC (*Sojourners* May/June 2000, p. 8 and May/June 2002, p. 2). In May of 2000 the Canadian Catholic bishops came out with a strong argument calling for the elimination of poverty, saying "It Can Be Done and We Want It Done" (Canadian Catholic Bishops 2000). Peter Henriot, SJ, provides a cogent analysis demonstrating how Catholic social teaching informs the effort to eradicate poverty (Henriot 2002). The eradication of poverty is not tilting at windmills (Sachs 2005). Poverty's eradication is the gospel call for this new millennium.

Bono calls the eradication of poverty this generation's moon shot (Bono 2005). At the National Prayer Breakfast in Washington on February 2, 2006, Bono addressed the movers and shakers of the United States:

> Look, whatever thoughts you have about God, who He is or if He exists, most will agree that if there is a God, He has a special place for the poor. In fact, the poor are where God lives. Check Judaism. Check Islam. Check pretty much anyone. I mean, God may well be with us in our mansions on the hill. I hope so. He may well be with us as in all manner of controversial stuff. Maybe, maybe not. But the one thing we can all agree, all faiths and ideologies, is that God is with the vulnerable and poor.
>
> God is in the slums, in the cardboard boxes where the poor play house. God is in the silence of a mother who has infected her child with a virus that will end both their lives. God is in the cries heard under the rubble of war. God is in the debris of wasted opportunity and lives, and God is with us if we are with them. "If you remove the yoke from your midst, the pointing of the finger and speaking wickedness, and if you give yourself to the hungry and satisfy the desire of the afflicted, then your light will rise in darkness and your gloom will become like midday and the Lord will continually guide you and satisfy your desire in scorched places" (Isaiah 58:9–11).
>
> It's not a coincidence that in the Scriptures, poverty is mentioned more than 2,100 times. It's not an accident. That's a lot of airtime, 2,100 mentions. (You know, the only

"If you keep your food in a fridge, your clothes in a closet, have a roof over your head and sleep in a bed you are wealthier than seventy-five percent of the world's population. If you have a bank account, you are among the wealthiest eight percent of the world."

(Privett 2003:12)

time Christ is judgmental is on the subject of the poor.) "As you have done it unto the least of these my brethren, you have done it unto me" (Matthew 25:40). As I say, good news to the poor. (Bono 2006)

In this next millennium, we can work to truly eradicate poverty, the way we have virtually eradicated hunger and slavery on our planet (although there is a drastic food distribution problem and various slaveries still exist, especially in the global sex industries). In the next thousand years will inequality persist and worsen? For the next hundred years, the choices are up to us who are living now. We can reach out with a message of love and justice to people like "Jane."

### The Story of Jane

*Jane (not her real name) comes to Holy Name rectory and "wants to talk to a priest." She tells me her father is dying in a hospital bed in her living room. He's a Baptist. Will I come? Of course. Here in Camden, all faiths work together.*

*Jane and I walk a few inner city blocks to her weather beaten, listing, dilapidated row house. The chances of the landlord fixing the place are about as good as your winning the lottery three weeks in a row.*

*I walk into an immaculately clean living room. The only furniture is a table, two chairs, and a hospital bed. The sixty-year-old black man and I chat about life, God, what happens when the cancer wins. He is serene. He greatly appreciates his daughter's taking him into her home in his hour of need. We read the Bible and pray. Jane thanks me for coming and says she'll stop by the rectory the next day.*

*Twenty-four hours later, she shyly knocks on the door, dressed up in a clean and pressed Goodwill outfit, her enormous black eyes betraying what I suspect, and what she readily admits: "I needed a little something to calm me down. I've never talked to nobody 'bout this before." I listen. It's a tale. A tale of pain and hurt. A story sad and sorrowful. I am hearing raw and naked suffering. Years of it. Constant. Raped as a little girl by brothers and cousins. Abused as a girlfriend/wife. Once, her sister's boyfriend*

*tore the back off the house as they were sitting at the kitchen table,
feeding the kids and drinking coffee. He drove a Mack truck cab
through the walls. Her voice goes on, mellow and articulate in the
lilting dialect of the poor. Constant, grinding poverty follows years
of little formal education, teen pregnancy, and drug abuse. Now,
I know, she doesn't have the money to care for her ailing father.
"Here it comes," I think to myself. But I'm wrong.*

*She speaks words I'll never forget: "I don't want money. I
want to know something. Is this it for me? Is this be what God
wants for me? Do I always got to live like this? God, he hate me
or what?"*

The love of money truly is the root of all evils (see 1 Timothy 6:10)
and the worship of Mammon, literally, ill gotten wealth, distorts the
fundamental fulcrum of our relationship to the true and living God.
Worse, the gross inequalities make the poor think God hates them.
Those of us who claim that faith in Jesus Christ shapes our life must
work to meet the challenge of making the justice God passionately
wants for our world real and operative in lives of people like Jane.

## PRACTICES TO MOVE TOWARD ECONOMIC JUSTICE

1. Organize "Simple Meal Thursdays." Invite Catholics to cut back a bit on Thursdays, the day of the Last Supper, by saving $3.50 for a Starbucks coffee, or $1.00 by giving up dessert at lunch, or $7.50 by doing without a meal altogether, etc., and donating the money saved. If 50 million out of 69 million Catholics gave $1 a week to such a fund, that would be $2.6 billion a year. It doesn't seem too optimistic to assume that each one could manage $5 a week. That would be $13 billion a year—quite a pot with which to eradicate hunger.

2. Form a worldwide, Catholic, non-profit bank. There was a reason why the church used to teach that usury was wrong: interest in many ways abuses the poor. But there can be sane and reasonable methods of extending credit. Micro-lending can be a concrete work of charity effecting social improvement for millions of people.

3. Institute progressive tuition for Catholic education. In Chile, the Jesuit K-12 school in Osorno costs less for the poor, more for the rich. At St. Joe's Prep in Philadelphia, tuition is $14,000 whether a family makes $35,000 or $3.5 million a year.

4. Reform the power of corporations. Support unionization of labor on national and global levels.

5. Understand and analyze politics and the economy for what they actually are: political economy.

6. Practice a simple lifestyle. Simplicity is so often praised, so little practiced. Making universal health care a right rather than a privilege would make this more feasible.

7. Invite people to practice poverty at the level and rate with which they are comfortable. St. Francis of Assisi reformed and transformed his world by showing thousands how to break out of the military industrial complex of his day. How about a religious order composed of Catholic families that vow to live on less than two or three times the median family income? That would mean a Catholic family would give away anything over $150,000 they make.

# 7
# Demography Matters
## Catholicism as the Practice of a Cross-cultural, Global Christianity

*Seven Deadly Social Sins:*

*Politics without Principle*
*Wealth without Work*
*Commerce without Morality*
*Pleasure without Conscience*
*Education without Character*
*Science without Humanity*
*Worship without Sacrifice*

*—Gandhi*

This book's analysis and arguments are rooted, to a large degree, in the experience of practicing Catholicism in the late twentieth- and early twenty-first-century United States. Still, as Philip Jenkins shows, the Catholicism of the future will more and more reflect the cultural assumptions and practices of the global South (Jenkins 2002, 2006a, 2006b). The newer manifestations and practices of Catholicism in Africa, Latin America, and Asia will be rooted in the Catholic traditions and heritage of Europe, but will transform and transmit life in Christ in ways as yet unforeseen and unpredictable. What will be needed in the future is discussion and dialogue between the older and newer churches. Although some intra-church battles may be looming on the horizon over theological interpretations of the gospel, there is widespread unanimity on the desire for social justice, at least in matters economic, on the part of Catholic church communities in both the Northern and Southern hemispheres. Just as Peter and Paul and so many others throughout the history of the church have had to confront and discern changing cultural conditions, so must we in the twenty-first century.

## Changing Demographics

Numbers matter. The world has changed more in the past fifty years than in the previous five hundred mostly because there are so many more human beings. One learning activity I use in my classes is to chart world population growth since Jesus walked the earth (this is the only way I get on such a list!)

POPULATION

| Person | Year | Earth's Population |
|---|---|---|
| Jesus Christ | 1 | 250,000,000 |
| Columbus | 1492 | 500,000,000 |
| Jefferson | 1776 | 1,000,000,000 |
| Malloy at 0 | 1955 | 2,500,000,000 |
| Malloy at 40 | 1995 | 5,000,000,000 |
| Malloy at 80 | 2035 | 9,000,000,000 |

The population of the United States has almost doubled in the fifty years since I was born (165 million in 1955 to 300 million in October 2006, <www.census.gov>). Increases in urbanization impact our communities and cultures. In 1800, 6.1 percent of Americans lived in cities; by 1900, this figure had grown to 39.7 percent, and by 2000, 79 percent of Americans were urban dwellers (Macionis 2007:591). Worldwide, in 1800, there was one city with a population over one million. By 1900 there were sixteen such cities; by 1975 there were 195; by 1995 there were 364; and by 2015 there will by 564 cities with a population of at least one million (Henslin 2007:595).

## THE WORLD'S TEN LARGEST URBAN AREAS, 1950–2000
(Population in Millions)

| 1900 | | 1950 | | 1980 | | 2000 | | 2015 | |
|---|---|---|---|---|---|---|---|---|---|
| London | 6.5 | New York | 12.3 | Tokyo | 16.9 | Tokyo | 28.0 | Tokyo | 28.7 |
| New York | 4.2 | London | 10.4 | New York | 15.6 | Mexico City | 18.1 | Mumbai | 27.4 |
| Paris | 3.3 | Tokyo | 6.7 | Mexico City | 14.5 | Bombay | 18.0 | Lagos | 24.4 |
| Berlin | 2.4 | Paris | 5.4 | São Paulo | 12.1 | São Paulo | 17.7 | Shanghai | 23.4 |
| Chicago | 1.7 | Shanghai | 5.3 | Shanghai | 11.7 | New York | 16.6 | Jakarta | 21.2 |
| Vienna | 1.6 | Buenos Aires | 5.0 | Buenos Aires | 9.9 | Shanghai | 14.2 | São Paulo | 20.8 |
| Tokyo | 1.5 | Chicago | 4.9 | Los Angeles | 9.5 | Lagos | 15.5 | Karachi | 20.6 |
| St. Petersburg | 1.4 | Moscow | 4.8 | Calcutta | 9.0 | Los Angeles | 13.1 | Beijing | 19.4 |
| Philadelphia | 1.4 | Calcutta | 4.4 | Bejing | 9.0 | Seoul | 12.9 | Dhaka | 19.0 |
| Manchester | 1.3 | Los Angeles | 4.0 | Rio de J. | 8.8 | Beijing | 12.4 | Mexico City | 18.8 |

(1950, 1980, 2000 in Curran & Renzetti 2000:520; 1900, 2015 in Brym and Lie 2007:589)

### Demographics and the Church

Most Catholics in the United States know how much, how fast, and how deeply things have changed in the past fifty years. Still, many of us are unaware of the global transformations in the Roman Catholic Church.

There are some 1.1 billion Roman Catholics. John L. Allen (2006) reports that the Catholic community in Africa grew from 1.9 million in 1900 to 130 million in 2000—a growth rate of 6,708 percent! The rest of the Catholic world has bloomed much more slowly, growing at 13.2 percent. Today there are 600 African bishops, 30,000 African priests, and 30,000 African seminarians. Asia had 11 million Catholics in 1900 and 107 million in 2000 for a growth rate of 861 percent. Note that 70 million of Asia's Catholics are in the Philippines. Estimates for the number of Catholics in China are around 13 million.

Latin America's 520 million Catholics constitute almost half of all Catholics in the world. Allen points out that Catholicism in Latin America is "under siege" as aggressive Protestant and evangelical proselytizers lure Catholics into their churches. Still, from my pastoral experience among Latinos in the United States, I know the fluidity and flux of people sampling and switching among denominations and churches. There is no sure way to know just how many Latino Catholics have truly left the church for the rest of their lives (and it is difficult to know what it means to say someone is "Catholic" when, having been baptized a Catholic, one may very rarely have seen the inside of a Catholic church before "joining" an evangelical sect or Protestant church). The Middle East has 2.1 million Catholics in union with Rome. Under severe stress on many fronts, these groups are in great flux. Allen reports there are "more Palestinian Catholics in Australia than in Palestine" (Allen 2006:88). Catholics in Europe total some 283 million, but church practice throughout the Western regions of Europe is in serious decline. (Allen 2006).

Looking at Christianity as a whole, Philip Jenkins, an astute observer of the shifting demographics of Christianity, tells the tale. Extrapolating the numbers, he predicts that by 2025, of the 2.6 billion Christians in the world, 595 million will be in Africa, 623 million in Latin America, 498 million in Asia, and 513 million in Europe. By 2050, "Christianity will be chiefly the religion of Africa and the African diaspora" (Jenkins 2006:12). In 2050, of the world's 3 billion Christians, only 20 percent at most will be non–Latino Caucasians (i.e., "whites").

---

### THE TEN MOST POPULOUS COUNTRIES IN 2006 AND IN 2050
#### Population in Millions

| 2006 Population | | 2050 Projected Population | |
|---|---|---|---|
| China | 1,311 | India | 1,628 |
| India | 1,122 | China | 1,437 |
| USA | 299 | USA | 420 |
| Indonesia | 207 | Nigeria | 299 |
| Brazil | 165 | Pakistan | 295 |
| Pakistan | 299 | Indonesia | 285 |
| Bangladesh | 124 | Brazil | 260 |
| Russia | 142 | Bangladesh | 231 |
| Nigeria | 135 | Dem Rep of Congo | 183 |
| Japan | 128 | Ethiopia | 145 |

(Population Reference Bureau 2006)

---

Of the countries in the world, the United States will have the largest number of Christians, many of Hispanic, Asian, and African origin. "By that point, one-third of all Americans will have Latino or Asian roots— roots that will be overwhelmingly Christian" (Jenkins 2006:12). The United States today is over 30 percent non-"white," and sometime rather soon in this century, we will see a "majority-less" United States, with no racial or ethnic category comprising 50 percent of the population. Such is the reality in California today. Globally, the coming shifts are even more dramatic. Jenkins notes that cultural and demographic shifts will transform, in the next quarter century, deeply held and cherished assumptions. "We can predict something of the beliefs and practices of the emerging Southern Christianity, but what of the future of God and the world? The greatest change is likely to involve our Enlightenment-derived assumptions that religion should be segregated into a separate sphere of life, distinct from everyday reality" (Jenkins 2002:140).

The churches of the global South read the scriptures with new eyes, new emphasis, new interpretations (Jenkins 2002:217 ff.; 2006a). Issues of persecution and forced conversion are all too real for those in lands beyond Europe and the Americas. The theme and experience of exile are a daily reality for millions. The Jesuit Refugee Service reports that in 2005, there were over 40 million refugees and displaced persons, mostly women and children and mostly in Africa and Asia (<www.jesref.org>, accessed January 2006).

For believers coming from the lands of Africa and Asia, the faith is vibrant and real, and is to be accepted with somewhat less hermeneutical suspicion than among Catholics in more developed and affluent countries. The growing number of priests imported from the global South to alleviate the pressing priest shortage in Europe and the United States will bring with them this new reading of the scriptures and interpretations of the faith. The cultural clashes between, for example, an African or Indian priest and his Catholic parishioners in the United States are greater and run much deeper than difficulties with his English pronunciation

"This global perspective should make us think carefully before asserting 'what Christians believe' or 'how the church is changing.' All too often statements about what 'modern Christians accept' or 'what Catholics today believe' refer only to what that ever-shrinking remnant of Western Christians and Catholics believe. Such assertions are outrageous today, and as time goes by they will become ever further removed from reality."
(Jenkins 2002:3)

during homilies. There is opportunity for both sides to learn from each other if both sides can overcome ethnocentric biases and open themselves to the wisdom and even wit of the other partner in the dialogue.

---

PROJECTION OF CATHOLICS WORLDWIDE IN 2025
(in millions)

| Continent | 2000 | 2025 |
|---|---|---|
| Latin America | 461 | 606 |
| Europe | 286 | 276 |
| Africa | 120 | 228 |
| Asia | 110 | 160 |
| North America | 71 | 81 |
| Oceania | 8 | 11 |
| TOTAL | 1,056 | 1,362 |

(Jenkins 2002:195 citing Barrett, et.al, 2001, World Christian Encyclopedia)

---

## Global Citizens: A Radical Re-imaging

At the start of the last century the famous African American sociologist, W. E. B. DuBois wrote, "... the problem of the Twentieth century is the problem of the color line" (Du Bois 1903:41,54). The problem of the twenty-first century may be the border line. Who gets into what country? Who gets to be considered a citizen of the first, the second, the third, or the fourth worlds? What will constitute membership in a society? I once met a German Jesuit who had spent the previous three years ministering to refugees in Bosnia in the late 1990s. He saw my blue United States passport and commented in a reflective manner, "There are so many who would give so much to have a passport like that."

> We assume an established group and a fixed population, and so we miss the first and most important distributive question: How is that group constituted? I don't mean how was it constituted. I am not concerned here with the historical origins of the

different groups, but with the decisions they make in the present about their present and future populations. The primary good we distribute to one another is membership in some human community. And what we do with regard to membership structures all other distributive choices. (Walzer 1983:31; emphasis added)

U.N. INDICATORS OF HUMAN DEVELOPMENT
Top Ten and Bottom Ten Countries, 2002

| Rank | | Life Expectancy (years) | Literacy (percent) | GDP per cap. |
|---|---|---|---|---|
| 1. | Norway | 78.9 | 99.0 | $36,600 |
| 2. | Sweden | 80.0 | 99.0 | $26,050 |
| 3. | Australia | 79.1 | 99.0 | $28,260 |
| 4. | Canada | 79.3 | 99.0 | $29,480 |
| 5. | Netherlands | 78.3 | 99.0 | $29,100 |
| 6. | Belgium | 78.7 | 99.0 | $27,570 |
| 7. | Iceland | 79.7 | 99.0 | $29,750 |
| 8. | United States | 77.0 | 99.0 | $35,750 |
| 9. | Japan | 81.5 | 99.0 | $26,940 |
| 10. | Ireland | 76.9 | 99.0 | $36,360 |
| 168. | Congo | 41.4 | 62.7 | $650 |
| 169. | C. Af. Rep. | 39.8 | 48.6 | $1,170 |
| 170. | Ethiopia | 45.5 | 41.5 | $780 |
| 171. | Mozambique | 38.5 | 46.5 | $1,050 |
| 172. | Guinea-Bissau | 45.2 | 39.4 | $710 |
| 173. | Burundi | 40.8 | 50.4 | $630 |
| 174. | Mali | 48.5 | 19.0 | $930 |
| 175. | Burkina Faso | 45.8 | 12.8 | $1,100 |
| 176. | Niger | 46.0 | 17.1 | $800 |
| 177. | Sierra Leone | 34.3 | 36.0 | $520 |
| World | | 66.9 | n.a. | $7,804 |

(Brym and Lie 2007:223)

To be born in the developed world grants advantages that the vast majority of people on earth can never have. Simply to live in a first world country gives one such a head start in the economic race, and in any race at all—and even in the amount of time one gets to run.

Who decides "who gets what" often is determined by the decisions concerning "who gets to live where." The national and societal mechanisms maintain the arbitrary divisions that affect the life chances of billions of persons. Could it be that as we enter the twenty-first century we have to re-think the way the planet's people are placed together (i.e., structured)? Does our Catholic faith call us to think in radically different ways about who is "us" and who is "them"? "Radical" comes from the Latin *radix*, meaning root. To be radical is to go to the roots. In what follows, I want to invite us to think about the roots of some of the problems noted in previous chapters and imagine new ways of being global citizens in light of our Catholic faith. The most radical response to Jesus is to truly love one another as Jesus loved us. Such love cannot be bounded by arbitrary borders imposed on the globe. At root, we are all connected in the realm of the human heart, the realm wherein we desire the best for all. In our hearts, on both the personal and societal levels, exists the kingdom where Jesus rules. We have rapidly entered the age of a globalized church, a church wherein the baptized navigate membership and community in the multicultural global village.

*"The basic structural problem of the twenty-first century is this: we have a nation-state political system, while the economy has become a supranational, global reality."*

The basic structural problem of the twenty-first century is this: we have a nation-state political system, while the economy has become a supranational, global reality. There is no political power that can counter and balance the globalized economic powers that dominate the well-being of peoples on the planet. The global village, in its infancy in the 1970s, has reached adolescence. This awkward stage is rough and disconcerting. Will the child grow to be a responsible adult, or will we fail to navigate the turbulent waters of growth and drown as a system and as a species?

As baptized Catholics, we have to ask: What is our relationship to those fellow Catholics who live beyond our nation-state borders? At the turn of the millennium, Los Angeles was 34 percent Catholic; Catholics will constitute 50 percent of the city's population by the year 2020 (Grossman 2002). Many of those Los Angeles Catholics will be of Mexican origin. In 1996, 42 percent of legal immigrants in the United States from fifty-two countries were Catholics (Grossman 2002). Over one billion people on earth are Catholic. Should we not strive to share the goods of the economy and the earth with our brothers and sisters in Christ?

The relationship between church and state has had a long and stormy history in the Western world. As we enter the twenty-first century, the question is no longer simply how the church relates to the nation-state, but how the church relates to the global economy. A truly world church can be a major influence on our ever more globalized planet. Since more and more it is businesses and corporations that call the shots, we as church will have to speak to and with them and call such institutions to use their power to form a world wherein all can grow happy and healthy and free.

> The modern global economy started in rural New Hampshire. There at the 1944 conference held at Bretton Woods, the soon to be winners of the Second World War conceived of an array of multinational institutions: the World Bank to promote economic development, the International Monetary Fund to support financial stability, the General Agreement on Tariffs and Trade to expand commerce.... If the world's political elite set the stage for globalization, it is the businesses that have written the script and played the lead roles. (Stewart 2003:8)

## Globalization: The New, Old Game in Town

Thomas Friedman, in his bestselling book *The Lexus and the Olive Tree* (2000), defines the new global reality being born.

> I define globalization this way: the inexorable integration of markets, nation-states and technologies to a degree never witnessed before—in a way that is enabling individuals, corporations and nation-states to reach around the world farther, faster, deeper and cheaper than ever before, and in a way that

is enabling the world to reach into individuals, corporations and nation-states farther, faster, deeper and cheaper than ever before. This process of globalization is also producing a powerful backlash from those brutalized and left behind in this new system. (Friedman 2000:9)

Friedman offers the images of the Lexus and the olive tree to help us comprehend what is going on in this rapidly emerging world. The Lexus represents the contemporary world of innovation and technological expertise; the olive tree, tradition and communities of meaning. Olive trees are important. They root us. One cannot be a complete person alone. According to Friedman, the Lexus versus the olive tree is the modern version of Cain versus Abel. Cain and Abel were fighting over who gets to control society (property, religious rites, etc.).

Friedman argues that the driving force of this new world is free-market capitalism. Whether we like it or not, free-market capitalism's values and practices are affecting everyone and everything. If not actually homogenizing cultures (Friedman 2000), capitalism's meaning and values nevertheless seriously affect all cultures (Friedman 2005). Capitalism's essence, "creative destruction," forces everyone to be involved in a world where innovation trumps tradition. The new anxiety of our age is terror at the effects that such rapid global changes will have on us and ours. The ever increasing urbanization of the planet exacerbates these tensions.

Friedman recognizes that power in this globalized world depends on the delicate balancing of three relationships: (1) the nation-state, (2) nation-states and global markets, and (3) individuals and nation-states. Super empowered individuals (e.g., Bill Gates; Osama Bin Laden) can have influence and power beyond that of entire blocs of nations.

---

Bill Gates is the richest person in the world, his wealth worth $51 billion in 2005, which is roughly equal to the economic output of the poorest forty-five countries on the planet (Maciones 2007:307). He also is the most generous person in history, having given away more to those in need than anyone else ever (Henslin 2007:269). But he made much of his money taking advantage of the structural inequalities and cultural attitudes and assumptions undergirding the economic system. When he was 29 years old, Gates said, "Well, let's hire two women because we can pay them half as much as we have to pay a man, and we can give them all this other 'crap' work to do because they are women."
(Brym and Lie 2007:352)

Thus the global system in which we all are immersed today consists of nation-states and Supermarkets and Super-empowered individuals (Friedman 2000:15). In this world, power morphs at the speed of light. It is no longer a world where hierarchies function well.

Everyone on earth is now feeling the effects of globalization. We've gone from a 10 miles-per-hour national rat race to a 110 miles-per-hour global rat race. Friedman realizes that this new world is a "Golden Straitjacket" (although in my view a straitjacket, even if golden, is still a straitjacket and a symbol of the insane asylum, not of a sane and sensible economic freedom). There is now only one game in town (all towns). There are no alternatives to free-market capitalism. There is no "third way" (Friedman 2000:103). Even those who would struggle against the new order of things stand little chance. The groups and nations Friedman names "turtles" and "wounded gazelles" have no organization. They're too disparate to challenge the system. "And," he adds, "don't kid yourself, the backlash is not just an outburst from the most downtrodden. Like all revolutions, globalization involves a shift in power from one group to another. In most countries it involves a power shift from the state and its bureaucrats to the private sectors and entrepreneurs" (Friedman 2000:336).

According to Friedman, the reason why everyone cooperates with the new order of things is that they like it this way. Most people are in favor of the globalized capitalistic economy. There is a groundswell bolstering the free market system. The "wretched of the earth" want to go to Disney World, not the barricades. They want the Magic Kingdom, not *Les Miserables*.

> What such stories teach us is that while globalization can produce a profound sense of alienation, as power keeps moving up to more and more abstract levels that are difficult to touch, affect or even see, it can also do the opposite. It can push down to the local level and to the weakest individuals more power, opportunities and resources to become shapers than ever before. (Friedman 2000:362).

Although he has not written a religious book, Friedman notes that God is in our choices (Friedman 2000:468). Within this new globalized world, we stand in danger of re-creating the tower of Babel.

Indeed, the reason God so wants to be in cyberspace, and the reason we should want him there, argues Israeli philosopher David Hartman, is because in some ways cyberspace is the world the prophets spoke about, "a place where all mankind [sic] can be unified and totally free. The danger is that we are unifying mankind in cyberspace—all speaking one language, all using one medium—but without God." And we certainly don't want to be unifying mankind through the Internet without any value system, without any filters, without any alternative conception of meaning other than business and without any alternative view of human beings other than as consumers looking for the lowest price. But these much needed values are best learned off-line, outside the Internet. The only way people are going to find God on the Internet is if they bring Him there in their own heads and hearts and behaviors—drawing on values they learn in the terrestrial world—in the olive groves of their parents' home or their community, church, synagogue, temple or mosque. (Friedman 2000:470)

Friedman's wildly popular *The World Is Flat 2.0* (2005) continues in the same vein, arguing the inevitability of globalization's penetration of our lives and communities and its overall beneficial effects. At the end of that book he again returns to the image of the tower of Babel, receiving counsel from his spiritual advisor, Rabbi Marx. Friedman's rabbi tells him that the meaning of the tower of Babel was that God was angry with the reason behind the tower's erection. People wanted to make themselves God. "The heresy is not that mankind works together—it is to what ends. It is essential that we use this new ability to communicate and collaborate for the right ends" (Friedman 2005:539). Beyond the irony of globalization's best-selling, popular champion accepting advice from a rabbi named Marx, there is a profound truth in the rabbi's observation. The discovery of right responses to the predicaments and problems,

---

**Globalization: One Case**

"Four Indonesian plants, owned by South Koreans, paid young girls as little as 15 cents an hour for an eleven-hour day. Nike shows that it costs $5.60 to make in Asia shoes sold in the West for $70 and up. Michael Jordan's $20 million endorsement fee was higher than the combined yearly payrolls of the Indonesian plants that made the shoes."

(LaFeber 1999:107)

the troubles and tribulations, of the world constructed by free market capitalism is found in the examination of ends. Friedman's take on globalization can be supported or attacked depending on whether one thinks globalization is good or bad for the vast majority of people on planet earth.

John H. Dunning, at the end of a set of provocative and erudite essays he edited, raises three salient questions: (1) How far does globalization "fall short" in its moral and ethical practices? (2) How much of any failure on the part of globalization is due to the inherent lack of "moral capital" in the processes of globalization's implementations? (3) What should be done to address the moral inadequacies of individuals and institutions as they re-create the social networks of the planet according to globalization's tenets? (Dunning 2003). Whatever the ultimate answers, the present state of affairs is unacceptable.

The 2005 United Nations Human Development Report (UNDP 2005) reveals the stunning levels of inequality across the globe. The richest 500 people on earth have a combined income larger than that of 416 million poor people. Forty percent of the planet, 2.7 billion of our brothers and sisters, barely survive on less than $2 a day. That bottom 40 percent gets 5 percent of the world's income; the top 10 percent get 54 percent. "An obvious corollary of extreme global inequality is that even modest shifts in distribution from top to bottom could have dramatic effects on poverty. Using a global income distribution database, we estimate a cost of $300 billion for lifting 1 billion people living on less than $1 a day above the extreme poverty line threshold. That amount represents 1.6% of the income of the richest 10% of the world's population" (UNDP 2005:4). The report recognizes that such a "static transfer" would not achieve long-term poverty reduction, but such a program would be a powerful catalyst toward meeting the Millennium Development Goals.

At the turn of the century, the United Nations issued "A Balance Sheet of Human Development 1990–1997" (UNDP 1999)

"The cultural environment associated with the latest era of capitalism, dominated as that environment is by the global culture industries, presents new and imposing barriers (beyond those of typical earlier eras) to the formation of deep religious convictions.... What is at risk is not any particular interpretation of the gospel or the tradition of the church but the capacity to think, feel and experience in ways formed by the Christian story."

(Budde 1997:15)

showing the condition of our world as we entered the twenty-first century. Between 1990 and 1997, adult literacy rose from 64 percent to 76 percent, but in 1997, 850 million adults were illiterate. Despite rapid population growth, food production per capita increased nearly 25 percent between 1990 and 1997, but about 840 million people were still malnourished. The overall consumption of the richest fifth of the world's people was sixteen times that of the poorest fifth. During 1990–1997, real per capita GDP increased at an average annual rate of more than 1 percent. Real per capita consumption increased at an average annual rate of 2.4 percent during the same period. Yet, in 1997 nearly 1.3 billion people were living on less than a dollar a day, and close to 1 billion could not meet their basic consumption requirements. The share in global income of the richest fifth of the world's people was 74 times that of the poorest fifth. During 1990–1997 the net secondary school enrollment for girls increased from 36 percent to 61 percent and women's economic activity rate rose from 36 percent to nearly 40 percent. Nevertheless, only 340 million women were expected to survive to age forty. A quarter to a half of all women had suffered physical abuse at the hands of an intimate partner. Between 1990 and 1997, the infant mortality rate was reduced from 76 per 1,000 births to 58. But, nearly 160 million children were malnourished and more than 250 million children were working as child laborers. Between 1990 and 1997 the share of heavily polluting traditional fuels in the energy used was reduced by more than two-fifths, but every year 3 million people were dying from air pollution—more than 80 percent of them from indoor air pollution—and more than 5 million were dying from diarrheal diseases caused by water contamination (UNDP 1999:22).

The United Nation Development Programme's 1999 report's findings were widely disseminated. One example of the popular press's treatment of the report comes from Melbourne's *The Age*, which reported most of the statistics in the preceding paragraph. *The Age* noted that the report says global in-

---

**The USA Is Not #1:**

The United Nations asks rich nations to give 0.7% of GNP to address extreme hunger and poverty. Ranked by rates of generosity, here's the percentage rich nations gave in 2003:

Norway, 0.92%
Sweden, 0.70%
France, 0.41%
UK, 0.34%
Germany, 0.28%
Canada, 0.26%
Japan, 0.20%
Italy, 0.16%
USA, 0.14%

(*Sojourners*
August 2005, p. 9)

equalities have increased in the twentieth century "by orders of magnitude out of proportion to anything experienced before." The gap between the incomes of the richest and poorest countries in 1820 was 3 to 1; by 1950, 35 to 1; by 1973, 44 to 1; by 1992, 72 to 1. "The report breaks new ground by asserting that human rights must include economic, social and cultural rights" (*The Age*, June 30, 2000).

As we entered the twenty-first century, Jim Hug, SJ, of the Center for Concern in Washington, DC, reported that "The wealthiest 20 percent of the world's population (about 1.2 billion people) receive over 86% of the world's annual income.... The poorest 1.2 billion are living on about 1%. These percentages are not static. Over the past 30 years, statistics reveal an increasing concentration of wealth in the hands of a shrinking percentage of the global population. In today's economy, wealth does *trickle*, but it trickles *up*, not down" (Hug 2000:17). People of nearly half the countries on earth (about 25 percent of the world's population in 2000) are poorer in real terms today than they were ten years ago. "More economic growth—at least of the kind we're experiencing now—will only make the problem worse." (Hug 2000:17). Hug argues that the poor do not have access to the processes by which wealth is created.

For transformation of the global economy to occur, more and more people will need to elicit in themselves and others a love for the poor and a desire to see things radically transformed. John Paul II teaches that our vision concerning Catholic social teaching must be more international in scope and must include:

> the option or love of preference for the poor. This is an option...to which the whole tradition of the Church bears witness. It affects the life of every Christian inasmuch as he or she seeks to imitate the life of Christ, but it applies equally to our *social responsibilities* and hence to our manner of living, and to the logical decisions to be made concerning the ownership and use of goods. (John Paul II 1987, *On Social Concern*, #42, in O'Brien and Shannon 1992:425)

PRACTICES TO ADDRESS INJUSTICE AND INEQUALITY

1.  Get informed. The overwhelming sense of being at the mercy of the forces of globalization leaves many exhausted and confused. Start by reading Friedman's books (2000, 2005). Or get a good Introduction to Sociology textbook and read the chapters on social and global stratification. Go online to <www.one.org>, <www.census.gov>, <www.worldbank.org>, and the United Nations Human Development Reports, <http://hdr.undp.org/>. Learn about Catholic social teaching from the superb websites set up by the Office of Social Justice of the Diocese of Saint Paul-Minneapolis, <www.osjspm.org/cst>.

2.  Attend a Eucharist celebrated in another language, in a section of the city where the poor live. Ride a bus on which you are the only person of your race. Go to a restaurant that serves ethnic food different from your own. Much of our economic inequality is rooted in our ethnocentric lifestyles.

3.  Travel. Get out of the United States and go to other countries, but not to the tourist destinations. Visit places in other countries where the poor live. Become a global citizen.

4.  Go on a service trip to a poor section of the the United States or beyond. Thousands of folks go forth on service trips each year. Such efforts help bridge the divides created between people by our global economy.

5.  Take steps to make sure that care for our planet and its people is included in all Catholic catechesis. Concern for both environmental and social ecology are central aspects of living and practicing the Catholic faith as a faith that frees.

6.  Question the dictates of globalized, corporate capitalism. The internal dynamics and logic of profit-driven corporations too often almost force those making decisions on the corporations' behalf to choose what they know is against the common good. Catholic social teaching can stand as a touchstone, offering an alternative to the profit-driven ideologies of the market.

7.  Make an option for the poor. St. Francis of Assisi transformed his social world by taking seriously the gospel's call to live in simplicity and harmony. Such practice is never out of date or ineffectual.

# 8
# Liberation Matters
## Jesus' Vision of God's Reign in the Twenty-first Century

*"You will know the truth, and the truth will make you free."*
    *—John 8:32*

Peter and Paul had to take the ideas and ideals of the preacher from Galilee and adapt them for audiences across the first-century Mediterranean world. We must do the same for the twenty-first century.

In this chapter, I want to call for a holistic approach to issues and topics in the light of the liberating and transformational energies pulsating through our prayer and service as the people of God. The energies of the people of God concentrated on the amelioration of matters economic, and on establishing justice between races, genders, and nations, will make authentic and credible our preaching of the gospel. This will necessitate placing the issues surrounding sexuality in their proper perspective. It will also necessitate the integration of the message of the cross into all we do as we and all of creation live in anticipation of the establishment of the reign of God.

### Loving Matters: Catholicism as the Practice of Sane, Sensual, Responsible, and Relational Sexuality

The more conservative Catholics focus exclusively on matters of sexual morality, the less we realize that our sexual practices play out in relation to the other cultural practices of our times. Jesus spoke much more about the dangers wealth and riches pose to our eternal salvation than about the seductions of sex. Jesus' message is all about love, love of God and love for neighbor. Like all Christians and people of good will, Catholics are called to love. St. Augustine said it best. *"Ama Deum et fac quod vis"* (Love God and do what you will). College students at first leap at the shallow implications of this central truth of our relationship with God. They exclaim, "You mean we can do whatever we want?"

> *Can you stand before God at the end of your life and, without shame, look Jesus in the eye and say, "This is what I did"?*

Yes, exactly. But then I add this caveat for the students: "If you love God, truly and really love God, all that you desire will be good and loving." Sexual relationships will be amazingly free from distress and disorder, sin and shame, violence and violations, if people really strive to love God in and through the ways they love others. Sexual relationships are no different from our economic and other social realtionships. Premarital sex, artificial means of birth control, abortion, divorce: these issues are subject to the same norm of authenticity articulated above. Is your practice in these areas congruent with your Catholic faith? Can you stand before God at the end of your life and, without shame, look Jesus in the eye and say, "This is what I did"? If you can, you are not far from the kingdom of God. If you cannot, reform and conversion are needed. The bottom line is clear: "Love one another as I have loved you.... This I command you: to love one another" (John 15:12, 17).

Our Lord's injunction to love extends to all the relationships of our lives. Still, a society like that in the United States in which more than twenty identified sexually transmitted diseases (STDs) are among the most common infectious diseases affecting more than 13 million men and women in this country each year, and costing well over $10 billion annually (National Institutes of Health, <http://www.nih.gov/>), in which there are 1.6 million abortions a year (P. Johnson 1997:964), in which one out of six women and one out of thirty-three men has experienced rape or attempted rape (Centers for Disease Control, <http://www.cdc.gov/ncipc/factsheets/svfacts.htm>, accessed January 2007), and in which the snatching and molesting and murder of small children is becoming commonplace news is a society spiraling downward, abysmally lost in the sexual chaos ushering forth from spiritual pain and confusion. To get all our relationships functioning in a manner that directs us according to the values of the kingdom of God will go far in fixing the mess our unbridled and unrestricted sexual passions have caused. But to address the sexual chaos, we must address all that is chaotic. My contention is that Catholicism is a sane alternative to those aspects of our culture that increasingly show signs of cultural mental instability, if not full blown insanity. The practices of full and flexible and freeing Catholicism offer a sane alternative to the confusions of our times.

Yet, far too many Catholics find the church's teaching on sexual morality somewhere between confusing to incomprehensible. One college student writes:

> In my experience many women find one-night stands emotionally unfulfilling and often hurtful. If the Church condemned this act because it is empty and damaging to all involved, I think a lot of young people would listen. It would certainly speak to their experience. Some might argue that this concern for our own dignity as well as our partners is, in fact, at the heart of the Church's wisdom on sexual matters. If so, at the age of 21 after 17 years of Catholic school, I've yet to hear it expressed in that way. Instead, young people are taught the act itself is wrong, which is often the only rewarding part. Until young Catholics are provided with a sexual ethic that reflects their experience, rather than what they perceive to be an ironclad list of unjustified rules, they will continue to make decisions about sexuality without religion as an authority. (Tier 2006)

The church does have a vision of authentic living to offer such a young person. Instead of a list of "dos and don'ts," we would do well to lead with a grounded, holistic, and challenging vision of chastity. We should also humbly realize that for most people sexual development and maturity are much like baseball: errors are part of the game. The Catechism teaches that chastity consists in "successful integration of sexuality within the person" (*Catechism of the Catholic Church*, #2337), which implies that one's growth as a human being takes time. Successful integration is worked at over a lifetime and is rarely easy. The church must support and guide people toward sexual integration rather than lay down unattainable edicts about premarital sex or artificial means of birth control. Cultural conditions surrounding those two matters have changed radically in recent times. Throughout much of human history, most people were married as soon as their sexual organs matured. In very recent times, the age of marriage has moved into the late twenties. The "pill" has been widely available for close to five decades. Changes of this magnitude need time to be assimilated into cultures. We have to allow for the presence of the Holy Spirit to work and lead us in these areas.

Allow me to make a provocative suggestion. It is time for the church to allow and urge as much freedom in matters sexual as we do in matters economic. In the same way that Catholics are urged to hear the church's call for economic justice and choose freely how they will respond to that call, I think we should urge people to live their sexual lives in ways that respect and take seriously the church's teachings on sexuality. People in their own responsible freedom will have to stand before God at the end of their days and render account of their lives.

Pelvic issues have caused incalculable controversy and confusion, even division, in Catholic circles. All the energy and effort the church has expended trying to control and complicate the sexual lives and actions of Catholics is worthwhile only if such efforts make us more authentic and vibrant followers of Christ. There is some evidence that those who strive for the sexual integration for which the church calls are happier and healthier than those who live hedonistic and sexually permissive lives. Priest and sociologist Andrew Greeley found that Catholics have better and more playful sex than other Americans and attributes this to the influence of the Catholic imagination on Catholics' lives (Greeley 2004:112). Still, culturally, many good and committed Catholics find themselves at odds with some official church teachings on matter of sexual morality. Maybe it is time for the church to enter into more open and transformative dialogue on these matters. It is quite possible that people are better at figuring out their sex lives than priests and bishops realize.

At best, what does living our sexual lives as Catholics look like? I was lucky to witness a fiftieth wedding anniversary at Holy Name Church in North Camden, New Jersey. Two members of the church had come to the mainland from Puerto Rico years before and had made a good life for themselves and their ten children. In this distressed inner city neighborhood, eight of the ten Ruiz children attended college. Don Cristobal managed all this by starting a small landscaping company that serviced people with large lawns who lived in the more affluent suburban communities surrounding the city. On the day of the anniversary, the couple's Puerto Rican priest nephew stood before them, ready to lead them in the renewal of their vows. He looked at Don Cristobal and asked, "*Tio, todavia la ama?*" (Uncle, do you still love her?), and Cristobal, some seventy-plus years of age, took Norberta's small, wrinkled, hands in his own, looked into her eyes, and said, "*Mas que nunca*" (more than ever). In that moment everyone in the church saw the grace of God made visible. Such a marriage confers on Cristobal and Norberta an authority about matrimony conferred only on truly married people.

PRACTICES TO HELP US LIVE OUR SEXUAL LIVES AUTHENTICALLY AS CATHOLICS

1.  Write out an answer to the questions "Why I Am Living my sexual life the way I am?"

2.  Read a good article or book on Catholic teaching on sexuality.

3.  Talk with your spouse or significant other about the relationship of your Catholic faith to the sexual choices you are making.

4.  Integrate prayer into your sexual life. Pray to God about sex.

5.  Make a list of your favorite movies. What are the messages they send about our sexual lives?

6.  List contemporary political issues that revolve around questions of sexuality. Employing Lonergan's transcendental method (Experience – Understand – Judge – Decide – Love) analyze your opinions and choices in response to these issues. Bring your conclusions to prayer. And then act. Write your elected representatives. Talk with those close to you about your stands on these issues.

7.  Integrate the practice of our faith with your sexual life. We pray before we eat. Ancient hunters thanked the gods for the animals they caught. We give thanks to God when we get a promotion and raise. Do we pray before having sex, and thank God for the gift of our lover?

8.  Talk with your children about matters sexual. Too often sex education is left to the TV and the peer group. Parents have to take on the task of forming the young as sexual persons, whose good choices in the sexual realm will make them all more happy and healthy and holy and free (and whose bad choices will make them unhappy, unhealthy, unholy and enslaved).

9.  Know that sex is like dynamite. Used wisely and well, sex can be creative, consoling and Catholic. Used indiscriminately and stupidly, sex can be incredibly destructive and dehumanizing.

10. Enjoy Sex. Practice the truth of our faith that all of creation is good and all the aspects of out lives give glory to God. Sex is God's gift. Let us use sex wisely and well. In doing so our respect for the other person will grow and sex will be both sacred and sweaty, joyful and just.

## Transformation Happens

All our confusions and difficulties in living our sexual lives and in making choices about matters of economic, gender, and racial justice are part of the existential state in which we find ourselves. The human situation is this: We are in a place we do not want to be, i.e., an existence threatened with death. We want to be transformed from people living in fear of death to people alive with the hope and faith of the resurrection. As a result of our faith in Jesus, we fear death no more (1 Corinthians 15:54–55). We want to be happy and healthy and holy and free, and live forever. The transformation promised by Catholicism and celebrated in the sacraments is the entering into that eternal life, now, "already," even if it is still, to some degree, "not yet." Living out of this faith vision of eternal life places all in relationship to God, and placing God at the center of our lives helps us live Lonergan's "Be-Attitudes" authentically. When we live authentically, things prosper; when we do not, things decline.

When we strive to place God at the center of or lives, transformation happens. A poignant example of transformation is the case of one of the most paradoxical personages in American history. Late in the spring of 1865, a black man challenged the cultural order in Richmond's St. Paul's Episcopal Church. He walked to the communion rail before the whites in the congregation. Before and during the war, blacks had always waited for the whites to receive communion, "a small but strictly adhered to ritual, repeated so often that to alter it was unthinkable" (Winik 2001:362). The bold move shocked the congregation. Transformation has a way of doing that. "It was one thing for the white South to endure defeat and poverty, or to accept that blacks were now free; it was quite another for a black man to stride up to the front of the church as though an equal. And not just any church, but here at the sanctuary for Richmond's elite, the wealthy, the well-bred, the high cultured" (Winik 2001:362). As the black gentleman knelt to receive the body of Christ before the clearly uncomfortable minister and the perturbed congregation, a white-haired, dignified man arose and walked up the aisle to kneel next to his fellow worshiper. The man was Robert E. Lee.

General Lee had led the Confederate armies in one of the bloodiest conflicts in history. A war fought with modern weapons in an antiquated style, it had led to virtual slaughter of thousands on hundreds of battlefields. After years of destruction and death, Lee surrendered the Army of Virginia to Grant, and led, by example, the surrender of other Confederates. Rejecting the call to continue the conflict by guerilla warfare, thus saving the nation from ongoing and endless hostilities, Lee cast his lot with reconciliation and peace. His deep faith in God, his unwavering commitment to the practice of truth and right as he came to understand those virtues, guided his entire life. After having fought for years to preserve the Southern way of life, a culture based to a large degree on the subjugation of fellow human beings in slavery and the extortion of their labor, General Robert E. Lee, just weeks after the war's end, was able and willing to accept and practice the transformations necessitated.

Ultimately, we are what we choose and do. And the good news is that God takes our efforts and magnifies their effects when we strive and struggle to align our hearts and actions with his divine action in history. Being Catholic is a way of aligning ourselves with the God who resides in the center of our existence. Being Catholic is something we are and become if we practice the faith, putting the love of Jesus and the power of the Holy Spirit at the center of our relationships with all of creation and the God who creates. None of us practice perfectly. None of us practice without backsliding and failure. But all of us are called to be continually converting ourselves and our world, consciously participating in the transformation of ourselves and all into the divine life to which we are oriented by the human nature that is given to us.

We cannot simply state the answer to the contemporary crisis of meaning meltdown. We cannot simply assert the truths of Catholicism as self-evident. What we can and must do is live that which we preach. We must be developing toward

> "What paralyses life is the failure to believe and the failure to dare.... What is difficult is not solving problems, but formulating them; as we see it now, harnessing passion to make it serve the spirit must—on biological evidence—be a condition of progress. Therefore, sooner or later, despite our incredulity, the world will take that step. For everything that is more true will come about and everything that is better is finally achieved. Some day, after mastering the winds, the waves, the tides, and gravity we shall harness—for God—the energies of love. And then, for the second time in history, man will have discovered fire."
>
> —Pierre Teilhard de Chardin, SJ
> (*La évolution de la chasteté*, 1943, quoted in Cuénot 1958:29)

that which Catholicism invites us to be. We must be willing to enter into the mystery of the cross. In their excellent explanation of the socio-cultural context of Jesus' life and ministry Richard Horsley and Neil Asher Silberman (1997) indicate that for Jesus, "the Kingdom of God meant a revolution in the way people behaved toward each other..." (Horsley and Silberman 1997:54). Jesus was immersed in a world occupied by the Roman Empire and ruled with harsh and hostile brutality. New Testament scholar Bruce Malina tells us that the Roman empire was a "power syndicate," a protection racket promising that your nation's enemies would not conquer your nation in return for your nation's taxes and services. Malina says the closest image in our time and culture is what is known in popular imagination as the Mafia (Malina 2001:29). Imagine Tony Soprano as Pilate. It may not be that far off the mark.

Jesus' entire public ministry was framed by the struggle between those faithful to the ideas and ideals of the kingdom of God and those who capitulated to the idolatrous practices and meanings of the Roman Empire (Horsley and Silberman 1997:2). From the start of Jesus' ministry, he was living under a death threat (Mark 3:6). His cleansing, or indictment, of the temple, which in the synoptic gospels occurs at the start of Holy Week, in the view of many scholars is what led to his crucifixion (cf. Borg 1994:233). The Herods were the tyrannical rulers of Jesus' time. King Herod built the temple and killed the baby boys while trying to murder the newborn Jesus and eliminate a threat to his power. Herod's sons took over after his death, and Herod Antipas colluded with Pilate to have Jesus crucified (Luke 23:12). The temple priests colluded with the Herods in order to preserve some slice of Jewish power in a Roman world. Jesus came to Jerusalem from Galilee, the Appalachians or hillbilly country of his world; Jerusalem was Tokyo, Mexico City, Paris, and New York all rolled into one. The Jesus movement threatened the political and economic powers of his society.

There were significant social changes going on during Jesus' lifetime. The poor were being taxed off their land. Herod Antipas took two hundred talents a year (something like nine tons of gold), in taxes from Galilee (Horsley and Silberman 1997:26). Jesus is best understood as a

> "The basic Christian message is basically nothing else than the transmission of the testimony that love has managed to break through death and thus has transformed fundamentally the situation of us all."
>
> —Benedict XVI
> (Ratzinger 2004:307)

prophet and "it was a true prophet's obligation to speak out against injustice" (Horsley and Silberman 1997:77). Jesus called for the establishment of the kingdom of God, an "alternative society" that would live according to the meanings of traditional village life, a way of life where all could depend on one another and share their goods, a way of life rooted in mutual aid and cooperation, a way of life that was disappearing under the rule of the Romans and the Herods as "Roman legal standards, not the Torah, began to take precedence" (Horsley and Silberman 1997:54–55).

> The simple fact was that the People of Israel were badly divided. Villagers who could have cooperated in their own liberation were at each other's throats. Jesus' healings and teachings must be therefore seen in this context not as abstract spiritual truths spoken between stunning miracles, but as a program of community action and practical resistance to a system that efficiently transformed close-knit villages into badly fragmented communities of alienated, frightened individuals. (Horsley and Silberman 1997:55)

The logic of the kingdom of God led Jesus to the confrontation with the powers of Herod, Herod's sons, and the Romans in Jerusalem (Horsley and Silberman 1997:62). Marcus Borg argues that Jesus' program was a realization of God's passion for justice (Borg 1994:185 ff.). According to Borg, Jesus prophetically denounced not only the rulers of his people but also the entire system of domination that oppressed the poor (Borg 1994:244). For this Jesus was crucified. The cross was the instrument of Roman oppression. It was that with which Romans controlled their empire. "Crucifixion was as much communal punishment and state-sponsored terrorism as it was judicial vengeance against a particular crime. The crosses planted outside the cities warned potential rebels, runaway slaves, and rebellious prophets of what could happen to them" (Horsley and Silberman 1997:86). Borg notes that crucifixion was "imperial execution," that those crucified were "engaged in armed resistance against Rome" and thought of as " 'terrorists' or 'freedom fighters' depending on one's point of view" (Borg 1994:265). The important point to note is that Jesus was killed by the Romans. He was crucified. If he had been killed by Jewish authorities, the penalty would have been stoning. Jesus was executed as an enemy of the Roman state (Borg 1994:271).

> There should be no question or mystery about the brutality of the Roman crucifixion.... All over the Mediterranean world, Roman emperors, governors, prefects and procurators had the power, and even the responsibility, to inflict unspeakable pain and physical suffering on any person whom their officers grabbed from the fields or the streets and identified—rightly or wrongly—as a threat to private property, public order or state security. The horrible, prolonged process of crucifixion was described in detail.... The condemned person would be stripped naked and humiliated in public and scourged soundly by soldiers with metal-tipped leather lashes. Then, forced to carry a heavy transverse beam, or *patibulum*, to the place of execution, the victim was brutally hung up on the vertical post. And he would remain there, guarded by soldiers, for as long as it took to die of his wounds or succumb to the asphyxiation caused by the sagging weight of his exhausted body—which was bound to the rough wooden cross with ropes or affixed there with jagged iron nails. (Horsley and Silberman 1997:85)

St. Paul's preaching of the cross reverses the Romans rulers' meaning of the practice of crucifixion. Instead of the cross being a symbol of oppression and terror, Jesus' willingness to accept death on the cross symbolizes his followers' refusal to cooperate with the injustice of the Roman world.

> [T]he vices he [St. Paul] railed against—immorality, impurity, licentiousness, idolatry, sorcery, enmity, strife, jealousy, anger, selfishness, dissension, party spirit, envy, drunkenness, carousing, and the like (Gal 5:19-21)—were the kinds of behavior that were all too common among the powerless subjects of the empire. Unless his followers abandoned them, they would remain helpless to effect or be part of any world transforming change. In that sense, the image of Jesus offered a model of practical self-sacrifice in the cause of the economic and spiritual resurrection for communities that were being scourged, mocked and

dismembered by imperial rule. The cross became the symbol both of Roman violence and of those who dared to resist its inevitability. (Horsley and Silberman 1997:160–61)

What do the cross, transformation, and liberation look like in our times? Back in the mid-1980s, I heard an African American Protestant pastor speaking in Roxbury, Massachusetts. He described himself as a liberation theologian and worked among the poorest of the poor in the Boston area. I'm not sure what denomination he was, or what the Eucharist meant for his brand of Christianity. But he certainly knew the deepest realities of Christ's presence among us. I'm not quoting him word for word, but this is the gist of what he said:

### Mrs. Cunningham

*It was back when I was studying for the ministry that I lost all faith in God. The evils and suffering of the world just made it all seem that either God didn't care or God didn't exist. Why didn't he do something? I was very perplexed and distressed, and was one year away from ordination.*

*I was also assigned to work with a pastor for the summer. I didn't know what to tell the man. Here I was supposed to work in his church, and I'd lost my faith in God. Didn't believe God existed. Wasn't sure I wanted to be a minister anymore, or even could be a minister. I felt I had to tell this pastor the truth. I walked into his office all nervous, not knowing what his reaction to my situation would be. To my surprise, he dismissed my doubts with a wave of his hand, saying all theology students go through something like this and that I should come and work in the kids' summer program. And I would be taking communion to an elderly shut-in, a Mrs. Cunningham.*

*So I started taking communion to Mrs. Cunningham. She was a little old black woman who always wore long skirts that reached below her ankles, right down to the floor almost. She was obviously crippled in some way, because she shuffled around her small apartment rather than walked. I'd bring her communion and we'd pray. Afterwards she always made me a cup of coffee and had me eat a piece of pie or some cookies. Over a few weeks, I got to know*

*her fairly well and really grew to enjoy her company. I found my-*
*self looking forward to my encounters with her.*

*Finally, I felt comfortable enough to ask her what had hap-*
*pened to her legs. She exclaimed, "Oh, I thought the pastor must*
*have told you." She stood up and turned around and lifted her*
*long skirts to reveal her calves. The backs of her legs were a mass*
*of thick, twisted scar tissue. She said, "It was the dogs. In Birm-*
*ingham. They gots me."*

*I was speechless. When I could talk I stammered out my*
*questions. How had this little, tiny woman been able to survive*
*such pain and suffering?*

*"It's that communion you brings me. Jesus resurrects me*
*every day for the struggle."*

*I had to go back and rethink all this stuff about how God is*
*with us in our suffering and how sacraments sustain and nourish*
*us in the living of our faith.*

The living of a freeing faith, a full and flexible Catholicism, will involve us in the difficult work of societal transformation. Sacraments are
signs that transform us and our world. Our prayer must surge forth in
action that ameliorates our world. The work of social justice is what
Jesus asks of us all. Transformation on the personal and social levels of
our being is the great promise made to us at our baptism, and the mission on which we are sent throughout our lives.

In the final analysis however, we must realize that social injustice
and unjust social structures exist only because individuals and
groups of individuals deliberately maintain and tolerate them. It
is these personal choices, operating through structures that breed
and propagate situations of poverty, oppression and misery. For
this reason, overcoming "social" sin and reforming the social
order itself must begin with the conversion of our hearts. As the
American Bishops have said, "The Gospel confers on each Christian the vocation to love God and neighbor in ways that bear
fruit in the life of society. That vocation consists above all in a
change of heart: a conversion expressed in praise of God and in
concrete deeds of justice and service." (John Paul II, quoting *Eco-*
*nomic Justice for All* in an address to Catholic Charities, California, September 19, 1987, in Bakalar and Balkin 1995:80)

## Practicing Peace

Conversion calls us to peace. It is the sign of our actualizing our faith, of our freely responding to God's love made manifest in Jesus, in the establishment of peace. Jerusalem means City of Peace, and it is for the New Jerusalem that we hope and labor. The cultural practices of our lives must express this desire for peace. Too often we leave the peacemaking to higher authorities and ignore the lack of peace in our world. Do we really want to know what is going on? The great apostle of peace, Jesuit John Dear, challenges us:

> What do we spend our lives seeing? We look at Dan Rather and *The CBS Evening News.* We watch Madonna's latest video on MTV. We sit glued to a football game and eat popcorn while watching the latest movie. We glance at the celebrity pictures in *People* magazine at the doctor's office or the *National Enquirer* while standing in line at the grocery store. But do we see anything worth seeing? In fact, what do we consider worth seeing? Do we want to see with the eyes of Christ, to see with the vision of God? Dare we look at the world from the perspective of Jesus? (Dear 2004:78)

We are sent to be peacemakers (Matthew 5:9) and we must dare to make a world of peace. Are we willing to see as Jesus sees, to pronounce peace, even when we are crucified? In the weeks following September 11, 2001, I stood in front of sociology and anthropology classes at Saint Joseph's University discussing with students what our response to the tragic events of that day ought to be. Students' shock, anger, and rage were indiscriminately aimed at the people whose images they had seen on CNN. "Those bastards hate us." Bewildered and confused, the students angrily stated, "They were dancing in the streets, all psyched because we'd gotten killed." "We should go over there and bomb them all to hell," was the predominant sentiment. I tried to gently suggest that there is only one way to stop terrorists, and that is to change them and/or us in ways that would ensure their wanting to live in peace with us rather

*"We are sent to be peacemakers (Matthew 5:9) and we must dare to make a world of peace."*

than their wanting to blow us all up. The students' response to this idea was to sit in silence, or argue how unrealistic such a strategy would be. They were little open to thinking about being peacemakers. They in no way, shape, or form thought that we should seek forgiveness for any wrongs we may have done or any suffering we may have caused. Their social imagination had no room for reconciliation.

Here in the United States, we unconsciously think that violence is normal and acceptable as a constitutive dimension of our lives and culture. We are raised on images of John Wayne and Harrison Ford destroying the "bad guys," be they "Indians" (i.e., Native Americans) or Arabs. When I was a little boy in the 1960s, we would run around the neighborhood playing army and "shooting" one another. Throughout my life, the quintessential American heroes have been the gunfighter, the detective/cop, and the soldier, all mythic characters who, usually alone, solve the problems of life by beating, shooting or in some manner dominating other persons (cf. Slotkin 1998). I now live in a nation where gun violence has been at epidemic proportions for years. Our thousands of deaths by handgun dwarf the murder rates in other nations. Our medals are given to those who wage war, not to those who struggle for peace. Mass media is rife with violent images. Over a decade ago, the U.S. Catholic bishops reported that "children see 8,000 murders a year and 100,000 other acts of violence before they leave elementary school" (USCCB 1994:423). Little has changed since then. Tragedies like the Columbine shootings in Colorado did little to challenge the ways we socialize our children. The debacle in Iraq has shown we too easily assume violent measures will improve situations. As 2007 begins, the bill for the war in Iraq stands at somewhere between $1.2 and $2 trillion dollars, for a war we were told would cost $50 billion! Violence costs us, costs us all a great deal (Kristof 2006). For those who have lost their lives (over three thousand U.S. troops and hundreds of thousands of Iraqis), the violence has cost everything. Still, we go about our daily business, assuming that such violence is "normal" and inevitable. We do not strongly demand an end to war. We too little imagine or value peace.

> "Here in the United States, we unconsciously think that violence is normal and acceptable as a constitutive dimension of our lives and culture."

Our culture didn't get this way overnight. It may take time, but we can change the way things are. The question is this: Do we really desire to do so? Do we want to choose a more peace-making rather than a war-waging culture?

A culture of peace will begin with cultural practices that foster and admire peace and peacemakers. Allowing ten-year-olds to sit for hours in front of a TV screen watching people getting stabbed and shot in scenes of graphic violence must be as unacceptable as letting them sit for hours watching sexual pornography. The whole world of video games has to be better analyzed and addressed because our children literally spend more hours playing these games than they do engaging in any other activity. The rise in violence in dating relationships and in the home is catastrophic.

Sports in America have become our new religions. If people were told they could not go to Mass from August to January, would they complain? But just think what would happen if we said people could not watch football. Disturbing is the degree to which violence has become acceptable and expected. Fans love to see hockey players' fists crashing into other players' rock-hard plastic helmets. Basketball originally was a non-contact sport. Today, if there's no blood on the playground, guys were taking it easy. How many summer nights a year do major league baseball teams' benches empty for pointless but dangerous brawls? The "vast majority" of NFL players have guns for their homes, cars, and lockers (Freeman 2003:1). Aren't NFL players big enough to intimidate people without using weapons? Increasingly we are a violent people who create and sustain a violent culture. Our coarse language and ubiquitous use of the "F" word imply that we are less and less nice and pleasant to one another, let alone charitable.

Our Lord said, "Peace I leave with you; my peace I give to you" (John 14:27). We need to change our violent, warlike culture. We need to become more peaceful and make more peace. The work of changing and transforming a culture and society happens at the group level. "To change the

**Military Spending 2004**
$13.0 billion: Cuba, Iran, Libya,
   N. Korea, Syria, and Sudan
$56.0 billion China
$65.2 billion: Russia
$399.1 billion: USA
(*Sojourners*,
September–October 2005, p. 9)

**What $1 Billion Means**
Spending $1,000 a day, you'd spend a million in almost three years. You'd need almost 3,000 years to spend a billion dollars.
(Brym and Lie 2007:214)

world, one has to change the ways of making the world, that is, the vision of the world and the practical operations by which groups are produced and reproduced.... The power to make groups [is the power] to manipulate the objective structure of society" (Bourdieu 1990:137–38). Many groups in the United States benefit from the war economy and have bought into the idea that the only way to handle global problems is by the use of massive force. We have millions of people serving in the military, and we have four military academies, institutions of higher education dedicated to producing highly trained warriors. We have no equivalent academy dedicated to helping young men and women become diplomats, reconcilers, and peace coordinators. How many schools have anything even like "peace studies" as a major? Martin Luther King, Jr., and Gandhi transformed our world. Where are the institutions and groups dedicated to carrying on and implementing their vision? This is not the work of individuals. Peace work is communal work, laboring together in community to transform our world. Lonergan is correct when he writes: "To grasp the contemporary issue and to meet its challenge calls for collective effort. It is not the individual but the group that transforms culture" (Lonergan Institute). We desperately need many more groups of people like Pax Christi and the Catholic Workers to boldly and prayerfully assert the truth of Christ's mission for peace. Jesus died rather than engage in violent revolt. Jesus became sacred to us, our sacrifice, rather than violently retaliate against oppressors (cf. Borg 1994:269). Jesus could have taken up arms, but he did not. When the soldiers came in great numbers to arrest him, Jesus told Peter to sheathe the sword, and healed the ear of the man Peter had harmed (Luke 22:50–51).

*"We have millions of people serving in the military, and we have four military academies, institutions of higher education dedicated to producing highly trained warriors. We have no equivalent academy dedicated to helping young men and women become diplomats, reconcilers, and peace coordinators."*

Paul VI declared, "If you want peace, work for justice." As one who lived through World War II, he begged the nations of the world to stop the conflicts: "War no more. War never again!" The USA spends trillions on war and war's byproducts. According to the War Resisters League, for FY 2008, the United States budgeted $1,188 billion for military expenditures, or $727 billion for current military costs and $461 billion for past military costs, such as veterans' benefits (<www.warresisters.org>, accessed June 2007). This is a more accurate count of military expenditures than the reported $622 billion defense budget for FY 2008 reported in the press (e.g., David S. Cloud, *New York Times*, February 3, 2007).

To stop the flow of money, Catholics should prayerfully consider withholding taxes that feed the war insanity. Our faith frees us and encourages us to do what Jesus did: to stand before the powers of empire and oppression and work for change.

Peace comes from peaceful people with peaceful hearts. As Gandhi said, "Prayer is not some old woman's idle amusement. Properly understood and applied, it is the most potent form of action." Our communal imagination follows our cultural practices.

The first word the resurrected Jesus speaks to the apostles is peace. "When it was evening on that day, the first day of the week, and the doors of the house where the disciples had met were locked for fear ... Jesus came and stood among them and said, 'Peace be with you.' Jesus said to them again, 'Peace be with you. As the Father sent me, so I send you.' When he had said this, he breathed on them and said to them, 'Receive the Holy Spirit'" (John 20:19, 21–22).

The missioning of the apostles and peace were intimately linked. So too is our mission and working to establish in our culture and times the peace God passionately desires for all peoples and all times.

SEVEN PRACTICES FOR PEACE

1.  Integrate peace studies into school curriculums, especially in Catholic schools.

2.  Establish peace study groups in parishes and schools.

3.  Study the ways in which most conflicts are, in origin, linked to issues of social injustice and the inequitable distribution of wealth and power.

4.  Study René Girard, who argues that Christianity is the antidote to the cultures of violence that have existed since the foundation of the world.

5.  Study those who have given their lives to peaceful non-violence (e.g., Gandhi, Dorothy Day, the Berrigans, Martin Luther King, Jr., and Bishop Desmond Tutu).

6.  Get involved with the peace groups in your area, such as Pax Christi and the Catholic Worker Movement.

7.  Pray. Crucial to any efforts at making peace is establishing peace in our own hearts and minds. Peaceful persons establish peace wherever they are—and prayer is the key to being a peaceful person.

# Conclusion: Mission Matters

*"Never doubt that a small group of thoughtful, committed citizens can change the world. Indeed it is the only thing that ever has."*
—*Margaret Mead*

The reality of Christian life is based on the trust and hope that the God revealed in the life, death, and resurrection of Jesus of Nazareth loves us and will fulfill the promise of our existence as baptized followers of Jesus forming the Body of Christ today. Our trust and hope is that Jesus will return, and that the reign of God will be fully established. It was that reign that Jesus preached and that reign for which he was crucified (1 Corinthians 15:28).

The searing question for those of us so many generations removed from the first communities of Christians, those Pauline churches that expected the imminent return of Jesus, is this: When will Jesus return? The eschatological both/and, the kingdom already here and still not yet completely realized, has been the standard theological answer to this question. Still, I wonder: Where is Jesus and what is he doing? To put it in simple terms: What is he waiting for?

One possibility that occurs to me, and I don't pretend to be speaking for anyone but myself, is that maybe Jesus is waiting for us. Taking seriously the notion that we are, with God, co-creators of human history, means that maybe Jesus is waiting for us, waiting for us to achieve a global culture that creates and sustains conditions like those for which we pray on the feast of Christ the King, ". . . a kingdom of truth and life, a kingdom of holiness and grace, a kingdom of justice, love, and peace" (Preface for the Feast of Christ the King). It is only by consciously creating cultures that foster and sustain human communities authentically dedicated to cultural practices that make a world wherein all can grow happy and healthy and holy and free that we can prepare the way for the second coming.

Many mainstream scripture scholars disagree with the idea that we have anything to do with the establishment of the kingdom. From their vantage point as scripture scholars, they assert that the kingdom is totally God's work alone. From the vantage point of systematic theology, I find this view quite problematic. If we have nothing to do with establishing God's reign, if our actions for, or against, justice and love do not really matter, then for what is God waiting? To assert that God alone brings the kingdom makes God the great cosmic underachiever. What's taking so long?

The early followers of Jesus imagined the Lord returning soon. Marcus Borg delineates two types of eschatology that developed in the history of the church. Imminent eschatology holds that God alone brings about the kingdom. Borg writes: "In short, imminent eschatology means that Jesus expected a dramatic supernatural intervention by God in the very near future that would establish the kingdom of God. It follows, of course, that Jesus was wrong" (Borg 2006:254). In order to explain this apparent misunderstanding on Jesus' part, many New Testament scholars do exegetical acrobatics. Borg proposes another solution. He describes participatory eschatology, another paradigm or framework for understanding who Jesus was, and what he was, and is, about. In contradistinction to imminent eschatology, Borg's participatory eschatology, "means that Jesus called people to respond and participate in the coming of the kingdom" (Borg 2006:260).

Jesus invites and encourages us to follow him in practices and ways of life that transform our societies, our cultures, and ourselves. Such transformation opens the way for the full and free establishment of the kingdom of God, and the free and participatory response of people to this initiative of God and God's people. Along with Borg, I argue that human agency does matter, and it is precisely in and through our free and freeing choices on personal and societal levels of our being that God is able to work toward the gradual establishment of the reign Jesus inaugurated.

Maybe it is no longer we who are waiting for God; maybe we should realize that God is waiting for us. God respects the freedom with which he has graced us. God cannot enter and transform us unless we freely choose to open our hearts to the transformation he wants to work in us.

Our prayers and religious practices dispose our souls, the center of our being, to allow God's liberating grace, the Holy Spirit, to enter our hearts, our deepest, truest self (Romans 5:5). It is in our hearts that we make the choices that form us for all eternity. In the same way that God waits for us to open our hearts on a personal level, I think God waits for us to open our cultures on the social level of our being. God will not enter and reign in the economic choices, sexual practices, media productions, and other aspect of our cultural communal selves unless we prepare the way and allow him to enter those realms. God is not an imposing dictator. God loves us and wants to be present in and through all that forms us as human persons. We are free to accept or reject, cooperate or not cooperate, with God's transformative presence.

St. Paul imagined a new creation, a new world, a world recreated in the light of the kingdom of God (Romans 8). Our mission is to form and contour the world so that the kingdom can come. That is God's will, that the kingdom come. That is what Jesus needs us to do in this life. When the world is readied, Jesus will return. Let us pray, and labor, for the coming of that glorious day.

# Bibliography

Allen Jr., John L.
    2006    "A Global Church in a Globalized World." In Brian Doyle, ed., *The Best of Catholic Writing* (pp. 83–96). Chicago, IL: Loyola Press.

Appleyard, Bryan
    1992    *Understanding the Present: Science and the Soul of Modern Man.* New York: Doubleday.

Arbuckle, S. M., Gerald A.
    1990    *Earthing the Gospel: An Inculturation Handbook for the Pastoral Worker.* Maryknoll, NY: Orbis Books.

Astin, Alexander W., Helen S. Astin, and Jennifer A. Lindholm
    2004    "The Spiritual Life of College Students: A National Study of College Students' Search for Meaning and Purpose." Los Angeles, CA: HERI (Higher Education Research Institute, UCLA). Available online at: <http://spirituality.ucla.edu/reports/index.html>; accessed January 2007.

Bakalar, Nick, and Richard Balkin, eds.
    1995    *The Wisdom of John Paul II: The Pope on Life's Most Vital Questions.* San Francisco: HarperCollins Publishers.

Barber, Benjamin R.
    1996    *Jihad vs. McWorld.* New York: Ballantine Books.

Barnet, Richard J.
    1994    *The Global War Against the Poor.* Washington, DC: Servant Leadership Press.

Baylor Institute for Studies of Religion
    2006    *American Piety in the 21st Century: New Insights to the Depth and Complexity of Religion in the U.S.* Waco TX: Baylor University. Available online at: <http://www.baylor.edu/content/services/document.php/33304.pdf>; accessed January 2007.

BBC News

    2007    BBC News in Depth. Factfile Roman Catholics Around the World. Available online at: <http://news.bbc.co.uk/2/low/in_depth/4243727.stm>; accessed January 2007.

Becker, Ernest

    1975    *Escape from Evil.* New York: The Free Press.

Beckmann, David, and Arthur Simon

    1999    *Grace at the Table: Ending Hunger in God's World.* New York: Paulist Press.

Behe, Michael J.

    1996    *Darwin's Black Box: The Biochemical Challenge to Evolution.* New York: The Free Press.

Bellah Robert, Richard Madsen, William M. Sulivan, Ann Swidler, and Steven M. Tipton

    1991    *The Good Society.* New York: Alfred A. Knopf.

Berman, Morris

    2000    *The Twilight of American Culture.* New York: W. W. Norton & Co.

Berry, Thomas

    1999    *The Great Work: Our Way into the Future.* New York: Bell Tower.

Bevilacqua, Cardinal Anthony

    2006    "Healing Racism through Faith and Truth." *Journal of Catholic Social Thought* 3/1 (Winter 2006). First published in 1998.

Bono

    2005    "This Generation's Moon Shot." *Time* Magazine (November 1, 2005). Available online at: <http://www.time.com/time/magazine/article/0,9171,1124333,00.html>; accessed January 2007.

    2006    "VERBATIM: In Fact the Poor are Where God Lives." *Philadelphia Inquirer* (February 26, 2006). Available online at: <http://www.data.org/archives/000774.php>; accessed January 2007.

Borg, Marcus

    1994    *Meeting Jesus Again for the First Time: The Historical Jesus and the Heart of Contemporary Faith.* New York: HarperSanFrancisco.

Bourdieu, Pierre

    1985    "The Social Space and the Genesis of Groups." *Social Science Information* 24:195–220.

    1990    *In Other Words: Essays Towards a Reflexive Sociology.* Stanford, CA: Stanford University Press.

Brooks, David
2000 *Bobos\* in Paradise (\*Bourgeois Bohemians): The New Upper Class and How They Got There.* New York: Simon and Schuster.
2003 "Bigger than the Nobel." *New York Times* (October 11, 2003): Op-ed page.
2004 *On Paradise Drive: How We Live Now (and Always Have) in the Future Tense.* New York: Simon and Schuster.

Brym, Robert J., and John Lie
2007 *Sociology: Your Compass for a New World.* Belmont, CA: Thompson and Wadsworth.

Budde, Michael
1997 *The (Magic) Kingdom of God: Christianity and Global Culture Industries.* Boulder, CO: Westview Press.

Budde, Michael, and Robert Brimlow
2002 "Christianity, Inc.: The Marketing of Pope John Paul II." *Sojourners* (May/June, 2002): 63.

Canadian Catholic Bishops
2000 "The Elimination of Poverty: It Can Be Done and We Want It Done." Message of May 1, 2000. Available online at: <www.eveques.qc.ca/aeqdoc_cas_2000_5_1_e_0.html>; accessed January 2007.

*Catechism of the Catholic Church*
1994 English translation of the *Catechism of the Catholic Church* for the United States of America. United States Catholic Conference, Inc.—Libreria Editrice Vaticana.

Chilton, Bruce
2000 *Rabbi Jesus: An Intimate Biography.* New York: Doubleday.

Chun Wah Tam, Patrick
2002 *Mellanguoq: The Awakening of the Yup'ik Catholic Imagination. The Making of Local Yup'ik Eskimo Theology in Southwest Alaska.* Master's Thesis. Berkeley, CA: The Franciscan School of Theology.

Coleman, SJ, John
1988 "American Catholicism." In Thomas M. Gannon, SJ, ed., *World Catholicism in Transition* (pp. 232–49). New York: Macmillan Publishing Company.

Coles, Robert
1999 *The Secular Mind.* Princeton, NJ: Princeton University Press.

Corporations.org
> 2007  "Of the world's 100 largest economic entities, 51 are now corpora-
> tions and 49 are countries." Compiled by Sarah Anderson and John
> Cavanagh of the Institute for Policy Studies in their Report on the
> Top 200 Corporations (2000). Available online at: <http://www.
> corporations.org/system/top100.html>; accessed January 2007.

Cote, Richard G.
> 1996  *Re-Visioning the Mission: The Catholic Church and Postmodern
> America.* Mahwah, NJ, Paulist Press.

Cozzens, Donald
> 2000  *The Changing Face of the Priesthood: A Reflection on the Priest's
> Crisis of Soul.* Collegeville, MN: The Liturgical Press.
> 2002  *Sacred Silence: Denial and the Crisis in the Church.* Collegeville,
> MN: The Liturgical Press.

Crossan, John Dominic
> 1995  *Jesus: A Revolutionary Biography.* San Francisco: Harper-
> SanFrancisco.

Cuénot, Claude
> 1958  *Teilhard de Chardin.* Baltimore, MD: Helicon Press.

Dawkins, Richard
> 2006  *The God Delusion.* New York: Houghton Mifflin.

Dear, SJ, John
> 2004  *The Questions of Jesus.* New York: Doubleday.

DeBerri, Edward P., James E. Hug, with Peter J. Henriot and Michael J. Schultheis
> 2003  *Catholic Social Teaching: Our Best Kept Secret* (4th ed.). Mary-
> knoll, NY: Orbis Books.

De Graaf, John, David Wann, and Thomas H. Naylor
> 2005  *Affluenza: The All Consuming Epidemic.* San Franscisco: Berrett-
> Koehler Publishers, inc.

Dennett, Daniel C.
> 2006  *Breaking the Spell: Religion as a Natural Phenomenon.* New
> York: Viking.

*The Documents of Vatican II*
> 1994  Edited by Walter M. Abbott, SJ. New York: America Press.

Dolan, Timothy M.
> 2000  *Priests for the Third Millennium.* Huntington IN: Our Sunday
> Visitor, Inc.

Domhoff, G. William

    2006    "Wealth, Income and Power." *Who Rules America?* Website of G. Willian Domhoff (professor of sociology, University of California Santa Cruz): <http://sociology.ucsc.edu/whorules america/power/wealth.html>; accessed January 2007.

Dorr, Donal

    1992    *Option for the Poor: A Hundred Years of Catholic Social Teaching* (rev. ed.). Maryknoll, NY: Orbis Books.

Dreyfus, Hubert L., and Paul Rabinow

    1983    *Michel Foucault: Beyond Structuralism and Hermeneutics* (2nd ed.). Chicago, IL: University of Chicago Press.

Du Bois, W .E. B.

    1995    *The Souls of Black Folk.* New York: Signet Classic. First published in 1903.

Dunne, Tad

    1985    *Lonergan and Spirituality.* Chicago, IL: Loyola University Press.

Dunning, John H.

    2003    *Making Globalization Good: The Moral Challenges of Global Capitalism.* New York: Oxford University Press.

*The Economist*

    2006    Special Report. Inequality in America: The rich, the poor and the growing gap between them. The rich are the big gainers in America's new prosperity. June 15, 2006. Available online at: <http://www.economist.com/world/displaystory.cfm?story_id= 7055911>; accessed January 2007.

Faludi, Susan

    1999    *Stiffed: The Betrayal of the American Male.* New York: Harper-Perennial.

Finley, James

    2003    *Merton's Palace of Nowhere* (25th anniversary rev. ed.). Notre Dame, IN: Ave Maria Press.

Fitzpatrick, Frank

    2005    "Pa. study shows gaps in Title IX compliance: The Women's Law Project found most colleges in the state are still treating male athletes better than women." *Philadelphia Inquirer* (December 21, 200): D1.

Flanagan, Joseph
   1997    *Quest for Self-Knowledge: An Essay in Lonergan's Philosophy.*
           Toronto, Canada: University of Toronto Press.

*Forbes* Magazine
   2004    "Wal-Mart and Sex Discrimination by the Numbers" (June 23,
           2004). Available online at: <http://www.forbes.com/2004/06/23/
           cx_da_0623topnews.html>; accessed January 2007.

Freeman, Mike
   2003    "More N.F.L. Players Turn to Guns for a Sense of Security." *New
           York Times* (December 26, 2003): D1.

Freeman, Steve, and Joel Bleifuss
   2006    *Was the 2004 Presidential Election Stolen? Exit Polls, Election
           Fraud, and the Official Count.* New York: Seven Stories Press.

Friedman, Thomas
   2000    *The Lexus and the Olive Tree: Understanding Globalization* (rev.
           ed.). New York: Random House, Anchor Books.
   2005    *The World Is Flat (2.0): A Brief history of the Twenty-First Cen-
           tury.* New York: Farrar, Strauss and Giroux.

Gadamer, Hans Georg
   1991    *Truth and Method* (2nd rev. ed.). Trans. Joel Weinshemer and
           Donald G. Marshall. New York: Crossroad Publishing Com-
           pany. First published in 1960.

Gallagher, SJ, Michael
   1998    *Clashing Symbols: An Introduction to Faith and Culture.* New
           York: Paulist Press.

Gans, Herbert
   1996    *The War Against the Poor: The Underclass and Antipoverty Pol-
           icy.* New York: Basic Books.

Gelles, Richard J., and Ann Levine
   1999    *Sociology: An Introduction* (6th ed.). New York: McGraw Hill.

GIA Publications
   1986    *Worship: A Hymnal and Service book for Roman Catholics.*
           Chicago, IL: GIA Publications.

Gibson, David
   2003    *The Coming Catholic Church: How the Faithful Are Shaping a
           New American Catholicism.* New York: HarperSanFrancisco.

Girard, René
> 1985    *The Scapegoat.* Baltimore, MD: Johns Hopkins University Press.

Gillis, Chester
> 1999    *Roman Catholicism in America.* New York: Columbia University Press.

Glenmary Research Center
> 2002    *Religious Congregations & Membership in the United States: 2000.* Nashville, TN. Glenmary Research Center. Available online at: <http://www.glenmary.org/grc/RCMS_2000/release.htm>.

Goodman, Ellen
> 1998    "Time to Hurry Along to Get First Woman President." *South Jersey Courier-Post* (September 28, 1998): 11a.

Greeley, Andrew M.
> 1988    *God in Popular Culture.* Chicago, IL: Thomas More Press.
> 2004    *The Catholic Revolution: New Wine, Old Wineskins and the Second Vatican Council.* Berkeley, CA: University of California Press.

Greene, Brian
> 2000    *The Elegant Universe: Superstrings, Hidden Dimensions, and the Quest for the Ultimate Theory.* New York: Vintage.
> 2005    *The Fabric of the Cosmos: Space, Time, and the Texture of Reality.* New York: Vintage.

Grossman, Cathy Lynn
> 2002    "A Changing Church: Immigrants, and active laity and thriving Catholic movements will lead the way." *USA Today* (August 29, 2002): 5D.

Hall, W.
> 1986    "Social Class and Survival on the *S.S. Titanic.*" In *Social Science and Medicine* 22:687–90, cited in David E. Newman (2006), *Sociology: Exploring the Architecture of Everyday Life* (p. 326). Thousand Oaks CA: Pine Forge Press, Sage Publications.

Harris, Sam
> 2005    *The End of Faith: Religion, Terror, and the Future of Reason.* New York: W. W. Norton.
> 2006    *Letter to a Christian Nation.* New York: Knopf.

Hartmann, Thom
> 2006    *Screwed: The Undeclared War Against the Middle Class and What We Can Do About It.* San Francisco: Berrett-Koehler Publishers, Inc.

Haviland, Paul
> 1982    *Anthropology* (3rd ed.). New York: Holt Rinehart and Winston.

Henslin, James M.
> 2007    *Sociology: A Down To Earth Approach* (8th ed.). Boston, MA: Allyn & Bacon.

Henriot, Peter J.
> 2002    "Catholic Social Teaching and Poverty Eradication: Key Concepts and Issues." Cafod Policy Papers. Available online at: <www.cafod.org.uk/policy/henriot_prsps.shtml>.

Henriot, Peter J., Edward P. DeBerri, and Michael Schultheis
> 1998    *Catholic Social Teaching: Our Best Kept Secret* (centenary ed.). Maryknoll, NY: Orbis Books (with Center of Concern, Washington, DC).

Hess, Beth B., Elizabeth W. Markson, and Peter J. Stein
> 1996    *Sociology* (5th ed.). Boston, MA: Allyn & Bacon.

Himes, Kenneth R. (ed.), Lisa Sowle Cahill, Charles E. Curran, David Hollenbach, and Thomas A. Shannon (associate eds.)
> 2005    *Modern Catholic Social Teaching: Commentaries and Interpretations.* Washington, DC: Georgetown University Press.

Hoge, Dean R., William D. Dinges, Mary Johnson, and Juan L. Gonzales
> 2001    *Young Adult Catholics: Religion in the Cultures of Choice.* Notre Dame, IN: University of Notre Dame Press.

Holland, Joe, and Peter Henriot, SJ
> 1983    *Social Analysis: Linking Faith and Justice.* Maryknoll, NY: Orbis Books (with Center of Concern, Washington, DC).

Horsley, Richard, and Neil Asher Silberman
> 1997    *The Message and the Kingdom: How Jesus and Paul Ignited a Revolution and Transformed the Ancient World.* New York: Grosset/Putnam.

Howe, Neil, and William Strauss
> 2000    *Millennials Rising: The Next Great Generation.* New York: Vintage Books.

Hug, SJ, James E. (ed.)
> 1983    *Tracing the Spirit: Communities, Social Action and Theological Reflection.* Washington, DC: Woodstock Theological Center.
> 2000    "Educating for Justice." *America* (May 20, 2000): 16–22.

Ignatius of Loyola, St.
    1992    *The Spiritual Exercises of St. Ignatius: A Translation and Commentary by George Ganss, S.J.* St. Louis, MO: The Institute of Jesuit Sources.

Jencks, Christopher
    1993    *Rethinking Social Policy: Race, Poverty, and the Underclass.* New York: Harper Perennial.
    2005    *The Homeless* (reprint ed.). Cambridge, MA: Harvard University Press.

Jenkins, Philip
    1996    *Pedophiles and Priests: Anatomy of a Contemporary Crisis.* New York: Oxford University Press.
    2002    *The Next Christendom: The Coming of Global Christianity.* New York: Oxford University Press.
    2006a   *The New Faces of Christianity: Believing the Bible in the Global South.* New York: Oxford University Press.
    2006b   "Believing in the Global South." *First Things* (December 2006): 12–18.

JFI (Justice for Immigrants)
    2007    Justice for Immigrants website. The Catholic Campaign for Immigration Reform: United States Conference of Catholic Bishops: <www.justiceforimmigrants.org>; accessed January 2007.

John Paul II
    1996    "Theories of Evolution: Address to the Pontifical Academy of the Sciences." October 22, 1996. *First Things* (March 1997): 28–29. Available online at: <http://www.firstthings.com/ftissues/ft9703/articles/johnpaul.html>; accessed January 2007. See also John Paul II (1997). "The Pope's Message on Evolution." *Quarterly Review of Biology* 72:377–83.

Johnson, Luke Timothy
    1997    *The Real Jesus: The Misguided Quest for the Historical Jesus and the Truth of the Traditional Gospel.* San Franciso: HarperSanFrancisco.

Johnson, Paul
    1997    *A History of the American People.* New York: Harper Collins.

Jones, Richard G.
    2007    "Threat and Harassment for New Jersey Town's First Black Mayor." *New York Times* (January 11, 2007). Available online at:

<http://www.nytimes.com/2007/01/11/nyregion/11bias.html?_r=
1&oref=slogin>; accessed January 2007.

Kammer, SJ, Fred
  1991    *Doing FaithJustice: An Introduction to Catholic Social Thought.*
          Mahwah, NJ: Paulist Press.

Kantor, Jodi
  2006    "Nanny Hunt Can Be a 'Slap in the Face' for Blacks." *New York
          Times* (December 30, 2006). Available online at: <http://select.
          nytimes.com/search/restricted/article?res=F30D1EFA35550C7
          58EDDAB0994DE404482#>; accessed January 2007.

Katz, Michael B.
  1990    *The Undeserving Poor: From the War on Welfare to the War on
          Poverty.* New York: Pantheon.

Kavanaugh, SJ, John Francis
  1981    *Following Christ in a Consumer Society: The Spirituality of Cul-
          tural Resistance.* Maryknoll, NY: Orbis Books.

Kenedy and Sons, P. J.
  2006    *The Official Catholic Directory.* New Providence, NJ: P. J. Kenedy
          and Sons.

Kennedy, Jr., Robert
  2006    "Was the 2004 Election Stolen?" *Rolling Stone* (June 2006). Avail-
          able online at: <http://www.rollingstone.com/news/story/
          10432334/was_the2004_election_stolen>; accessed January 2007.

Kindlon, Dan
  2006    *Alpha Girls: Understanding the New American Girl and How She
          Is Changing the World.* New York: Rodale Books.

Korten, David C.
  2001    *When Corporations Rule the World* (2nd. ed). San Franscisco,
          CA: Berrett-Koehler Publishers, Inc.

Kristof, Nicholas D.
  2006    "Iraq and Your Wallet." *New York Times* (October 24, 2006):
          Op-ed page.

Krugman, Paul.
  2002    "The End of the American Middle Class." *New York Times Mag-
          azine* (October 28, 2002).

Kunstler, James Howard
  1998    *Home from Nowhere: Remaking Our Everyday World for the 21st
          Century.* New York: Simon and Schuster, Inc. Touchstone Book.

LaFeber, Walter
   1999   *Michael Jordan and The New Global Capitalism*. New York: W. W. Norton & Co.

Lamott, Anne
   1999   *Traveling Mercies: Some Thoughts on Faith*. New York: Anchor Books.

Lefkowitz, Bernard
   1997   *Our Guys: The Glen Ridge Rape and the Secret Life of the Perfect Suburb*. Berkeley, CA: University of California Press.

Levy, Ariel
   2005   *Female Chauvinist Pigs: Women and the Rise of Raunch Culture*. New York: The Free Press.

Lewis, Claude
   2007   "Women, minorities making inroads." *Philadelphia Inquirer* (January 10, 2007): Commentary page, A15. Available online at: <http://www.philly.com/mld/inquirer/news/editorial/16422832. htm>; accessed January 10, 2007.

Lewis, John (with Michael D'Orso)
   1998   *Walking with the Wind: A Memoir of the Movement*. New York: Harcourt, Brace and Company.

Lonergan, SJ, Bernard J. F.
   1957   *Insight: A Study of Human Understanding*. London: Longmans, Green and Co.
   1972   *Method in Theology*. New York: The Seabury Press, 1972.
   1985   "The Dialectic of Authority." In Frederick Crowe, SJ, ed., *Third Collection: Papers by Bernard J. F. Lonergan, S.J.* (pp. 5–12). New York/Mahwah, NJ: Paulist Press.

Lonergan Institute
   Website of Boston College Lonergan Institute: <www.bc.edu/ bc_org/avp/cas/lonergan/default.html>.

Macionis, John J.
   2007   *Sociology* (11th ed.). Upper Saddle River, NJ: Pearson Prentice Hall.

Malina, Bruce J.
   2001   *The Social Gospel of Jesus: The Kingdom of God in Mediterranean Perspective*. Minneapolis, MN: Fortress Press.

Martin, SJ, James
   2000   "Anti-Catholicism in the United States: The Last Acceptable Prejudice?" *America* (March 25, 2000): 8–16.

Marsh, Charles
    1997    *God's Long Summer: Stories of Faith and Civil Rights.* Princeton,
            NJ: Princeton University Press.

Massa, SJ, Mark S.
    2003    *Anti-Catholicism in America: The Last Acceptable Prejudice.*
            New York: Crossroad Publishing Company.

Massaro, SJ, Thomas
    2000    *Living Justice: Catholic Social Teaching in Action.* Kansas City,
            MO: Sheed and Ward.
    2005a   "Poverty: A Concrete and Tragic Reality." In *All Things: A Je-
            suit Journal of the Social Apostolate* (Winter 2005–2006): 1–6.
            Available online at: <http://www.jesuit.org/images/docs/91
            pfXA.pdf>; accessed January 2007.
    2005b   "Welfare Reform and Our National Commitment to Poverty
            Reduction." In *All Things: A Jesuit Journal of the Social Aposto-
            late* (Winter 2005–2006): 9. Available online at: <http://www.
            jesuit.org/images/docs/91pfXA.pdf>; accessed January 2007.

McBrien, Richard
    1981    *Catholicism: One Volume Study Edition.* Minneapolis, MN:
            Winston Press.

McLaughlin, Martin
    1998    "Racial Violence and the Social Forces in America that Fuel It."
            Cited in "The Murder of James Byrd, Jr." Posted online at
            "Lynching and Violence in American Culture (An Online Col-
            lection of Essays Examining the New Lynch Mobs in America)":
            <http://amath.colorado.edu/carnegie/lit/lynch/byrd.htm>; ac-
            cessed January 2007.

Merton, Thomas
    1948    *The Seven Storey Mountain.* New York: Harcourt, Inc.
    1961    *The New Man.* New York: Farrar Straus & Cudahy.

Miller, Rowland S., Daniel Perlman, and Sharon S. Brehm
    2007    *Intimate Relationships* (4th ed.). New York: McGraw Hill.

Moyers, Bill
    2006    "America 101." A talk given October 27, 2006, in San Diego,
            CA, to the Council of Great City Schools, an organization of
            the nation's largest urban public school systems. Posted online
            at: <http://www.tompaine.com/articles/2006/11/01/america_
            101.php>; acessed January 2007.

Muhammad, Dedrick, Attieno Davis, Meizhu Lui, and Betsy Leondar-Wright
    2004    "State of the Dream 2004: Enduring Disparities in Black and White." United for a Fair Economy. Posted online at: <http://www.faireconomy.org/press/2004/StateoftheDream2004.pdf>; accessed January 2007.

Muhammad, Dedrick, Betsy Leondar-Wright, Meizhu Lui, Gloribell Mota, and Mara Voukydis
    2005    "State of the Dream 2005: Disowned in the Ownership Society." United for a Fair Economy. Posted online at: <http://www.faireconomy.org/press/2005/StateoftheDream2005.pdf>; accessed January 2007.

National Review Board for the Protection of Children and Young People
    2004    *A Report on the Crisis in the Catholic Church in the United States.* Washington, DC: United States Conference of Catholic Bishops. Available online at: <http://www.nccbuscc.org/nrb/nrbstudy/nrbreport.pdf>; accessed January 2007.

NEA (National Endowment for the Arts)
    2004    *Reading at Risk: A Survey of Literary Reading in America.* Research Division Report #46. Posted online at: <http://www.nea.gov/pub/ReadingAtRisk.pdf>; accessed January 2007.

Neuhaus, Richard John
    1987    *The Catholic Moment: The Paradox of the Church in the Postmodern World.* San Francisco: Harper and Row.

Newman, David
    2006    *Sociology: Exploring the Architecture of Everyday Life* (6th ed). Thosand Oaks, CA: Pine Forge Press, Sage Publications.

New York Times Correspondents
    2001    *How Race Is Lived in America: Pulling Together, Pulling Apart.* New York: Times Books. Henry Holt and Company.
    2005    *Class Matters.* New York: Times Books. Henry Holt and Company.

Nussbaum, L. Martin
    2006    "Changing the Rules." *America* (May 15, 2006). Accessed at <www.americamagazine.org>, May 2006.

Norris, Kathleen
    1996    *The Cloister Walk.* New York: Riverside Books.

O'Brien, David J., and Thomas A. Shannon
    1992    *Catholic Social Teaching: The Documentary Heritage.* Maryknoll, NY: Orbis Books.

Office of Social Justice, Diocese of St. Paul-Minneapolis
    2006    Catholic Social Teaching website (an excellent resource, in-dexed and well organized, for accessing Catholic social teaching documents on the Internet): <http://www.osjspm.org/catholic_social_teaching.aspx>; accessed January 2007.

O'Malley, SJ, William J.
    1990    *Converting the Baptized: A Survival Manual for Parents, Teachers and Pastors.* Allen, TX: Tabor Publishing.

*One: The Campaign to Make Poverty History*
    2007    "Fact Sheet: AIDS and Extreme Poverty." Posted online at: <http://www.one.org/aids_poverty>; accessed January 2007.

Page, Clarence
    1996    *Showing My Colors: Impolite Essays on Race and Identity.* New York: HarperCollins.

Parks, Sharon Daloz
    2000    *Big Questions, Worthy Dreams: Mentoring Young Adults in Their Search for Meaning, Purpose, and Faith.* San Francisco: Jossey-Bass: A Wiley Inprint.

Paul, Pamela
    2005    *Pornified: How Pornography Is Transforming Our Lives, Our Relationships, and Our Familes.* New York: Times Books.

Pilch, John J.
    1995    *The Cultural World of Jesus: Sunday by Sunday, Cycle A.* Collegeville, MN: The Liturgical Press.
    1996    *The Cultural World of Jesus: Sunday by Sunday, Cycle B.* Collegeville, MN: The Liturgical Press.
    1997    *The Cultural World of Jesus: Sunday by Sunday, Cycle C.* Collegeville, MN: The Liturgical Press.
    2002    *Cultural Tools for Interpreting the Good News.* Collegeville, MN: The Liturgical Press.

Population Reference Bureau
    2006    *World Data Sheet.* Posted online at: < http://www.prb.org/pdf 06/06WorldDataSheet.pdf>; accessed January 2007.

Postman, Neil
    1985    *Amusing Ourselves to Death: Public Discourse in the Age of Business.* New York: Viking.
    1988    *Conscientious Objections: Stirring up Trouble about Language, Technology and Education.* New York: Knopf, Inc.

Privett, SJ, Stephen A.
    2003    "The View From Outside." *Conversations on Jesuit Higher Education* 23 (Spring 2003): 12–16.

Radcliffe, OP, Timothy
    2005    *What's the Point of Being a Christian?* London: Burns & Oates.
    2006    "Overcoming Discord in the Church." *National Catholic Reporter* (May 5, 2006): 5–8. Available online at: <http://ncronline.org/NCR_Online/archives2/2006b/050506/050506a.php>; accessed January 2007.

Rahner, SJ, Karl
    1984    *Foundations of Christian Faith: An Introduction to the Idea of Christianity.* Trans. William V. Dych, SJ. New York: Crossroad Publishing Company.
    1986    *The Practice of Faith: A Handbook of Contemporary Spirituality.* New York: Crossroad Publishing Company.
    1997    *The Need and Blessing of Prayer.* Trans. Bruce W. Gillette. Collegeville, MN: The Liturgical Press.
    1999    *Encounters with Silence* (2nd rev. ed.). Trans. James M. Demske, SJ. South Bend, IN: St. Augustine's Press. First published in 1938.

Ratzinger, Joseph Cardinal (Pope Benedict XVI)
    2004    *Introduction to Christianity.* San Francisco, CA: Ignatius Press, Communio Books.

Rawls, John
    1971    *A Theory of Justice.* Cambridge, MA: The Belknap Press of Harvard University Press.

Reiser, SJ, William
    1997    *To Hear God's Word, Listen to the World: The Liberation of Spirituality.* Mahwah, NJ: Paulist Press.

Reitman, Janet
    2006    "Sex and Scandal at Duke: Lacrosse players, sorority girls and the booze-fueled culture of the never-ending hookup on the nation's most embattled college campus. *Rolling Stone* (June 2006). Available online at: <http://www.rollingstone.com/news/story/10464110/sex__scandal_at_duke>; accessed January 2007.

Renzetti, Claire, and Curran, Daniel
    1998    *Living Sociology.* Boston, MA: Allyn and Bacon.
    2000    *Living Sociology* (2nd ed.). Boston, MA: Allyn and Bacon.

Ritzer, George
    1999    *Enchanting a Disenchanted World: Revolutionizing the Means of Consumption*. Thousand Oaks, CA: Pine Forge Press.
    2000    *The McDonaldization of Society* (3rd ed.). Thousand Oaks, CA: Pine Forge Press.
    2002    *McDonaldization: The Reader*. Thousand Oaks, CA: Pine Forge Press.

Rilke, Rainer Maria
    1995    *Ahead All Parting: The Selected Poetry and Prose of Rainer Maria Rilke*. Stephen Mitchell, ed. and trans. New York: The Modern Library.

Roberts, Sam
    2006a    "The 300 Millionth Footprint on U.S. Soil." *New York Times* (October 8, 2006): Sunday Week in Review section. Available online at: <www.nytimes.com>; accessed Oct 8, 2006..
    2006b    "It's Official: To Be Married Means to Be Outnumbered." *New York Times* (October 15, 2006). Available online at: <www.nytimes.com>; accessed October 15, 2006.

Robertson, Ian
    1989    *Sociology: A Brief Introduction*. New York: Worth Publishers.

Rohr, Richard
    1999    *Everything Belongs: The Gift of Contemplative Prayer*. New York: Crossroad Publishing Company.

Rolheiser, Ronald
    2002    "Faith Today: The Struggle, the Invitation." *Church* (Fall 2002): 5–8.

Roof, Wade Clark
    1993    *A Generation of Seekers: The Spiritual Journeys of the Baby Boom Generation*. San Francisco: HarperSanFrancisco.
    1999    *Spiritual Marketplace: Baby Boomers and the Remaking of American Religion*. Princeton, NJ: Princeton University Press.

Roof, Wade Clark, and William McKinney
    1987    *American Mainline Religion: Its Changing Shape and Future*. New Brunswick, NJ: Rutgers University Press.

Sachs, Jefferey D.
    2005    *The End of Poverty: Economic Possibilities for Our Time*. New York: Penguin Books.

Sagan, Carl
    1994    *Pale Blue Dot: A Vision of the Human Future in Space.* New York: Random House.

Schaefer, Richard T.
    2001a    *Race and Ethnicity in the United States* (2nd. ed.). Upper Saddle River, NJ: Prentice-Hall
    2001b    *Sociology* (7th ed.). New York: McGraw Hill.
    2005    *Sociology* (9th ed.). New York: McGraw Hill.

Schiff, Stacey
    2006    "Know It All: Can Wikipedia Conquer Expertise?" *The New Yorker* (July 31, 2006). Posted online at: <http://www.newyorker.com/fact/content/articles/060731fa_fact>; accessed July 31, 2006.

Schneiders, Sandra M.
    1999    *Written That You May Believe: Encountering Jesus in the Fourth Gospel.* New York: Crossroad Publishing Company.

Schreiter, Robert J.
    1985    *Constructing Local Theologies.* Maryknoll, NY: Orbis Books.

Selznick, Philip
    1992    *The Moral Commonwealth: Social Theory and the Promise of Community.* Berkeley, CA: University of California Press.

Shipler, David K.
    1998    *A Country of Strangers: Blacks and Whites in America.* New York: Random House

Simmons, Rachel
    2002    *Odd Girl Out: The Hidden Culture of Aggression in Girls.* New York: Harcourt, Inc.

Singer, Peter
    2006    "What Should a Billionaire Give—and What Should You?" (a philosopher's case for donating more than you're comfortable with). *New York Times Magazine* (December 17, 2006): 60 ff. <http://www.nytimes.com/2006/12/17/magazine/17charity.t.html>; accessed December2006.

Sklar, Holly
    1995    *Chaos or Community: Seeking Solutions, Not Scapegoats for Bad Economic Policies.* Boston, MA: South End Press.

Slotkin, Richard
    1998    *Gunfighter Nation: The Myth of the Frontier in Twentieth-Century America.* Norman, OK: University of Oklahoma Press.

Smith, Christian, with Melinda Lundquist Denton
    2005    *Soul Searching: The Religious Lives of American Teenagers.* New York: Oxford University Press.

Sobrino, SJ, Jon
    1978    *Christology at the Crossroads.* Maryknoll, NY: Orbis Books. Originally published as *Christologia Desde America Latina,* 1976.
    1984    *The True Church and The Poor.* Maryknoll, NY: Orbis Books. Originally published as *Resurreción de la Verdadera Iglesia: Los pobres, lugar teológico de la eclesiología,* 1981.
    1986    "Poverty Means Death to the Poor." *Cross Currents* 36/3 (Fall 1986): 267–76
    1987    *Jesus in Latin America.* Maryknoll, NY: Orbis Books. Originally published as *Jesús en América Latina: Su significado para la fe y la cristología,* 1982.
    1988    *Spirituality and Liberation.* Maryknoll, NY: Orbis Books, 1988. Originally published as *Liberación con espíritu,* 1985.

Society of Jesus 32, 33, and 34
    1977    *Documents of the Thirty-First and the Thirty-Second General Congregations.* Saint Louis, MO: Institute of Jesuit Sources.
    1995    *Documents of the Thirty Fourth General Congregation of the Society of Jesus.* Saint Louis, MO: Institute of Jesuit Sources.

Soros, George
    2000    *Open Society: Reforming Global Capitalism.* New York: Public Affairs.

Southern Poverty Law Center
    2007    Intelligence Project. Posted online at < http://www.splcenter.org/intel/intpro.jsp>; accessed January 2007.

Sperber, Murray
    2000    *Beer and Circus: How Big-Time College Sports Is Crippling Undergraduate Education.* New York: Henry Holt & Co.

Spence, Jonathan D.
    1985    *The Memory Place of Matteo Ricci.* New York: Penguin.

Steinfels, Margaret O'Brien, ed.
    2004a    *American Catholics and Civic Engagement.* American Catholics in the Public Square, Vol. 1. Lanham, MD: Rowan and Littlefield Publishers, Inc. A Sheed and Ward Book.
    2004b    *American Catholics, American Culture: Tradition and Resistance.* American Catholics in the Public Square, Vol. 2. Lanham,

MD: Rowan and Littlefield Publishers, Inc. A Sheed and Ward Book.

Steinfels, Peter
    2003    *A People Adrift: The Crisis in the Roman Catholic Church*. New York: Simon and Schuster.

Stewart, Thomas A.
    2003    "Mending Walls?" *Harvard Business Review: Leadership in a Changed World* (Special Issue, August 2003): 8.

Swartz, David
    1997    *Culture and Power: The Sociology of Pierre Bourdieu*. Chicago, IL: The University of Chicago Press.

Tacey, David
    2000    *ReEnchantment: The New Australian Spirituality*. Australia: HarperCollins, Pty Limited.

Tier, Julia
    2006    "Sex and the University." Bustedhalo.com. Posted online at: <http://www.bustedhalo.com/features/SexandtheUniversity.htm>; accessed March 2006.

Thompson, J. Milburn
    2003    *Justice and Peace: A Christian Primer* (2nd rev. and expanded ed.). Maryknoll, NY: Orbis Books.

Thompson, William E., and Joseph V. Hickey
    2005    *Society in Focus* (5th ed.). New York: Pearson/Allyn and Bacon.

Twitchell, James B.
    1992    *Carnival Culture: The Trashing of Taste in America*. New York: Columbia University Press.
    1999    *Lead Us into Temptation: The Triumph of American Materialism*. New York: Columbia University Press.

UNDP (United Nations Development Programme)
    1999    "A Balance Sheet of Human Development 1990–1997." In *United Nations Development Report 1999: Globalization with a Human Face* (p. 22). New York: Oxford University Press. Available online at: <http://hdr.undp.org/reports/global/1999/en/pdf/hdr_1999_front.pdf>; accessed January 2007.
    2005    *Human Development Report 2005: International Cooperation at a Crossroads: Aid, Trade and Security in an Unequal World*. Available online at: <http://hdr.undp.org/reports/global/2005/pdf/HDR05_overview.pdf>; accessed January 2007.

U.S. Census
2005    "Income Stable, Poverty Rate Increases, Percentage of Americans Without Health Insurance Unchanged." Press release (August 30, 2005). Posted online at: <http://www.census.gov/Press-Release/www/releases/archives/income_wealth/005647.html>; accessed December 2005.

2006    "Income Climbs, Poverty Stabilizes, Uninsured Rate Increases." Press release (August 29, 2006). Posted online at: <http://www.census.gov/Press-Release/www/releases/archives/income_wealth/007419.html>; accessed December 2006.

USCCB (United States Conference of Catholic Bishops)
1979    *Brothers and Sisters to Us: A Pastoral Letter on Racism.* Washington, DC: United States Catholic Conference.

1986    *Economic Justice for All.* Washington, DC: United States Catholic Conference.

1989    *For the Love of One Another: A Special Message on the Occasion of the Tenth Anniversary of "Brothers and Sisters to Us."* Washington, DC: United States Catholic Conference.

1991    *Marketplace Prophets: Voices for Justice in the 20th Century* (60 min. video). Washington, DC: The Catholic Communication Campaign, United States Catholic Conference.

1993a   "The Challenge of Peace: God's Promise and Our Response." Washington, DC: United States Catholic Conference.

1993b   "Communities of Salt and Light: Reflections on the Social Mission of the Parish." Washington, DC: United States Catholic Conference. Available online at: <http://www.nccbuscc.org/sdwp/saltandlight.htm>; accessed December 2006.

1994    "Confronting a Culture of Violence." *Origins* (December 1994): 423 ff.

1998    "Sharing Catholic Social Teaching: Challenges and Directions." Reflections of the U.S. Catholic Bishops. Posted online at: <http://www.usccb.org/sdwp/projects/socialteaching/social-teaching.htm>; accessed December 2006.

2000    "Responsibility, Rehabilitation, and Restoration: A Catholic Perspective on Crime and Criminal Justice. A Statement of the Catholic Bishops of the United States." Posted online at: <http://usccb.org/sdwp/criminal.htm>; accessed December 2006.

2006a   "The Catholic Church in the United States at a Glance." Posted online at: <www.nccbuscc.org/comm/satisti.shtml>; accessed December 2006.

2006b   "Poverty in the USA: The State of Poverty in America," quoting the U.S. Census Bureau, *Income, Poverty, and Health Insurance*

Coverage in the United States: 2004. Posted online at: <www.usccb.org/cchd/povertyusa/povfacts.shtml>; accessed December 2006.

2007a.    CCHD (Catholic Campaign for Human Development). Posted online at: <http://www.nccbuscc.org/cchd>; accessed January 2007.

2007b    "Themes of Catholic Social Teaching." Posted online at: <http://www.usccb.org/sdwp/projects/socialteaching/excerpt.htm>; accessed January 2007.

Vitillo, Robert J.
2002    "Who Are the Poor in the Richest of Nations?" New Theology Review 15/2 (May 2002): 5–15

von Balthasar, Hans Urs
1957    Prayer. Trans. in 1961 by A. V. Littledale. New York: Sheed and Ward.

Walzer, Michael
1983    Spheres of Justice: A Defense of Pluralism and Equality. New York: Basic Books, Inc.

West, Cornel
1993a    Prophetic Thought in Postmodern Times: Beyond Eurocentrism and Multiculturalism. Vol. 1. Monroe, ME: Common Courage Press.

1993b    Prophetic Reflections. Notes on Race and Power in America: Beyond Eurocentrism and Multiculturalism. Vol. 2. Monroe, ME: Common Courage Press.

1994    Race Matters. New York: Vintage Books.

2004    Democracy Matters: Winning the Fight Against Imperialism. New York: The Penguin Press.

Whitehead, Barbara Defoe
2006    "Role Reversals: Hazards of College Party Culture." Commonweal (September 8, 2006): 8.

Williams, CSC, Oliver F., and John W. Houck (eds.)
1993    Catholic Social Thought and the New World Order: Building on One Hundred Years. Notre Dame IN: University of Notre Dame Press.

Wilson, William Julius
1996    When Work Disappears: The World of the New Urban Poor. New York: Alfred A. Knopf.

Winik, Jay
2001    April 1865: The Month that Saved America. New York: HarperCollins Perennial.

Wolfe, Alan

    1989    *Whose Keeper? Social Science and Moral Obligation.* Berkeley,
            CA: University of California Press.

    2001    *Moral Freedom: The Search for Virtue in a World of Choice.* New
            York: W. W. Norton & Co.

Wolfe, Tom

    1987    *Bonfire of the Vanities.* New York: Farrar, Straus and Giroux.

    1998    *A Man in Full.* New York: Farrar, Straus and Giroux.

    2004    *I Am Charlotte Simmons.* New York: Farrar, Straus and Giroux.

World Bank

    2007    "Overview: What Is Poverty? Understanding Poverty." World
            Bank Website. Posted online at: < http://web.worldbank.org/
            WBSITE/EXTERNAL/TOPICS/EXTPOVERTY/0,,content-
            MDK:20153855~menuPK:373757~pagePK:148956~piPK:2166
            18~theSitePK:336992,00.html>; accessed February 2007.

Wright, N. T.

    1996    *The New Testament and the People of God.* Christian Origins
            and the Question of God, Vol. 1. Minneapolis, MN: Augsburg
            Fortress Publishers.

    1997    *Jesus and the Victory of God.* Christian Origins and the Ques-
            tion of God, Vol. 2. Minneapolis: MN: Augsburg Fortress Pub-
            lishers.

Zahn, Gordon

    1986    *In Solitary Witness.* Springfield, IL: Templegate Publishers.

# Index